WHEN A GIANT STIRRED

WHEN A GIANT STIRRED

SHEFFIELD WEDNESDAY 1976-1993

GARETH PLATT

DB PUBLISHING

First published 2021 by DB Publishing, an imprint of JMD Media Ltd,
Nottingham, United Kingdom.

ISBN 9781780916125

Printed in the UK

CONTENTS

INTRODUCTION

TO SAY that Sheffield Wednesday have underachieved in recent times is a bit like saying Benny Hill's treatment of women now appears a bit outdated.

In the last 50 years, Wednesday have spent only 15 seasons in England's top division. For the biggest team in one of England's biggest cities, the place where the first football club was formed anywhere in the world, that's pretty damning.

For a brief period in the 1980s and '90s, however, Wednesday *did* live up to their potential. They established themselves in the top flight and regularly reached the latter stages of both cup competitions.

And, miracle of miracles, in 1991 they actually won a trophy.

It almost seems like a trick of the mind now, doesn't it. Wednesday claimed the scalp of Manchester United, one of the most glamorous clubs in the world – and they didn't just beat them, they actually outplayed them. Of all the giant-killings that have taken place at Wembley down the years, it's hard to remember David ever outwitting Goliath so comprehensively.

This book will look in detail at how Wednesday pulled off that result. How Ron Atkinson first moulded a team that could compete at the top of English football, and then orchestrated a tactical masterpiece to completely bewilder Alex Ferguson and his all-star team.

But we won't just look at the miracle of '91, fun as that would be. The book will explore Wednesday's entire golden era, from Jack Charlton's arrival to the Wembley marvels of 1993.

We'll look at how this golden age began and ended, and explore all points in between. From Big Jack's key signings to the capture of Chris Waddle, and the effect his signing had on the club. From the boozy nights out that forged team spirit to the dressing-room tear-ups that helped turn defeats into victories.

This whistlestop tour will be narrated by the players who made it happen, including Mick Lyons, David Hirst, Mel Sterland, Carlton Palmer, Andy McCulloch, Roland Nilsson and Chris Bart-Williams. These men have shared some amazing stories, not just about their time at Wednesday but what came afterwards.

The book will also look at the four managers who shaped this period: Charlton, Atkinson, Howard Wilkinson and Trevor Francis. Wednesday fans will no doubt have strong opinions about each of them, but we'll let the players give their view on each man's strengths and weaknesses.

Of course, one member of this managerial quartet has sullied his reputation with a tirade that no football fan of any stripe could condone. In 2004 Atkinson was heard using a racist epithet to describe Chelsea player Marcel Desailly during a Champions League match in Monaco. His legacy will forever be shaped by that outburst.

Atkinson's language that night was, unacceptable, and this book makes no attempt to condone it. When discussing him in this book, and reporting what the players have said about him, we are talking about the manager and not the person.

For those Wednesday fans who were lucky enough to witness this period first-hand, we hope you enjoy this guided tour down memory lane. At the time of writing the team are slumming it in League One, and with all the other madness going on in the world right now, it feels like a good moment to delve into the memory bank.

So enjoy the book, and let's hope we don't have to wait another 30 years for Wednesday to get back to where they belong.

Gareth Platt
September 2021

1
THE TURNING OF THE TIDE

Chris Turner could barely bring himself to watch. He'd turned down Manchester United, European Cup winners just a few years earlier, to sign for his boyhood heroes. Now he and his fellow Sheffielders watched on, powerless to affect what was happening in front of them. The biggest crowd in weeks had turned up to lend their support but at times you could hear a pin drop, such was their anxiety.

Out on the pitch, Wednesday and Southend United slugged it out with all the dignity of two sloshed brawlers at closing time. The Hillsborough turf, churned and congealed by a season's football, might as well have been quicksand; the match was effectively a play-off and the loser would be dragged down into the Fourth Division.

'It was do or die,' Turner says, looking back on that dogfight in April 1976. 'If we'd gone down, Wednesday might not have survived.

'We'd had financial problems for years. I'd been to places like Halifax as a fan and watched people marching round with buckets for the Save Our Owls campaign. You never know what would have happened had we gone into Division Four.

'The tension around the ground was unbearable. But everyone wanted to be there because we knew what was at stake.

'We knew this was it.'

* * *

EVEN LOOKING back with half a century of hindsight, the very fact Wednesday ended up in such a mess is staggering. Almost exactly a decade before that cliff-edge shoot-out against Southend in April 1976, they'd reached the FA Cup Final with one of Britain's most enterprising young teams.

Unlike the England heroes who would shimmer on that same baize a couple of months later, Wednesday weren't able to hang on for victory. Still, the fans who accompanied them down to the Empire Stadium must have thought that the good times would keep on rolling for years to come.

The squad was chock-full of quality, from World Cup-winner-to-be Ron Springett in goal to flying fledgling David Ford in attack. Manager Alan Brown was regarded as one of the shrewdest tactical minds in the country and Hillsborough was unquestionably one of the best grounds, about to host several matches in the World Cup.

So where did it all go go wrong? How did one of the country's best sides, with one of its leading stadiums, end up sliding to the brink of the Fourth Division in just ten years?

In truth, the wheels of that savage decline were set in motion even before the visit to Wembley. In January 1965 two Wednesday players – defender Peter Swan and striker David 'Bronco' Layne – were jailed for agreeing to fix a match at Ipswich with their former team-mate Tony Kay. It remains the most high-profile betting scandal in the history of British sport and it ripped the heart out of the team at a stroke.

Swan, who sadly died a few months before this book went to press, was a lion-hearted defender and inspirational leader, an England regular once described by the Italian media as 'the best centre-half in the world' after a match in Rome. Layne was a local lad who had moved back to Wednesday from Bradford and become one of the country's leading goalscorers. They were the 1960s equivalents of Nigel Pearson and David Hirst. The FA banned both of them for life.

In an age when football was still shaking off the shackles of the maximum wage and transfers were far rarer than they are today, it was practically impossible to replace such gifted players. In the five seasons prior to their incarceration, Wednesday had finished in the top six every year (even coming second in 1961); they would not repeat the feat again for more than a quarter of a century.

But Wednesday could have regrouped. They were still one of the country's biggest clubs and had spent the majority of their existence in the top division. They still had a clutch of excellent young players. They still had a blue-riband stadium. All that was needed was a bit of patience and clarity at boardroom level and the storm would pass.

Unfortunately, patience and clarity proved to be severely lacking as the '60s slowly lost their sheen.

In the years that followed the cup final, key players such as Jim McCalliog and John Quinn were sold off and replaced with pale imitations, draining the quality from the squad. When Brown jumped ship in 1968, the problems were compounded by a string of bone-headed managerial appointments. For fans of today, it must all sound so grimly familiar.

In 1970, Wednesday slipped out of the First Division after somehow losing at home to Manchester City, who were desperately trying to avoid injuries ahead of their European Cup Winners' Cup Final. The scorer of City's goals, Ian Bowyer, was only on the field because of a shocking tackle on Mike Summerbee by Wednesday left-back Colin Prophett – whose name seems somewhat appropriate given the momentous nature of his intervention. One hopes, for Prophett's sake, that he didn't foresee the consequences of his X-rated lunge.

As crowds dwindled in the second tier, Wednesday's financial problems mounted. Having spent a fortune getting Hillsborough ready for the 1966 World Cup the board were left with a huge stadium which was only ever full when FA Cup semi-finals came round. Instead of bouncing back into the top flight, Wednesday just drifted further and further away.

In 1973 the club plumbed a new depth of callous ineptitude by sacking Derek Dooley on Christmas Eve. Dooley had been a legendary post-war player before suffering a horrific broken leg, which subsequently became gangrenous and required amputation. He had quite literally bled for the blue and white stripes, yet the board couldn't even wait until the Christmas trees were down to get rid of him.

* * *

Turner was forced to watch all this with a sense of childish bewilderment. A brickie's son from Stannington, his parents were Wednesday-mad. They took him to his first game when he was just four years old in 1962, just after Wednesday had pushed Tottenham for the league title.

'For people like me, there was no choice about who you supported,' Turner recalls. 'I was going home and away with my mum and dad. We used to stand on the Kop at Anfield, stand on the Stretford End, rain or shine. So it hurt to watch us make such a mess of things.

'Even at the time the financial problems were obvious. People used to say "we've got the greatest ground but the shittiest team" and that sums it up really. What's the point of having a great ground if you can't find the money for decent players?

'Then the managers started coming and going. There were no solid foundations and we could never seem to get a team together.'

Turner vividly recalls the match against City in 1970. By this time he was turning out for Sheffield Boys and appearing in Wednesday's junior sides, yet still turning up to Hillsborough as a fan.

'It almost felt like they were going easy on us. Maybe they were mates with the Wednesday players, or they just enjoyed the easy trip along the Snake Pass for away games, I don't know! We just missed chance after chance. It summed everything up.'

But nothing could prepare him for the departure of Dooley – a man who'd just persuaded him to sign schoolboy forms for Wednesday.

'That was the worst thing for me, what they did to Derek, He was a lovely guy, one of the best.

'I'd had a few clubs after me, including United, who invited me to watch a game at Old Trafford, back when Best, Law and Charlton were on the go, and put me in digs. But then Derek came over to Stannington to meet my mum and dad and there was nowhere else I was ever going to go. What a man. I was desperate to do well for him.

'It's clear results weren't great. No one could deny that. But it just shows how badly the club was being run. What are you going to achieve by sacking someone on December 24? Why not have the decency to leave it until after Christmas? That sort of humiliation would live with you for the rest of your life, wouldn't it?'

*   *   *

Dooley's sacking achieved nothing, at least in the long term. Wednesday avoided relegation that season but they went down the following year. And by the spring of 1976 they were down near the foot of the Third Division, a depth to which the club had never previously sunk in its entire history.

When Southend arrived for the last game of the league season, everyone knew what was at stake. Wednesday had 38 points and their opponents 37. Whoever lost was down.

Some fans had already given up by this point, which is hardly surprising: Wednesday were so bad that they'd recently lost to Mansfield, Chesterfield and Rotherham, three local clubs which until recently wouldn't have been visible through a microscope. Nonetheless, thousands still answered the call in their team's hour of need. Nearly 26,000 turned up, three times as many as the previous home gate (although, to put this into context, 55,000 had packed in to watch Manchester United beat Derby in the FA Cup semi-final earlier that month).

It was not a classic but, of course, it was never going to be. Wednesday opened up a two-goal lead but then they allowed Southend to nick a goal with the sort of amateur-hour defending that had characterised much of the previous decade. The last few minutes seemed to last an eternity.

Eventually the referee's whistle blew. Fans ran on to the pitch and mobbed local lad Mick Prendergast, scorer of the decisive goal and a 100-per-center who deserved to be playing in happier times. But despite the jubilation, the overall feeling was one of relief.

Turner remembers 'thinking we'd got away with it' as he walked away from Hillsborough. Indeed, for many supporters of that period, it felt that the tide had turned. New manager Ken Ashurst, who had taken over from Burtenshaw earlier in the season, could now begin to rebuild. And rebuild he certainly did.

Working in tandem with the recently arrived chairman Bert McGee, Ashurst, a genial Scouser still in his 30s, began overhauling the squad. They weeded out the cloggers and has-beens and replaced them with shrewd signings such as Ian Porterfield, while also promoting a raft of young players.

One of the first to receive the call was Turner, who made his debut at the start of 1976/77. It turned out to be an inspired decision; Turner won the club's player of the year award in his first season.

'I remember that first game, Walsall at home, 0-0,' Turner says of his debut campaign. 'I played 45 out of 46 games that season. At first it was a bit daunting, but you soon get used to the pace and physicality of the game.

'Len started sorting things out. I really appreciated him. He gets forgotten by Wednesday fans these days but trust me, he was a good manager. He brought in players he knew – guys like Jeff Johnson, Neil O'Donnell from Gillingham, Richard Walden from Aldershot. You could see the squad beginning to improve.'

Just as important was the addition of Tony Toms, a former Royal Marine who was hired to whip the Wednesday lads into shape.

To describe Toms as a 'character' would be the grossest of understatements – this is a man who once taught combat skills to young squaddies and would eventually find work as Madonna's minder. His muscular power struck the fear of God into his charges, but they came to love his brutish bonhomie.

'Tony Toms was great,' Turner says. 'Massive character, total ladies' man, but a great coach too. He and Len demanded hard work – we'd have to run up and down the Kop for ages, and trust me that's one seriously big stand – but it really helped me personally.

'Tomsy got me on the weights, made me strengthen my legs. Not only did that mean I could kick the ball further, it made me more able to hold my own when the ball was coming into the box. You used to get absolutely buffeted in those days. I can't thank him enough.'

With the slide arrested, the mood around the squad soon began to pick up – even when Ashurst and Toms forced them into those quad-busting runs up and down the Kop all day.

'Great lads, all of them,' Turner recalls with a chuckle. 'People like Roger Wylde, Paul Bradshaw, Dave Cusack; it was a young squad and we all went out together, which was great for team spirit. You could feel things coming together.'

As Turner suggests, Ashurst is often overlooked when Wednesday fans fire up the 'best manager' debate. But surely no one has played a more significant role in Wednesday's history than the genial Liverpudlian. Ashurst took on a job that no one else wanted and performed as well as anyone could have expected.

By the time he moved on, in October 1977, the foundations had been laid for a very different kind of manager to take Sheffield Wednesday forward. The appointment would have profound consequences, both for Turner and his beloved club.

2
JACK THE REDEEMER

Living With Jack Charlton.

In the reality-TV boom that blitzed Britain at the turn of the millennium, it would have been the perfect pitch: Britain's most eccentric World Cup winner at home in his natural habitat.

*For Andy McCulloch, though, it **was** reality. For six whole months.*

Back in the winter of 1979 McCulloch had just signed for Wednesday from Brentford, and he and his wife needed somewhere to stay as they settled up north. So Charlton offered them a place at his country pile in Worsbrough, a leafy hamlet in the Barnsley suburbs.

What was it like sharing a house with a man famed for his eccentricity? 'It was fine,' McCulloch says, with a chuckle. 'But Jesus, he did nothing around the house. His wife, Pat did everything. She cooked, she cleaned, she'd even put the coals on the fire. We'd feel so guilty we'd end up doing it ourselves! He was always getting things dirty and she'd have to clean up after him.'

It's just one of many stories of Charlton gleefully recounted for this book. Peter Shirtliff recalls being ordered to turn up at the great man's house at 6am, complete with flask and sandwiches, to go off 'beating' – chasing birds out of the trees on the nearby moors so his manager could shoot them. After a few ales in the local hostelry, Shirtliff ended up driving Charlton's car home, its owner snoozing away in the back.

Then, of course, there's the tale we've all heard about Charlton: the one where he goes to a pub and hands the barman a cheque because he knows it will never be cashed. The man himself always denied the story but plenty of players were happy to confirm its veracity.

But for all the chaos and derring-do, the players are clear on one thing. For all his idiosyncracies, Charlton was a brilliant football manager. If Len Ashurst had righted the ship and plugged the holes in the hull, it was Charlton who set it on a path to glory once again.

* * *

THE TALE of how Jack Charlton became Wednesday manager in October 1977 has gone down in Sheffield folklore. And like so many of the yarns surrounding Big Jack and his life, it's hard to know where the truth ends and the legend begins.

It is claimed that Charlton was besieged by desperate Wednesday fans while attending a game at Hillsborough at the start of the 1977/78 season. They begged him to take the job, which, at that time, was still occupied by Len Ashurst, and guide the club back to the land of milk and honey. Charlton supposedly agreed and then marched up to the boardroom to present his candidature, which was accepted by the star-struck directors on the spot.

Of course, the real story may be slightly more nuanced than that. It may be that Charlton's visit that fateful day wasn't motivated purely by his love of Third Division football. Maybe he had already been in contact with Wednesday even before the fans surrounded him. Maybe he'd been in touch with the Hillsborough power-brokers ever since he left Middlesbrough the previous April.

What is undeniable, however, is that Charlton's appointment was a huge coup. He had won the World Cup in 1966, just a few weeks after Wednesday's players cast their own golden shadows on the Wembley turf. Since then, however, their football trajectories had gone in opposite directions.

Following the World Cup, Charlton had cemented his reputation as England's toughest centre-half, the obsidian cornerstone of that great Leeds team which dominated English football at the start of the 1970s. Then he'd gone into management with Middlesbrough and won promotion at his first attempt, beating Wednesday 8-0 along the way.

As for Wednesday themselves, Ashurst had done a fine job in refitting the squad but by autumn 1977 they were on the canvas again, bottom of the Third Division having lost to Bury, Chester and Shrewsbury.

Charlton would have been forgiven for passing up this poisoned chalice. But, like the proud contrarian that he was, Big Jack decided to take a gulp. No doubt he saw the potential of the club, and the fact that it was so close to his home may have sweetened the deal.

Even so, it was a massive gamble for a man who had so recently been managing in the First Division. In fact, just months before Charlton pitched up in S6, he'd gone for the England job – although his application was rather overshadowed by that of Brian Clough, who was passed over in the same round of interviews.

Old Big 'Ead would soon make mugs of the FA by winning the league and then the European Cup with Nottingham Forest. But the job Charlton would do at Hillsborough, in its own way, would be just as impressive.

* * *

When Charlton got to Wednesday, he realised it wasn't a time for flair or frippery. And in truth those were never his strengths anyway.

So he invited Maurice Setters, one of football's hardest midfielders in his playing days, to be his assistant. And of course he inherited Toms, whose background made him the ideal man to prepare Wednesday for the trench warfare of the Third Division. Together they toughened the team up and imposed the same direct style of play that had brought Charlton success at Middlesbrough.

Wednesday would have won few beauty contests that season but slowly, surely, things began to improve. They ended the season with a run of one defeat in 12 games, which was enough for a 14th-placed finish, well clear of the relegation mire that had threatened to engulf them.

The following season, 1977/78, was really one of consolidation – or stagnation, depending on how full a fan's glass was. Wednesday again finished 14th, with 13 wins, 14 defeats and a goal difference of exactly 0. Mediocrity has rarely been more symmetrical.

There was one shining light, however: the marathon FA Cup run against Arsenal. Having already slugged their way through five matches to get to the third round, Wednesday took their illustrious opponents to five games, four of them going to extra time. Eventually they were downed 2-0 in the final replay at neutral Filbert Street, drenched in the blue and white of Wednesday rather than Leicester.

Chris Turner played in every single match. 'That first game at Hillsborough was bloody freezing,' he remembers. 'I played in tracky bottoms and people threw snowballs at Pat Jennings when he came down to the Kop in the second half!

'Eventually we ran out of steam after so many games. But what stands out is the memory of Wednesday filling the ground at Filbert Street. Arsenal came from one of the wealthiest parts of the country and we outnumbered them about four to one. After such a long period of mediocrity it felt like the start of a new era.'

Arsenal would go on to reach the FA Cup Final that year and then win the trophy the following season. The fact that Wednesday were able to match such an excellent side showed the potential that lay within their ranks.

But Charlton was clear: if Wednesday were going to get promotion, he needed to make some changes. So he set out on an ambitious retooling programme – and Turner, surprisingly, was one of the first to make way.

In the summer of 1979 the fiery young stopper was shipped off to Sunderland because Charlton wanted the appropriately named Bob Bolder to fill the Wednesday goal. Having just been named in the PFA Team of the Season, Turner would have been forgiven for feeling miffed. However, looking back with 40 years of hindsight, he's phlegmatic.

'It was gutting, for sure,' says Turner. 'It was the club I'd supported all my life, and I'd thought I'd done enough to cement myself in the team having won the player of the year award the year before, and then made the PFA team.

'But Jack was clear: he wanted a physically imposing goalkeeper for Division Three and Bob Bolder was the man he chose. It was nothing personal.'

* * *

As well as the change in goal, Charlton wanted some fresh faces up front. And in the spring of 1979 he signed two players who would go on to become folk heroes in South Yorkshire.

Andy McCulloch's signing was the more unorthodox. A strapping centre-forward who had started out with Rodney Marsh at Queens Park Rangers and settled at Brentford, he wasn't at his best – in any sense – when Wednesday came in for him.

'I've scored a goal, I've got concussed and I'm on a stretcher,' McCulloch recalls. 'As I'm recovering in the back of the stand, I get a shake. It's Ian St John, who was working as Jack's assistant manager at the time. He just said, "Do you fancy a move?"'

'I was definitely interested – I'd got frustrated at Brentford, there were no signings coming in and the team was stagnating. So I agreed to go and meet Jack.

'We met in the gantry at Wembley, up in the heavens, before the England-Scotland match. It might seem quite unorthodox now, but that's how it was!

'We agreed on everything, but the problem was that I had a plaster on my nose. I used to get bangs on the nose all the time with the way I played, it could have been any game that it happened.

'But when I went up to see Jack at his mansion to get all the final details sorted out, I had the plaster off. I rocked up and he asked, "Who the fucking hell are you?" His wife even told him off for swearing.'

Andy McCulloch's bravery and selfless running made him the perfect foil for his partners to play off.

Terry Curran's signing was every bit as remarkable. He was approached by Charlton and Setters at Peter Stringfellow's Cinderella Rockafella nightclub in Leeds, in the company of his Southampton team-mate Alan Ball. When the Wednesday duo made their intentions clear, Ball told them they were crazy. And he was right.

Curran was at the peak of his powers at the time. Literally hours before that encounter, he'd created both goals in Southampton's 2-2 draw with Leeds in the first leg of the League Cup semi-final, a tie they would go on to win. Curran played in the final at Wembley but within days he was completing a deadline day move to Hillsborough and swapping the First Division for the third.

One might imagine that Curran would have needed some persuading to take such a leap of faith. In fact he was desperate for the move. As the deadline-day clock ticked down, stuck in a traffic jam in central London, Curran leapt from his vehicle and sprinted towards the FA's headquarters to ensure he signed the paperwork in time.

But why? Well there was the attraction of reuniting with Setters, who'd nurtured him at Doncaster. But there was another, even bigger pull factor at work: Curran was a mad Wednesday fan.

'I'd been brought up in Kinsley, a mining village in between Leeds and Sheffield,' Curran says. 'From my area you had John Radford who played for Arsenal, the Knowles brothers, and Geoff Boycott. It was about 28 miles from Hillsborough.

'Towards the end of my time at Southampton I really started to play again. But Wednesday was my club.

'Maurice offered me the chance to help Wednesday get back up, and I wanted to get them up again.'

Curran's life at Wednesday wouldn't always go smoothly. Other players remember him having a scrap with Charlton in the Hillsborough gymnasium one morning due to a dispute about playing positions. But he formed an instant relationship with McCulloch, despite their markedly different characters.

'Tel was crazy,' McCulloch recalls. 'He'd always try wacky things in training, or he'd turn up in daft clothes, the sort of stuff you'd get down in London – but in the middle of Yorkshire on a wet Monday morning! You wouldn't see me dead in that kind of gear.

'We were very different lads – I'd be happy with a quiet pint, didn't like the attention at all – and we didn't socialise much because we lived in opposite directions. The only thing we had in common was that we both liked a flutter on the horses.

'But we just clicked on the pitch. He was a good player, really good player, and we just got on. Never fell out. I'd played with players who were really selfish, I'd make them loads of goals but they wouldn't make me one back. But we made goals for one another and we appreciated one another.'

*   *   *

But the dream partnership would take time to gel. Wednesday started the 1979/80 season slowly; on the second Saturday they went down 3-0 at home to Blackburn. By Christmas, the Hillsborough crowd had only seen four home league wins. Their city rivals were riding high, five points clear at the top.

On Boxing Day United slooped over to Owlerton, the first derby for eight years and the final match either side would play in the 1970s. For Wednesday it had been a decade of near-unrelenting misery, while their neighbours had lorded it in the top two divisions until the previous season. Now, as the decade faded into wintry blackness, the blue half of Sheffield had one final chance to give their local rivals a shoeing.

The kick-off was brought forward to 11am, denying the two sets of supporters the chance to get bladdered beforehand. Despite the early start, and Wednesday's decision to charge the princely sum of 75p for entry (a decision that caused uproar among the fans) a crowd of 49,000 packed into Hillsborough to see the game, many with a stale yeasty tang to their breath.

As the stands began to hum and rattle in anticipation, the tension mounted in the bowels of the stadium. The Wednesday lads had been salivating over the match for weeks. They had even taken to plotting in the nearby greasy spoon after training, mapping out their schemes to nullify the United players – by fair means or foul.

But the visitors had their own plans for skullduggery, too. As the teams gathered in the tunnel (some bigwig had clearly thought it would defuse the tension if they walked out side by side) the United players began whispering in Curran's ear, telling him what they were going to do to him out on the field. Suffice to say they were picking on the wrong bloke.

'They couldn't put me off,' says Curran. 'A lot of players get nervous, a lot of players find it hard to play it in front of a crowd, but I had that confidence about me.'

On winning the toss, United chose to turn round and defend the Kop in the first half. But if their hope was to disrupt Wednesday's rhythm, ride out the early storm and gradually silence the feverish crowd, suffice to say the plan didn't work.

Ian Mellor opened the scoring with a 25-yard-screamer, and then came the crucial moment of the match; a horror miss by John MacPhail, United's no-nonsense defender. With the goal at his mercy, MacPhail somehow contrived to fire the ball straight at Bolder, who was still lying prostrate on the ground from the initial shot.

As the ball flew towards the goalkeeper's giant chest, the sliding doors crossed. From that moment on Wednesday pulled away from their bitter rivals and the balance of power began to shift. In one moment, the pattern for the 1980s had been set.

In the second half Curran decided to put on a masterclass. First he doubled the lead by heading home a McCulloch cross, then he set up Jeff King after a coruscating run down the right-hand side. Finally the moustachioed marvel won a penalty, gleefully converted by Mark Smith.

Before that game, the Wednesday fans had appreciated Curran. By the end they adored him. As if his footballing brilliance wasn't enough, he endeared himself to them by sliding on his knees in front of the United fans to celebrate his goal (for which he was rewarded with a shower of coins) and then lying down on the ball as he waited to take a corner, as if he was sunbathing by the Mediterranean.

Looking back now, Curran says his behaviour may have been slightly over the top but euphoria had well and truly taken over. As he sat in the bath afterwards, rehashing the Boxing Day song that had peeled down from the Kop during the game, the player realised he'd just fulfilled a childhood dream.

McCulloch, the Batman to his Robin, the Toshack to his Keegan, had no such affiliation. But he enjoyed the victory every bit as much.

'It was a day I'll never forget,' he recalls now. 'I didn't really get the conflict back then, not being from Sheffield, but you soon realise the effect. I remember having a glass of milk to line my stomach before getting on the beer that day. Terry even came up and thanked me. He didn't have to do that.

'It was a great celebration after the match, and it's an amazing memory. Even now people still ask me about it.'

*   *   *

The ripple effect wasn't immediate as Wednesday took only a point from their next two games. But then came a purple patch of seven wins in eight, during which 25 goals were scored. Charlton's team soared towards the promotion places as United, broken by their Hillsborough experience, headed in the opposite direction.

Wednesday stuttered during the run-in, winning only four of their final 12 games, but they'd done enough. Promotion was eventually secured with a 0-0 draw at home to Carlisle United. Curran was the King of the Kop and even released a pop record – although he proved rather less adept with a microphone in his hand than a ball at his feet.

'It was a golden time for both of us,' McCulloch recalls. 'For me and for Tel too, I think. After that United game we started believing in each other and it just fell into place.

'We had some big characters in that team. Terry could make you laugh sometimes – God, I still remember that pop record – but then we had guys like Mike Pickering at the other end of the scale. It was a lovely balance and a great set of lads.'

A decade on from relegation, the decline had finally stopped. Wednesday had heroes again and a true inspiration in the dugout. People remember that season for a massacre but ultimately, it brought a resurrection.

3

LYONS BRINGS THE PRIDE

Tears ran down Mick Lyons's face as he wallowed in his cups, contemplating what he'd just done. After 14 years at Everton, during which he'd become a granite-hewn hero of the Gwladys Street End, the day of reckoning had finally arrived.

Now he was about to move to a club that had not competed in the top division since he'd made his debut. He'd been the kingpin at Everton, the man who organised all the social nights and commanded the unconditional respect of every single player. Now it was time to start again.

'I was gutted,' Lyons said. 'I'd been an Evertonian since I was born. I was from the same council estate as Wayne Rooney, went to the same school. Dad worked down the docks, Mum worked for Littlewoods – you couldn't get more Scouse than that. Now I had to move away.

'So I was on my way home from signing for Wednesday and I was listening to the radio. "I'll Find My Way Home," by Jon and Vangelis, came on and I started getting tears in my ears. I'd been at Everton for over ten years, and I'd been a season ticket holder before that. I was upset.'

Unfortunately, the pub would not offer the solace he'd hoped for.

'So I'm sitting there with a pint – I was supposed to get home to the wife, but I needed a beer – and this bloke comes up to me and says, "I hear you're leaving." I said, "Yeah, that's right."

"Ah right", he goes. "Well, I always thought you were shite anyway."'

Suffice to say Lyons's new public wouldn't share this opinion. During his three and a half years at Wednesday, he would lead them back into the First Division and help them breach some of the most redoubtable footballing fortresses in the land. He would mould a group of youngsters into hardened professionals, and help catapult his team to one of the most successful periods in their history. His commitment, bravery and force of personality would set standards by which all future Wednesday players would be judged.

*   *   *

BUT ANYWAY, we're getting ahead of ourselves.

Lyons's arrival in the summer of 1982 was actually the final piece of Charlton's jigsaw, the last step in the three-year rebuilding project which was supposed to fashion a top-flight team.

The first season back in the Second Division, 1980/81, was one of consolidation. At home Wednesday won 14 games and lost only three but the problem came away, where the record was neatly reversed. That season's most memorable moment came not on the pitch but in the stands of Oldham Athletic's Boundary Park where a group of Wednesday fans went on the rampage, prompting the authorities to close part of Hillsborough for the subsequent home games.

The second season was better. Throughout that nine-month slog, Wednesday looked like First Division material. But the promotion push was scuppered by a defence that leaked goals like a rusty tug. In a crucial match at Vicarage Road in April, Graham Taylor's Watford cruelly ripped open the flaws, scoring four times in the first half and showing Wednesday just how far they still needed to go.

Throughout this two-year period, however, Charlton kept tinkering. Ever the footballing alchemist, he gradually phased out the lads who weren't quite up to the higher tiers and added a series of promising youngsters who'd caught his eagle eye.

Two of the best signings both abandoned top-division football to join Big Jack's project. Gary Shelton had been part of Aston Villa's title-winning squad of 1981; Gary Megson, son of Wednesday legend Don, had made a string of appearances for Everton. Ultimately, however, neither had really cut it at the top level.

At Hillsborough they created one of the best midfield partnerships in the entire league, let alone the Second Division. Shelton brought the perspiration, Megson the inspiration. In a league dominated by thuggish plodders, Wednesday's new pairing glittered like sapphires in a sump.

Up front there was another new signing, another Gary who, like Megson, had emerged from the muck and bullets of suburban Manchester. Setters convinced the boss to sign Gary Bannister, an 11st winger with one leg shorter than the other who'd left Coventry City because the club wanted to sign a player from America instead.

Many would have flinched at the idea of signing such a diminutive player for such a physical league. But Charlton and Setters knew that Bannister's waif-like frame hid an iron will. This was a lad who, growing up in Warrington, had taken to swinging across the Manchester Ship Canal, then as foul as an open sewer, in games of 'Tarzan' with his mates. A lad who had broken his leg so badly as a teenager that the bone had grown the wrong way – and yet still convinced Coventry to take him on.

'I was desperate,' Bannister recalls now. 'I'd grown up in a family of six, my three siblings and me in the same room. I wanted to get out of there – not many people are desperate to get to Coventry, but I was!

'By the time Wednesday came in for me, I was properly strong. I'd come up through Manchester pub football, which was no mean school, and I'd been hitting the gym every day at Coventry, building up my legs. I doubt Maurice Setters would have taken a punt on me if I wasn't able to hold my own.'

Bannister would only stay for three years at Hillsborough but he would score 20 goals in each of them, and become one of the most feared strikers outside the top flight. Of all the clubs he played for in his nomadic career, Wednesday is the one he remembers with the most fondness.

'I'd had reservations about dropping down from Division One, but I saw straight away that this was a much bigger club. I thought Highfield Road was a good stadium, but Hillsborough was on a different level. And the people – wow!'

*   *   *

These new signings didn't just gel on the pitch; they formed the tightest of units off it too. Megson and Bannister were particularly close, living together in a club house and sharing car journeys back to Manchester after games in Megson's Lancia Beta, with *Bat Out Of Hell* blaring out of the car window. Sometimes Charlton would even lob them his own car keys and tell them to take the motor for a spin (whether they were insured is a question lost in the mists of time).

But the real core of the squad were the Sheffield lads. Charlton had skilfully nurtured a fine crop of local players and together they became the beating heart of the club.

The Shirtliff brothers would travel everywhere together in Peter's old banger, and they'd often be joined by Mark Smith, now the fulcrum of the defence, and Charlie Williamson, a dependable left-back who never let the side down when he was called upon.

Together the local lads would go out after games, often for a good steak at the Berni Inn, where they'd pick one another's brains and help one another through the growing pains of professional football. Outsiders were welcome, too, although the accent was tricky for some. 'It was like they were speaking a foreign language!' Bannister recalls with a laugh.

Wherever that early-'80s team went, one man would invariably be holding court – a man who was on his way to becoming one of Wednesday's best-ever players.

Even by footballers' standards, Mel Sterland had risen from tough circumstances. He'd been reared on Sheffield's infamous Manor Estate, which would soon be dubbed the worst council sprawl in Britain by local MP Roy Hattersley, and taken his licks playing for The Three Feathers in Darnall, where Wednesday's scouts had picked him up. A lifelong Wednesday fan, he'd grown up idolising Tommy Craig and had run on the pitch to celebrate survival back in 1976.

To a man, the players interviewed for this book say that Sterland was a marvellous character, the sort of lad who'd do anything for anyone. But his tough upbringing had forced him to develop a streetwise cockiness. As he himself recalls, this had nearly got him into bother when he came to sign his first professional contract.

'I walked into the room and Jack was there with a flat cap, glasses, cigarette in his mouth and a copy of the racing post,' Sterland says. 'When I asked him for 250 quid a week, the whole lot fell off!

'He eventually shoved a contract under my nose and said "sign it or get out." So I signed! It was for about 60 quid a week plus bonuses.'

But Charlton came to love Sterland, as much for the player's jack-the-lad charm as his buccaneering approach to football. And in September 1981 Sterland's career was jumpstarted when Charlton's scout John Harris convinced him to have a go at right-back after an injury to Ray Blackhall. Soon he was voted into the PFA team of the year and starring in the England under-21 side.

Charlton had taken Mel Sterland and turned him into Zico.

*   *   *

But in the summer of 1982 Wednesday's likely lads were still raw. They had to be knocked into shape and hardened, so they could truly thrive among the knees and elbows of Second Division football.

'Zico! Zico!' Mel Sterland's all-action style and jack-the-lad personality made him a hero of the Kop.

There was certainly plenty of tough love to be found on the training field. Sterland recalls that Setters was 'a very, very hard man' but Toms was 'a different level altogether'. He adds, 'I remember going down injured in one game and I was holding my shin. Tomsy ran on and he just said, "Get up you soft fucker or I'll really break it." Jack and Maurice loved that!'

But Toms and Setters couldn't go on to the pitch with their young charges. Charlton, who'd been one of about half a dozen enforcers in that all-conquering Leeds team, was acutely aware that they needed a mentor, someone who would talk them through games and show them how to win.

In Lyons the manager recognised a fellow warrior. Still only 30, he had played nearly 400 games for Everton and won universal respect throughout the game, as much for his human decency as his bravery.

Although his rugged playing style had some detractors (like that bloke in the pub), Lyons's impact at Goodison had been so great that he would eventually be named an Everton Giant, a member of the club's illustrious hall of fame which, at the time of writing, includes only 30 names.

However he'd fallen out of the side as new manager Howard Kendall began introducing the young players who would eventually win him the league championship. For a man as passionate and dedicated as Lyons, that stung.

'I was still in the first team right up until I left Everton, but sometimes I'd be left out because we had really good young centre-backs like Billy Wright, Mark Higgins and Kevin Ratcliffe,' he remembers.

'So Howard called me in one day and said, "Listen, we've had offers for you from Sheffield Wednesday, would you fancy it?" We chatted in the office, and we decided I'd go to Sheffield and talk to them.

'Jack was away on international duty as a commentator [the World Cup was taking place in Spain at the time], so it was Maurice Setters I saw. He asked if I'd like to come to the club, we chatted about a few different things, and I said yes to the move.'

For all his sadness about leaving Everton, Lyons says he was 'made up' by the prospect of joining Charlton's upwardly mobile outfit.

'The ground was great, Jack was in charge and I thought it was really well-organised. Everyone made you feel welcome and all the lads mixed. It was a little bit different to Everton but there was a good atmosphere in the club. Everyone just seemed down to earth, ready to get on and do it.'

As soon as he arrived, Lyons began to inspire awe and affection in equal measure. Peter Shirtliff recalls that 'he was an inspiration for a young guy playing alongside him. He had such good habits. He trained hard, he took the job so seriously.'

Sterland, for his part, says that Lyons was 'magnificent. Great captain. Great guy. He was a winner. Even in five-a-side games he wanted to win. He did it in training and in the matches.

'If I went out and I wasn't defending properly he'd have a right go. "What are you fucking doing?" he'd shout. "Stop the cross." I used to think "yeah, whatever Lyonsy," but then I'd sit back after the game and think "yeah, he was right."'

Bannister, who was still learning his own trade at the other end of the pitch, gives an equally glowing testimony.

'Mick was just a leader,' he says. 'We had a young side and he brought them all together. Never stopped talking the whole time. And we all just had massive respect for him.'

Lyons didn't have to rant and rave to earn that respect. His former team-mates say he was a laid-back character in the dressing room, always happy to go with the banter. Shirtliff recalls with a chuckle that he'd often try on a foreign accent after a few drinks to make the lads laugh.

But his bravery was more than sufficient to win their loyalty. This is a man who, after all, once headed Norman Hunter's foot during a game. And when he wasn't nutting boots he was throwing his head at the dressing room ceiling before games, putting himself in harm's way before he'd even stepped on to the field. It's an act so tough, so foolish, that it makes you wince even thinking about it.

Lyons is remarkably blasé about his masochistic pre-match routine. 'It was just a superstition really, nothing more,' he explains, as if he were talking about putting his left boot on first or wearing a pair of lucky briefs. 'It wasn't a hard ceiling. I just used to flick the ceiling to visualise getting headers.

'At Everton we'd had a wall where you'd go and head the ball, so I took it a stage further and headed the wall itself. Psychologically, you'd do your warm-up and it was an extra stage to the warm-up, to help you get going.'

Sometimes he'd even rope other players in. Mel Sterland remembers one game where Lyons demanded a team-mate 'volunteer' to give the ritual an extra edge. 'He put one of the lads in front of him, and then he made me throw him the ball. The other lad had to jump with him.

'So they went up together and, of course, they banged heads. He had five stitches before he even got on the fucking pitch. Then he went out and performed. Fucking tremendous.'

Lyons, of course, thinks people make far too much of a fuss over him.

'People talk about the heading the wall and that kind of stuff, but I don't really think that I was an especially hard player. A fair player, sure. A player who gave his all, yeah. But a hard player? Nah.'

But his former Wednesday team-mates know the truth. They know that he was the epitome of everything a football captain should be, a man you would run through a brick wall for – if he hadn't smashed it down with his own head first.

By bringing Lyons to Hillsborough, Charlton hadn't just signed a player. He'd signed an extension of his own personality, a man who could take his own footballing values out on to the pitch.

With his new captain on board, Charlton's five-year rebuild was complete. Wednesday had a team worthy of the First Division. Now all they had to do was get there...

4

A TEARFUL GOODBYE

Jack Charlton sat sobbing in a corner of the dressing room, utterly inconsolable. After all those titles and cup finals, all those epic battles and glorious triumphs, losing still cut to the very quick of his being. And, as football pundits since time immemorial have reminded us, no defeat hurts more than an FA Cup semi-final.

Wednesday shouldn't even have lost. They hadn't been at their best but they'd still created better chances than Brighton. In the end, a combination of bad finishing and bad defending had cost them. The road to Wembley, which had lain so invitingly open a couple of hours earlier, had ended up going nowhere.

Little did any of those gathered in the dressing room know at the time but Charlton's journey with Wednesday would soon be over, too. After six highly eventful years, his time at Hillsborough was about to come to an abrupt end.

It had been a successful tenure by anyone's yardstick. Charlton had turned Wednesday from Third Division trundlers into Second Division promotion challengers, and created the nucleus of an excellent young side. In the end, however, the summit remained tantalisingly out of reach. Another man would have the privilege of reaching the peak.

Charlton, of course, would go on to do brilliant things with the Republic of Ireland, leading the Emerald Isle to its first World Cup and becoming a national treasure all over again.

It's just a shame he didn't enjoy that kind of glory at Hillsborough.

* * *

AT THE start of the 1982/83 season, everything seemed in place for Wednesday to push on to promotion. Mick Lyons's arrival had given the team a bedrock while Gary Shelton, Gary Megson and the chain-smoking Yugoslav Ante Mirocevic provided an ideal blend in midfield. Like all good Charlton teams, Wednesday were well-organised and hard-working; no one was going to be able to better them for effort or discipline.

Up front, Wednesday didn't have quite the firepower of some of their rivals (Clive Allen, Kevin Keegan and Gary Lineker all played in the Second Division

At the start of the 1982/83 season, Wednesday appeared ideally placed for glory.

that season) but they still looked a team full of goals. Andy McCulloch and Gary Bannister provided the classic 'big-man-little-man' combo, and Charlton had added David Mills, who'd been Britain's most expensive footballer just three years earlier.

There was one rather large fly in the ointment, however. Terry Curran had decided to leave, and as if that wasn't enough, he'd agreed a move to Sheffield United. It was an even bigger surprise than Charlton's own departure would be 12 months later.

Curran may never quite have recaptured the blistering form of his first full season at Hillsborough but he'd still been bloody good. In September 1981 Jimmy Hill had even suggested England manager Ron Greenwood should give him a call.

Controversy had never been far away, however. That infamous riot at Oldham in 1980 had actually been sparked by a fracas between Curran and Simon Stainrod, although Wednesday fans who were there that day will swear blind that their man was blameless in the exchange. Throughout his time at Wednesday, the fiery forward had clashed repeatedly with his manager. Their relationship reached a nadir when Curran tried to give Charlton advice on transfer targets, prompting a complete breakdown in communication. In the end United offered Curran a hefty signing-on fee to jump the fence.

Today, however, Curran admits he was wrong to leave. Although he would play a bit-part in the great Everton team which conquered England and Europe in the mid-'80s, the Goodison crowd never took to him as Hillsborough once had.

Curran should have been part of the Wednesday team that reached the big time again, the goal he'd set himself back in 1979. Instead he was condemned to watch from the outside.

When asked about his decision to leave Wednesday, Curran is clear. It remains his biggest regret in football.

*   *   *

As Curran readjusted to life in the Third Division, Wednesday started the new season like a train. The first eight league games brought six wins and by the end of October they were top of the table.

In their first two years back in the Second Division, Wednesday had struggled to score goals. But now they were flying in: in those first eight games they netted 21 times. McCulloch was as good a target man as there was in the Second Division at that time (in truth he was better than many in the top tier) and Bannister gorged on the knock-downs.

And in case those big guns failed to fire, Wednesday now had a secret weapon – one that was moulded from Sheffield steel.

John Pearson's school had overlooked Wednesday's training ground. As a youngster, playing for the Owls had dominated his every waking thought. Now he was forging a reputation as a reliable, versatile forward, and scoring the goals he'd rehearsed so often on the playing field.

'I didn't want to be a footballer,' Pearson says now. 'I wanted to be a *Sheffield Wednesday* footballer. I remember writing a letter to the secretary, Eric England, offering to help when we had an injury crisis. I was about six years old at the time!

'Other clubs had been interested in me but, really, there was never a choice. I was Wednesday through and through, and once they asked me to sign, that was it.'

Like many other young lads coming through the Wednesday system, Pearson was exposed to his manager's maverick streak from an early age.

'When we were apprentices he'd take us up on the Yorkshire Moors shooting. I hated it! He used to take me and Gavin Oliver up. Him and Tomsy would go off for a few pints and we'd eat this game pie.

'Then on a Wednesday everyone would have the day off, so Jack would make apprentices come and do jobs for him. We'd all go down, do his garden and paint his fence. I remember him showing me his World Cup medal. God it was heavy.'

Perhaps Charlton used these bonding rituals as a kind of rite of passage, to see whether youngsters were made of the right stuff to play in his team. If so, then Pearson clearly passed with flying colours and made his debut just a few days after his 17th birthday.

'I got my chance in the first team after Terry Curran had that fracas at Oldham, and scored on my debut. My dad was on holiday in Majorca and he didn't even know about it until he read it in the paper!

'From there it was a case of establishing myself in the team. By that 1982/83 season, I was very much part of the first team. It was a dream come true.'

Pearson wasn't the only local hero living out his dreams. The dressing room was built around the gang of Sheffield smartarses, led by clown prince Sterland whose repertoire of japes ranged from snipping socks to peeing in the shampoo bottles.

There were other jokers in the pack, too. Megson had installed himself as pisstaker general, flaying all and sundry with his one-liners, while McCulloch and Bolder were always game for a laugh.

But the players knew not to overstep the mark. If they did, they were painfully aware that Tony Toms would gladly step in to give them a kick up the arse – usually literally.

'He was a hard, hard man,' McCulloch recalls now. 'He was ex-SAS. If anyone ever tried to attack him in the street, he would have them on the deck before they had the knife out.

'Sometimes we'd try jumping him but it would never work. Three or four of us would try and sneak up on him and drag him down, but we never could. And if he ever caught you, God you were in trouble: if you did anything wrong to him, he'd make you walk round the training pitch, in agony, holding your wrist. Oh my God, the pain!

'He made us go on an SAS training course once, doing things like abseiling and stuff like that. We had to go through a Smartie tube full of water, right to the top, pull ourselves out the other side and wriggle free. You look at it and think "for God's sake!" I remember turning round when we were running and seeing Mirosevic going the other way, halfway up the hill! He just couldn't handle it. It was a great bonding trip though.'

But despite Toms' best efforts to instil fitness in the squad, Wednesday couldn't sustain their early momentum as the nights drew in and the pitches clogged up. A 1-0 loss at Shrewsbury heralded a run of nine league games without a win and a nadir was reached on New Year's Day with a 4-1 thumping at Burnley, who were on their way down to the Third Division.

Bannister was still finding the net regularly but for Pearson and McCulloch the goals had dried up. Mills was enduring a particularly rotten time, utterly unable to recapture his former glories. In fact during those grim months of November and December, Wednesday managed just eight goals.

How Charlton missed the craft of Curran. Perhaps, had he been given the freedom to move into the transfer market, he might have found another point of difference to reignite the promotion drive. Mick Lyons, for one, believes some fresh blood would have made all the difference.

'The standard of all the lads was really high,' he recalls now. 'I played alongside two excellent centre-halves, Peter Shirtliff and Mark Smith. I just thought we needed a few signings, a shot to get us going again.'

Sterland, typically, puts it more bluntly when he talks about the backing Charlton received from his paymasters.

'I thought Sheffield Wednesday shat on Jack. They didn't give him enough money to get the players he needed. Simple as.'

To add a further note of misery to that cheerless midwinter, Wednesday were knocked out of the League Cup at the quarter-final stage just when expectation was starting to bubble. Not for the first time (or indeed the last) it was Arsenal who snuffed out their hopes, winning 1-0 on a chilly January evening in a half-empty Highbury. At that stage it seemed the season was going to peter out.

Little did the players know, however, that they'd be treading the famed marble halls again before the season was out. And this time they'd be greeted by a full house.

*   *   *

Wednesday's FA Cup run began slowly. They needed three games to overcome Southend; the performance in the first replay, a 2-2 draw at Hillsborough, was so lacking in guile and cohesion that one fan, 35-year-old Bob Montgomery, complained to the South Yorkshire Consumer Protection Department that his team had violated the Trade Descriptions Act.

Wednesday eventually won through, however, and further victories over Torquay and Cambridge brought them a tie with Burnley in the sixth round, and a chance to avenge that New Year's Day battering.

After a 1-1 draw at Turf Moor, secured through a piece of typical Bannister opportunism, Wednesday produced arguably their best performance of the season to thrash their cross-Pennine rivals 5-0 in the replay.

And so on to the semi-final, Wednesday's first since 1966. Their opponents, Brighton & Hove Albion, were no mugs. They had a former Liverpool player in Jimmy Case and a future one in Michael Robinson. But Wednesday had nothing to fear. Their strapping young side was a match for most first division teams; they certainly had enough quality to deal with Brighton, who were on their way down.

There was a problem, though. Bannister, the man Charlton depended on so heavily for goals, had taken a knock in the Burnley game.

'I got a fractured cheekbone and was out for five weeks,' he recalls. 'I had the shape of the guy's elbow in my cheekbone! I had to sit around the whole match, wait for everyone to get changed and then go back to Hallam hospital. By the time the Brighton match came round, I'd missed a few games and was lacking match practice.'

As if that wasn't enough, Lyons was struggling too. Instead of girding his loins for the match with Brighton, readying himself for one final herculean effort, Wednesday's inspiration was barely able to raise a gallop.

'I desperately wanted to play in that Brighton game, but my knee was in bits,' Lyons says. 'In fact I ended up having surgery. I can't jog now because of that knee.

'In the end we went to do a last-minute fitness test – on Hampstead Heath! It must have been the nearest place we could get to from the hotel. I just had to get out there, even if I was only half-fit. As a football player, if you waited until you were 100 per cent fit, you'd never play.'

Lyons's injury meant a reshuffle of the squad. Instead of John Pearson, Charlton had to put defender Peter Shirtliff on the bench as cover. If the match went against his team, the manager had no one to throw on and get him a goal.

The mood in the camp was still pretty good. Most of the lads were blissfully untarnished by previous failures; they knew not the pain of losing on English football's cruellest stage.

Sterland remembers being in high spirits when he roomed with Ante Mirocevic the night before the game. 'For some reason, Jack put me and him together. I thought, "Fucking hell fire, I like a laugh and a joke!" He'd point to the radiator and say "Mel, Mel, this is a radiator" and I would tell him "yeah". Then some hostages came on the TV and he said "sausages", and I had to correct him. In the end I just said "bed" and put my hands over my eyes and said "sleep".'

But the jovial mood was punctured by a farcical moment the next day, as the players made their way to the stadium. In a truly bizarre oversight, Pat Heard and Simon Mills were left behind at the hotel and had to get to the ground in a taxi, a self-inflicted distraction that Charlton could ill afford. 'You'd think they'd do a head count, wouldn't you?' asks McCulloch, still incredulous after all these years.

Things were just as frenetic when the team arrived at Highbury. Sterland remembers his room-mate Mirocevic leaning out the window, trying to pass tickets to his family. Instead of providing an oasis of calm, the dressing room was jumping with nerves.

Perhaps it was understandable, then, that Wednesday started so poorly. Brighton went ahead early on with a screamer from Case and they could easily have had more, such was the confusion in the Owls' defence.

The second half brought a significant improvement, however, and Wednesday equalised when Mirocevic profited from a goalmouth scramble. But the back four never really looked comfortable, and one particularly hellish piece of defending allowed Robinson to tap home in front of the mortified Wednesday hordes on the North Bank.

'If we're honest with ourselves, we just didn't play well,' Sterland concludes. Lyons believes his team were the better side but they only had themselves to blame for the defeat. 'We had a chance to get to the biggest game in football and we blew it,' is his assessment.

For Lyons, the defeat was doubly (well, triply) painful given he'd already lost two semi-finals during his time at Everton.

'I was distraught. Some reporter came to me and asked, "Well, how do you feel?" I know he had a job to do, but really, come on! How do you think I feel?! If you've lost three semi-finals in a row, it seems like a lot more than a game.

'I knew I wasn't going to get many more chances, and I knew we were a better side than Brighton. We might not have beaten United in the final but we wouldn't have collapsed like they did in that replay.

'More than anything, I felt guilty. All our supporters wanted to go to Wembley and it's like we'd let them all down. We had the best support in that division.'

The dressing room, scene of such chaos a couple of hours earlier, was frozen in despair as the players wallowed defeat. John Pearson recalls the club's medical man, Dr Passell 'telling some awful gags – real knock-knock stuff, to try and lift the players. It was just really weird.'

In the middle of it all sat the manager, unable to hide his despair.

'The thing that really sticks with me is Jack Charlton crying,' Pearson continues. 'I remember glancing over at him in the changing room, bawling his eyes out. He went up in my estimation even more then. A guy who'd won the World Cup, won the league, won God knows what else with Leeds and he was affected like that. It made me realise just what it all meant to him.'

* * *

Indeed, it's obvious that Charlton held the respect of all his players.

'Some people had presence and he was one of them,' Shirtliff says. 'He'd make you scared, he'd give you praise but very sparingly. You were wary of him.' Sterland may have had his run-ins with Charlton, but he describes his former manager as 'a fantastic bloke. You knew exactly where you stood with him.'

Bannister is perhaps the most effusive of all. 'I was Jack and Maurice's man. They brought me in, I had a lot to thank them for. They put a lot of confidence in me. I was gutted we missed out on promotion when Jack was there, because I would have loved to get up with him.'

But why did Wednesday fall short? Was there anything in Charlton's managerial make-up that prevented him and his team from getting the promotion they so craved?

As a team builder he was as good as anyone. He knew exactly what was needed at each stage of his team-building project and he generally found the right piece to fit the puzzle. From McCulloch to Lyons, the signings usually delivered.

It was the same in his backroom staff. McCulloch says that 'he had the knack of finding the right people round him. He had the right people for coaching, motivation, [and] he had John Harris, who would look after the money side and had a gift for spotting talent, like he did by converting Mel into a full-back.'

Charlton was no slouch on the training ground either. Peter Shirtliff remembers him as, 'a really good coach, an amazing coach for young players really. He was really good at passing on certain tips and bits of advice, what to do in certain situations. We had a young back four and Jack helped us gel.

'I remember playing against someone who was really good at jumping and I was struggling with it. So Jack pulled me aside and said, "He wants to feel you and jump just before you. Keep moving your feet and he won't know when to jump. He'll look towards you and the ball will hit him." And do you know what, he was right!'

If things weren't working on the training ground, the manager was more than happy to go on and show them how to do it. Various players recall one particular day when a free-kick drill was going wrong. Charlton, in his brogues, strode on to the pitch, spotted the ball down and hammered it into the top corner from 25 yards. 'That's how you do it,' he said as he walked off.

If any fault can be found with Charlton the manager, it is his occasional lack of attention to detail.

Lyons says Charlton would 'do what he wanted' and occasionally leave the training ground to go fishing, although he insists this happened far less often than some might imagine. Sterland, meanwhile, suggests the manager would often just smoke on the side of the training pitch, 'coming up with mad stuff.'

'Once, we played Charlie Williamson at left-back all week and then he picked Pat Heard on the Saturday. Another time he picked the teams for a practice match and we ended up with 12 players on one side. When someone pointed this out to him he just told us to get on with it!'

Then there's the one about the great Shirty switcheroo. John Pearson tells the story with particular fondness.

'Once, before a game, when we had Paul Shirtliff and Peter Shirtliff, Jack came up with an idea to just write "P Shirtliff" as sub on the team sheet and put both of them on the bench. He said, "If a defender gets injured, we'll put Pete on. If a midfielder gets injured, we'll put Paul on." In the end Maurice had to talk him out of it!'

Peter Shirtliff remembers the story too, although he says he isn't sure Charlton would ever have dared try such a thing. Pearson, however, is adamant, 'Jack would have gone through with it, no question.'

Looking back nearly 40 years on, these stories engender only mirth and merriment. They're wrapped into our memory of Charlton, a genial nonconformist brimming with outlandish charm.

But might they have hindered Wednesday at crucial moments?

Bannister, for all his affection for Charlton, says, 'We didn't always prepare ourselves, fitness-wise, and it showed in the last ten or 15 minutes of games. Just a 1-2% extra would have done it.' This aspect of Wednesday's preparation would certainly be stepped up under the next managerial regime.

Viewed on the whole, however, Charlton's reign was a tour de force. He got Wednesday out of the quagmire of the Third Division and created the nucleus of a team that would eventually stun Liverpool and Manchester United. After all those years of hurt, he gave Wednesday back their pride – and, of course, he gave them Lyons.

Above all, he was a marvellous man. And his players will never forget that.

'Even when he was leaving, he sorted me out,' John Pearson says. 'He gave me a new contract, with extra security. That was just typical of the bloke.

'Wednesday will never have another manager like him.'

5
HOWARD FINDS A WAY

It had been a boozy few days for John Pearson. After a season in which he'd carved a niche in the first-team pecking order and established himself as a beloved jester in the dressing room, he was enjoying a lads' holiday in Benidorm with Peter Shirtliff, Kevin Taylor and a few of the other Wednesday roustabouts.

Then there was a rude awakening.

'I remember Kevin picked the paper up while I was on my morning beer and it said that Howard Wilkinson had been appointed,' Pearson recalls. 'My first thought was "Oh Christ!"'

'The other players around the table didn't even know who this bloke was. But Pearson certainly did.

'I remembered back to when I'd been picked for the England under-21s and he was there at the time. Jack had told us to report injured. He'd dropped us off at the bottom of the M1 and said, "Go in and tell him you're not fit to train. If you do train, you'll get fined."

'So I told Howard I had a groin strain and he just shrugged his shoulders and walked off, like I was a piece of dirt on his shoe.'

For Pearson, the holiday suddenly took a rather serious turn. His dream of playing for Wednesday, nurtured so tenderly since childhood, appeared to be in jeopardy.

'When I got home from Benidorm, my mum told me Howard had been on the phone and I needed to go and see him. So I went to the ground, without having a clue what he wanted. All I knew is that he hated me.

'So I tap on his door really gently. He marches out, opens his door and says, "Fucking hell, are you my fucking centre-forward?! Go and knock on that fucking door again!"

'So he shuts the door again. This time I batter hell out of it. He comes out again. "Right, that's fucking better, now go and fucking get changed."'

The new manager would spend the next ten days working alone with his young striker on fitness. Looking back now, Pearson says, 'He taught me how to be a professional footballer.' And he'd teach many others, too.

* * *

IT'S HARD to find two people more different than Jack Charlton and Howard Wilkinson. Jim Davidson and Germaine Greer, perhaps. Or maybe David Dimbleby and Paddy McGuinness. At a push, you might reach for Boris Johnson and Jeremy Corbyn.

But Charlton and Wilkinson were from totally different streams of the football management school. While both preached the gospel of direct, physical play, their sermons sounded remarkably different. Charlton was all about intuitive decisions and keep-it-simple-stupid thinking; Wilkinson relied on rigorous planning and preparation.

In today's football world, defined as it is by directors of football and long-term strategies, few clubs would countenance such a radical change of approach. But that's exactly what Wednesday did in the summer of 1983. And it was a move that would soon bring rewards.

Like Derek Dooley, Wilkinson had been reared on the Kop. Although he'd inexplicably trained with Sheffield United as a youth, it was Wednesday who gave him his debut back in 1962.

Like a lot of great managers he was a fairly ordinary player, appearing only 22 times for the first team during the halcyon days of the mid-'60s. Eventually he settled at Boston and became a titan of the lower leagues.

After training as a PE teacher in Sheffield he soon showed he had a gift for management. In 1982/83, the year before taking the Wednesday job, he guided Notts County to the dizzy heights of 15th in the First Division.

Nonetheless, it's fair to say his new players were underwhelmed by his appointment.

Mel Sterland recalls, 'I was on holiday with my wife. We didn't even know Jack had gone! I had to ring my dad to find out who'd got the job and he said "someone called Howard Wilkinson". I didn't know who he was.'

But Wilkinson knew the players. And, even more importantly, he knew what he needed to take them up.

Right from the start, Wilkinson's strategy was simple. Wednesday would control the controllables. Other teams might be more skilful, but none would be fitter or better-organised.

They could press high, play a tight offside trap and make sure every set-piece was orchestrated to perfection, in both boxes. They might not be a dream team but they could be everyone's worst nightmare.

This meant endless repetition in training. Lyons recalls that, 'Howard would always practise set-pieces. Half an hour, three quarters of an hour… as long as it took. We even practised long throw-ins, that's how detailed it was. Nothing was left to chance.

'But he really was a top manager. And straightaway you could see that he knew what he was about.'

To capitalise on all the centre-backs in his squad, Wilkinson decided to go 3-4-3. A decade on, at the start of the Premier League boom years, many of England's top sides, as well as the national team, would start playing three defenders. Back then the move was pretty much unheard of.

The decision made Wednesday hugely solid in the centre of the pitch but it placed major demands on the full-backs (well, the wing-backs) as well as the forwards. Wilkinson has since said that he wouldn't ask of a dog what he demanded of them.

To play this way, the new boss needed to freshen up his squad. He'd need players who would follow his instructions to the letter, conformists who would accept his intense physical demands without complaint. Dilettantes and iconoclasts were not welcome.

Ante Mirocevic had agreed a deal to return to Yugoslavia before Wilkinson even took over, which is probably just as well; the midfielder was blessed with flair to spare but he also liked a pint and a fag, and had even incurred the wrath of Charlton (no stickler for the rules himself) by trying to light a cigarette inside the stadium on one occasion. It's hard to imagine him fitting into Wilkinson's monastic regime.

A far more painful departure, for both the players and the fans, was that of McCulloch, who moved to Crystal Palace after a hugely popular four-year stay at Hillsborough.

'Howard said I could stay if I wanted, but I just felt I was coming to the end,' McCulloch recalls. 'I wanted to be able to give 100 per cent to Sheffield Wednesday and I knew I wasn't able to do that. It's always better to leave on top than go on too long. Plus I got a few bob out of the deal.

'Looking back, though, it was a mistake. I didn't enjoy the move to be honest. Wednesday was a high point of my career.

'I loved the area. We lived out in the country in a place called Millthorpe, near Chatsworth, and there was a guy whose dad owned a big club in Sheffield. I got to take this horse out twice a week – thank God the club didn't find out!

'But the fans were what made it for me. Even now they come up to me. There's a fella called Scott Rowlinson, very well educated, lovely kids, in his 40s, and he's got a tattoo of me scoring a hat-trick. It's amazing, I can't even remember the games! If you give the Wednesday fans 100 per cent, they give it back.'

*   *   *

Another man ready to fly the Owls' nest was Bob Bolder, who was out of contract and unhappy with the money Wednesday were offering. In the end he got an offer out of the blue from Liverpool, who were looking for an understudy for Bruce Grobelaar.

At the time, Bolder's decision to leave was seen as a major blow. This was a guy who'd played over 200 times for the club and become a senior player under Jack Charlton. He'd never been a world-beater but neither had he let anyone down.

However, Wilkinson knew the perfect man to replace him. Or rather Mick Lyons did.

'I recommended Martin Hodge to them,' says Lyons. 'He was my best mate, and I was happy to tell them he was a top lad.

'He was in the reserves at Everton and wasn't getting much of a look in ahead of Neville Southall. To be honest, though, I thought there wasn't much between him and Neville. Hodgey was miles better than reserve football and he'd show that later on.'

Lyons realised that Hodge fitted the Wilkinson mould perfectly. His journey to the top had been fuelled by an insatiable work ethic, ever since he'd been spotted by a bloke who worked as a lifeguard on Southport beach and did a bit of scouting for Plymouth in his spare time. Even when he'd run into the brick wall of Big Nev at Everton, Hodge had continued to throw himself into training like a trojan.

'It hadn't really happened for me at Everton,' Hodge himself recalls. 'I had a serious chest injury that kept me out for a long time, I'd got my knee stuck in the sand messing around on the beach. But Neville played me the ultimate compliment when he said in his book that he'd never seen anyone work as hard. My dad would have been proud of that. That's what he instilled in me.

'So I got a call from Mick, saying, "We've got a goalkeeper here, Iain Hesford, but he's the only one. I've told Howard [Wilkinson] how good you are." I said, "Well, I need to speak to Howard," so he got in touch and asked if I wanted to come for a month. I said not really – I'd rather sign, if that could be sorted out. So I signed and the rest is history. Best five years of my career.'

Now Lyons had his pal by his side. He and Hodge would share digs, not to mention car journeys back to Merseyside. Hodge didn't just prove an amazing goalkeeper; he allowed Lyons to become even better, and set an example alongside him in training.

'People like Mel, Mick, Meggo, maybe myself… we had that winning mentality. It went hand in glove with Howard,' Hodge recalls fondly.

In fact the Wednesday dressing room was becoming something of a refuge for former Evertonians. Gary Megson, of course, had played at Goodison before swapping Merseyside for South Yorkshire. And, just in case they needed any more cohorts, Wilkinson decided to move for Imre Varadi, a striker who had also played at Everton (and, like the manager himself, had actually started his professional career on the wrong side of the tracks at Bramall Lane).

The Londoner had faced his own struggles breaking into Everton's first team but had made a much bigger impression at Newcastle, scoring 39 goals in 81 games before Wednesday came calling. Blessed with both pace and power, this son of Hungarian immigrants would provide the perfect foil for both Pearson and Bannister.

To stiffen the other end of the pitch, Wilkinson plumped for another young Cockney who would go on to become one of Wednesday's most consistent players of the 1980s.

Lawrie Madden, by his own admission, didn't really look like a footballer. But he was another 100-per-center, possessed of both leadership skills and a burning intellect; like Varadi, who has established his own football agency, Madden has enjoyed considerable success since hanging up his boots, becoming a journalist and university lecturer.

Raised in the bustling Irish enclave of Bethnal Green, Madden had already shown his independent streak by turning down the chance to sign professional forms with Arsenal to go to university. 'Bob Wilson, who was first-team goalkeeper at the time and had also gone to uni, said I should sign for Arsenal, but I decided otherwise,' he says.

'I was from a big working-class family. My dad was one of ten siblings, mum one of seven. She worked as a cleaner and a conductress for London Transport, he worked in the booking office at King's Cross Station. No one in the family had been to university. That was a big thing.'

Lawrie Madden wasn't your typical footballer, but he was one of Wednesday's most reliable players of the 1980s.

In his final year studying at Manchester, Madden was persuaded to come and play for Boston. No formal contract, just expenses to cover the train fare. There he met Wilkinson, taking his first steps as a manager.

The relationship blossomed. Although they were never close – Madden recalls that Wilkinson could be 'aloof' with his players – they appreciated one another's intelligence and professionalism. Most importantly, Wilkinson looked beyond Madden's lumbering style and saw that there was a serious player buried beneath those sloping shoulders.

In fact Madden was deceptively quick – at Millwall he'd played alongside Sam Allardyce, picking up the runners while Big Sam grappled with the target men. At Hillsborough he would do the same job for Mick Lyons, giving the backline an ideal blend of muscle and finesse. With Hodge behind them, and Chris Morris now ready to challenge for the full-back berths, Wednesday would boast the most solid defensive unit in the division.

*   *   *

But before they could test themselves against the rest of the Second Division, Wilkinson was determined to knock his squad into shape. Maurice Setters and Tony Toms were eased out and in their places came Peter Eustace and Alan Smith. Together with Wilkinson, they implemented the most brutal pre-season regime the players had ever known.

Charlton's training sessions, which had focused heavily on sprints, gave way to endless long-distance runs in the valleys around Sheffield. Wilkinson, a keen runner himself, would join them and would usually end up near the front of the pack.

'Oh my god, I hated it,' Bannister says. 'People were going down like flies, being sick everywhere. Sit ups, star jumps – the whole lot. Howard and Alan Smith, the physio, pushed you to your absolute limits.

'There's always a lot of fitness work in pre-season. As a footballer, you expect it. But this was something else. Howard would go out on his own around the hills and reservoirs, usually in the Rivelin Valley or around Ewden Reservoir, and plot these brutal ten or 12-mile runs. Then we'd have to follow him.

'When we'd come back from these runs, we'd have to run up and down the stands. It felt like it went on for months, like a prison sentence.'

Wilkinson would tone down the running when the season started, but he'd never stop completely. Some of the players, like Lyons and Shelton, took to it like ducks to water. For others, though, it was a daily ordeal that no amount of repetition would dilute.

'I moved to Sheffield and when my family come over they said, "How come you know all these walks?"' Hodge says. 'I told her, "Because I've run every single one."

'We would go on five, six, seven-mile runs and in between that you'd go up steep hills for six to ten miles. You couldn't get away with cutting corners. Howard would have spotters everywhere, so you had to run every metre. Nobody could walk.

'We'd do all the dams, we'd go on an 11-miler down to Ladybower Reservoir. You'd get to where you thought you were finishing, after a 90-minute run, and he'd say "right, 30 minutes' extra time".

'The lads hated it and they hated Howard for making us do it. It was horrible. You'd be sliding down these freezing hills on your backside. But it made you a team. Without us doing that, we wouldn't have been the team we were. It would be scorned today, but to win games and have a successful team, that was part of it.'

Wilkinson's approach certainly paid dividends when the season finally kicked off. His team went a full 18 games unbeaten, swatting fellow promotion challengers like Leeds and Chelsea aside. The defence, which had been sound under Charlton, was now inpenetrable, conceding only one goal in the first four matches.

As the success began to flow, so did the criticism. Wednesday were written off by the media as a long-ball team, an insult to the traditions of English football and the players who had made it great.

Looking back now, the players don't refute the criticisms. Lyons admits 'we normally played a bit long' under Wilkinson. But context is important here.

'The long ball was in vogue back then,' Lawrie Madden points out. 'Watford were playing that way under Graham Taylor, who was very good pals with Howard. The year before Howard joined Wednesday, Watford had finished second in the league. Then they reached the FA Cup Final. So it's understandable that other teams thought that was the way forward.'

But if Wilkinson was to emulate the success Taylor had enjoyed at Watford, he knew he would need a big squad. Specifically, he would need a roster of forwards who could deliver the high-energy pressing his system relied on. They had to keep chasing long balls into the corners and keep closing down the defenders. It was a thankless task, requiring real strength in depth.

So in November Wilkinson decided to bolster his ranks with a player whose physicality would have made even Mick Lyons wince.

Tony Cunningham fit Wilkinson's template perfectly. Like Madden and Varadi, he'd been moulded by an immigrant upbringing having moved from Jamaica at the age of seven to join his parents in Wolverhampton. He was humble and hardworking, the sort of guy who'd do whatever his gaffer asked of him. And he was a seriously bright bloke who, like many others interviewed for this book, would flourish when his football career was over.

Back then, though, Cunningham was a hugely imposing man, blessed with leonine bravery and a physical frame that enabled him to dominate the burliest centre-half. He never went out looking for trouble on the field but he would never back down if it got in his way.

'I wasn't a dirty player,' Cunningham says, 'I only ever crossed the line to respond to the aggression I was being subjected to. But I was forceful and robust. I wanted to get to the top and nothing would intimidate me. Football was very, very serious to me.

'I poured everything into my training so I knew that, come matchday, I would be as prepared as I could be. Once I had a smile on my face, that was it, you were in trouble. I was all confidence and aggression. You couldn't intimidate me.'

Cunningham's power had stood out ever since he was spotted by Lennie Lawrence while playing amateur football for Kidderminster. 'A ball came over in the game and I went up with the two centre-halves. The ball ended up in the net, they ended up on the floor. Lennie told me later that he didn't need to watch any more!' Lawrence took Cunningham to Lincoln, where he was cutting his teeth as a coach, and the new signing made his league debut against Barnsley, whose defence was anchored by Norman Hunter. Far from being intimidated by the great man, Cunningham played so well that Hunter would make him his first signing when he became manager at Oakwell.

By the time he arrived at Hillsborough, Cunningham was 26 and entering his prime. Wilkinson knew that his strength and speed would make him the perfect battering ram to blast a way out of the Second Division. That fast-twitch physique, however, was hardly suited to the daily grind of Wednesday's training sessions.

'I was quick,' Cunningham says. 'I was once approached by the England athletics manager to become a sprinter. I could run the 100 metres and do it again and again, with minimal recovery. In that respect, I was the fittest player at the club. But I'm not a cross-country runner, never have been.'

This much became apparent when the squad went for a Monday run at Ewden soon after he joined. With winter beginning to set in, the ground was soggy and the light fading. Cut off at the back of the group, Cunningham inevitably got lost.

'Howard said "leave him",' Madden recalls. 'So we all got back to Hillsborough and were just getting changed when TC turned up - on the back of a tractor! Some local farmer had taken pity on him and given him a ride.

'It was a bit of a joke from Howard, but a lesson as well – this is how fit you've got to be to play for me.'

*   *   *

But if Cunningham didn't quite cut it in the boggy foothills of the Peak District then he certainly did on the turf of Hillsborough. On 19 November a Newcastle side featuring Kevin Keegan, Chris Waddle and Peter Beardsley arrived with 10,000 fans in tow. Wednesday simply ran riot with Varadi scoring against his old club and Cunningham marking his home debut with a goal.

By now, the players realised they had a real chance of going up. And their initial resentment towards Wikinson's fitness methods began to morph into real respect. They could see their body shapes changing because of all the running and they could see that it was bringing results on the field.

'People might turn their nose up at some of the stuff Howard did, all the repetition of set-pieces, but what's wrong with that?' John Pearson asks. 'What's wrong with practising free kicks if you score goals from them and win games? I don't understand why you wouldn't practise free kicks and work on things like that.

'The level of detail was incredible. We'd work on what would happen if the opposition crossed the ball and Martin Hodge collected it. Who would he throw it to? How could he get it to the full-back so the full-back wouldn't have to take a touch?

'Even the ball boys were brought into it. We were one of the first to get the ball boys to throw the balls back quickly to us and slowly to the opposition. Howard literally thought of everything.'

Some players were more obliging than others, of course. Gary Bannister admits that he would speak out if he thought Wilkinson was going too far. 'I wasn't difficult, but I didn't mind saying my piece if I thought something was wrong. I was confident that I was a good player and I wasn't afraid of answering back to the manager.'

But the squad was so tight that they basically controlled themselves; any dissent would be swiftly nipped in the bud and minds refocused on the collective goal.

The pranksters and the thinkers, the Sterlands and the Maddens, took the piss out of one another relentlessly but always had one another's backs. All those dark, cold mornings out on the moors forged an *esprit de corps* that no one could break.

'That group of lads that got promoted, we went through everything,' Peter Shirtliff says. 'It was an amazing group of lads. We got each other through.'

Other teams may have been out every night of the week, pissing their wages up the wall. But on Wilko's watch the Wednesday lads were barred from going out after Tuesday. In Lyons he had the perfect man to enforce the rule; the skipper might join the lads at Josephine's on Monday, after their longest run of the week, but after Tuesday he wouldn't touch a drop. He loved a party as much as anyone, but only when the time was right.

'After Tuesday night that was it,' Martin Hodge, Lyons's digs buddy, recalls. 'Wednesday, Thursday, Friday we'd stay at home or we might go for a game of snooker at the police club on Niagara Road just round the corner.

'Off the pitch, Mick lived life to the full. But he knew when it was pleasure and when it was business, and he was the ultimate pro. Brilliant, brilliant, brilliant.'

Of course, the lads would try and break the rules now and again. But it rarely worked out well.

'I got injured in that Newcastle game and ended up getting stretchered off,' John Pearson recalls. 'So I knew I was out of the next game, at Crystal Palace. It was a real blow — we were still unbeaten and everyone wanted to play.

'I went out to the Park Hotel, close to where I live and near the ground, on the Wednesday. It seemed fine as I was definitely out of the game. I bumped into one of the directors, who asked me if I was going to the game. I said I wasn't sure so the director said he'd speak to Howard. All he did was land me in the shit!

'In the dressing room at Selhurst Park before the game, Howard bollocked me in front of anyone. Really tore strips off me about being unprofessional, even though I wasn't playing. He fined me, too.

'But then, when the lads had gone out, he whispered to me, "If we win today, you're on a win bonus with the rest of the lads." Turns out he was only using me to prove a point!'

Doubly frustratingly for Pearson, Wednesday lost – their first defeat in over three months of football.

Others would have been rocked by this setback but Wilkinson and Lyons ensured their charges stayed focused. They bounced back straight away with a brilliant win at First Division Stoke in the League Cup, then secured a crucial victory at Manchester City with a double from Varadi, prompting City boss Billy McNeill to declare them the best team in the division. As if to prove his point they then went and thrashed Cardiff 5-2 in the final game before Christmas.

For once, Wilkinson decided to let his lads off the leash. And his captain decided it was time for Mad Mick to come out.

'Mick Lyons organised a Christmas party,' John Pearson recalls. 'We told him we were all going in fancy dress, but we all chatted among ourselves and decided we weren't going to do it – we'd just let him come on his own!

'So he came in this caveman outfit, like Fred Flintstone. He had all his muscles painted on; he'd even gone to the extent of getting that big bone that Fred had.

'So we went to one of the clubs in Sheffield. As the only one in fancy dress, you might think he'd be a bit sheepish. But no, not Lyonsy. He was up in the DJ booth, putting tunes on, getting the crowd dancing. He was absolutely wrecked!

'He ended up crashing at a mate's house that night, woke up in the morning and realised he didn't have his car, didn't have any money, all he had was his outfit. He had to walk back from his mate's on the edge of town to the training ground, freezing, dressed as a caveman. What a guy.'

Lyons himself says he doesn't remember the night. But he does concede it sounds like the sort of thing he might have done.

* * *

Despite a couple of annoying defeats over the festive period, Wednesday soon regained their composure. And as if the promotion push wasn't enough to excite the fans, there was the visit of Liverpool in the fifth round of the League Cup, which saw the Reds, who would go on to win the trophy as well as the First Division and the European Cup, lucky to escape with a 2-2 draw.

The replay, however, wasn't so evenly contested. Wednesday were hammered 3-0. Soon enough they'd be knocked out of the FA Cup even more convincingly by Southampton, who triumphed 5-1. It was the worst defeat of the season and it also produced one of the biggest bust-ups, with Cunningham at the heart of it.

'I wasn't fully fit but Howard wanted me to play,' Cunningham recalls. 'I had a bit of an injury, I told Howard, but he reiterated that he wanted me to play.

Mark Wright would have been marking me for Southampton so they needed a big striker up against him.

'So I played, and in the second half I dislocated my shoulder. I was literally holding my arm. The centre-half could see that, so he pulled it down! The pain was excruciating.

'I waved to the bench halfway through the second half, and said I needed to come off. I was substituted and we lost the game. When I got back to the dressing room, Howard said, "You let me down today." On reflection Howard was probably angry that we'd lost the game and his emotions took over.

'I said to him, "Listen, you knew I was injured, you knew I was struggling to play, and you asked me to play. I went on the pitch to play – for you. If I didn't play to the standard expected, that's because I was injured, and you knew that. You've got no right to be shouting at me. I didn't let you down, you let yourself down." And we had this big argument.'

Cunningham is a huge admirer of Wilkinson but he maintains he was right to rail against the criticism.

'I'm no shrinking violet. Managers don't buy me, don't pick me because I'm a shrinking violet. They expect me to stand up to whatever's thrown at me. But sometimes they don't like it when they throw things at you and you stand up against it.'

Thankfully the two men, and their team, soon patched things up. Grimsby, Portsmouth and Derby were all seen off, and a stunning Shelton overhead kick sealed victory at Newcastle in front of thousands of travelling fans. Easter still hadn't arrived but Wednesday's ascension already felt like a formality.

With each passing week, Wilkinson revealed another part of his managerial repertoire. Every trick in the book was pulled out to ensure the players stayed fresh.

'I remember before the game against Portsmouth, and he started this team talk,' Pearson says. 'He said, "Well the goalkeeper's six foot three, comes out and catches everything. The right-back never stops, he's up and down all day. The centre-halves head everything that comes near them." And he kept going on like that. We're thinking, "Christ, who are we playing this afternoon?"

'So then he turns round and says, "That's what their manager's just been telling them in there. Just think how scared they are now." He was so clever like that.'

The squad continued to improve, too. Wilkinson went back to Notts County to sign Nigel Worthington, a player he trusted implicitly. Worthington was a seriously good player, a guaranteed seven-out-of-tenner every week. He was also a seriously decent bloke and exactly the sort of character you need to build a successful side.

'I guess I was a bit of a goody two-shoes,' Worthington says. 'Howard knew exactly what he was going to get from me and he knew that he could trust me.

'The dressing room was great. Right from the start, the lads did everything they could to make me feel welcome. Mel Sterland was always running around causing chaos, but he became a great mate of mine – we just clicked straightaway.'

Indeed, everything was clicking smoothly into place. When Crystal Palace visited Hillsborough on 28 April, Wilkinson's players knew that victory would take them up.

Andy McCulloch was given the Palace captaincy to mark his return to Sheffield. It was a sentimental gesture which prompted a rousing reception from the Wednesday fans, but it did nothing to douse the enthusiasm of the players. Wednesday tore into Palace with controlled fury, winning every 50-50 and second ball. But despite all their pressure, they couldn't score.

Then, midway through the second half, a long diagonal from Worthington was flicked on to Cunningham, who wrestled his way between two defenders before being brought down by Palace centre-half Billy Gilbert. A penalty in front of the Kop.

Perhaps fittingly the responsibility fell to Mel Sterland, who'd been through the club's grimmest days as a fan. With three goals in his previous five games, 'Zico' was a man in form; even more importantly, he possessed balls of steel. The kick was placed unerringly into the corner, beating the despairing dive of the Palace goalkeeper. 'An unbelievable feeling,' is how Sterland describes it now.

Suddenly it all came in a blur... the final whistle, the lap of honour, Lyons shoeing fans off the pitch, the interviews in the dressing room, and then another amazing night out in Sheffield – with Lyons, of course, holding court.

'I don't think I was sober for five days,' Sterland recalls. 'We went everywhere – all the local pubs, and Josephine's of course. It was just constant drinking.'

Perhaps unsurprisingly, the players lost a bit of focus with promotion secured. Wednesday lost at Shrewsbury and drew at home to Manchester City, allowing Chelsea to sneak into top spot on goal difference.

In truth, the fans didn't really care. The final game, at Cardiff, turned into a giant party with hordes of giddy Wednesdayites making the 200-mile trek down to South Wales. One fan unfurled a banner with the message 'The Hibernation Is Over. The Owls Are Back'.

Looking back now, however, some of the players say they wish they'd seen the job through and won the title they so patently deserved. Martin Hodge says, 'We led the league for ages and then Chelsea pipped us at the end. We'd been promoted in April so we basically threw it away, and I really regret the fact that we didn't win it.'

But if there was any gloom around the camp, it didn't last. To celebrate their promotion the players booked themselves on a flight to Mallorca, which would go down in club folklore as one of the all-time great trips.

'It was basically a non-stop drinking contest,' Gary Bannister recalls. 'Mick Lyons made us all drink a bottle of brandy on the plane, and that was before we'd even taken off. These days you'd probably get kicked off the flight for being as rowdy as we behaved.

'Then, one day, we started playing this daft game where a person would be drinking a bottle of beer and you'd push it up from below, so the bottle would smash up into their teeth. The number of lads who went home with bruised cheeks and chipped teeth was unbelievable.

'It was one of the most stupid things I've ever seen. But who cared? We'd finally done it.'

As if that wasn't enough to infuriate the locals, Cunningham provided an unforgettable send-off.

Pearson recalls, 'On the last morning there was this scream from one of the bedrooms and it went on and on for about ten minutes. It was Tony. He might have been dreaming, I don't know, but he was screaming at the top of his voice. It woke the entire hotel up. They were glad to see us go!'

But the players had more than earned their few days in the Spanish sun. They'd slogged their guts out all year and created a unit that was so much more than the sum of its parts. There've been more talented teams in Wednesday's history, but there haven't been any more resilient.

'We were a bunch of misfits,' Hodge says. 'I couldn't get into the Everton team, neither could Gary Megson. Gary Shelton couldn't get into the Villa team, Mick Lyons was coming towards the end.

'But all these lads came together for a period of time, and it was just brilliant.'

6

BLOODYING THE NOSES OF GIANTS

It's 29 September 1984. Wednesday are playing at Anfield in the league for the first time in 14 years. In the intervening period Liverpool have won eight league titles, two UEFA Cups, an FA Cup and four European Cups, the last of which came just a few weeks ago. Wednesday have won... well, let's move on.

The first part of the match goes to script. Liverpool, kicking towards the Kop, force their unfancied visitors on to the back foot and create a string of chances. Surely a goal is inevitable.

The goal duly comes. But it's Wednesday who grab it. Bruce Grobbelaar races out of his goal, attempting to intercept a through ball, but only succeeds in tapping it into the path of Varadi. Where others might flay the opportunity into the stands, Varadi rounds Grobbelaar and strokes home from the corner of the area, sparking a mini pitch invasion by the Wednesdayites mobbed up at the Anfield Road End.

Then, in the second half, Mel Sterland and Brian Marwood combine beautifully down the right. Zico fires in a shot, Grobbelaar commits another howler and Shelton pokes the ball in under the flaming nostrils of the Red hordes.

Liverpool huff and puff but the best chance falls to Lee Chapman, who is denied by Grobbelaar. Wednesday run the clock down with little fuss. Then the whistle goes.

*   *   *

LOOKING BACK now, it's hard to quantify just how remarkable that victory at Anfield was. Wednesday hadn't claimed such a scalp since the days of Twiggy and Carnaby Street, when Richard Nixon was still an honest man and there wasn't a single footprint on the surface of the moon. When football, and the world, was still black and white.

But several more notches would be added to the Wednesday belt in the two years that followed the glorious assault on Anfield. Wilko's wonders would take further points off the Merseyside giants and become the scourge of Manchester

United, subjecting Ron Atkinson to the sort of tactical masterclasses that would later become his own calling card at Hillsborough.

For the people of Sheffield, still reeling from the miners' strike, the football provided a source of pride. For two years they would be able to channel their socioeconomic frustrations into sporting excellence. Rival fans would taunt the Sheffielders all season, but their heroes would usually have the final word.

'I thought Division One would be a lot harder,' Mel Sterland recalls now. 'But we knew we had a manager who knew what he wanted to do. The fitness, organisation, discipline… all that stuff.

'Then when the matches came, we'd just go out and demolish teams in the first 25 minutes. It was amazing what we did, really.'

*   *   *

For scores of Wednesdayites, the summer of 1984 was a time of unremitting turmoil.

On 19 April, nine days before their team sealed promotion against Crystal Palace, the National Union of Mineworkers met in Sheffield and called on its members to come out on strike. For months the mines around the city remained at a standstill as a high-stakes game of brinkmanship with Margaret Thatcher's government dragged on.

On 18 June the tension finally erupted into a full-scale battle between police and miners at Orgreave, a coking plant just seven miles from Hillsborough. Police were caught on camera charging at their opponents and beating them with truncheons, but the only ones to be prosecuted were the ones behind the pickets. A day after the clashes, Thatcher made her infamous reference to 'the enemy within.'

But in all this misery and anger, football provided a chink of light. Just like on Merseyside, where Everton and Liverpool were giving thousands of unemployed Scousers reason to cheer with their dominance of the First Division, Wednesday fans could occasionally forget about their ordeal and look forward to returning to the top flight.

For over a decade they had had to watch smaller clubs such as Ipswich, Derby and Nottingham Forest grinning down from the top of the football pyramid, winning titles and getting to cup finals. Now, finally, they had been allowed back to the top table.

The players knew how much promotion meant to their followers. The Shirtliff brothers had been raised in a mining family and even the outsiders, the ones not privileged to have been born within the seven hills, were amazed by the dedication of the fans. Lawrie Madden, for one, recalls that the Wednesday away support was huge during this period and credits this as a major factor in the club's success.

If anyone forgot the significance of the badge they were playing for, Wilkinson would soon remind them. A born-and-bred Sheffielder himself, he was keen for his players to be meshed into the local community and has since spoken of his pride at the way the club helped their fans during those grim days of the mid-1980s, when many were wondering where their next wage packet was coming from.

But, as he plotted his team's return to the First Division, the manager knew he could not afford to be swept away by emotion. Wednesday may have belonged in the top flight but he realised that some of the players that had got them there weren't quite up to the highest standard.

No decision was more ruthless than the one to call time on Tony Cunningham, who had given his all to get Wednesday over the promotion line.

'Wilko called me into his office at the end of the season and told me he was buying someone else. He told me I wouldn't be playing in the First Division,' Cunningham recalls.

'It was a horribly uncomfortable conversation, devastating really. Playing in the First Division was all I wanted to do. I had dedicated my entire life to getting to the top, then I'd finally got to the top, and had it taken away from me.

'But I understand Howard's job is to do the best he can for Sheffield Wednesday. If he thinks someone else can play my position better than me, he's got every right to make that call.'

If the sale of Cunningham was harsh, the departures of Megson and Bannister seemed downright barmy. The two Mancunians weren't just best mates off the pitch, they were the heartbeat of the team and clearly possessed the quality to step up.

In the end, though, it was just business. Together the two sales raised £450,000, a significant profit on the fees Jack Charlton had paid to bring them to Hillsborough. And while Megson got on well with Wilkinson, whom he has cited as the biggest influence on his managerial career, Bannister's relationship with his boss was more tetchy.

Looking back now, in fact, Bannister believes Wilkinson was looking for an opportunity to get rid of him.

'I went in to renegotiate my contract after we'd won promotion and Howard offered me 25 quid a week more,' he recalls wistfully. 'Twenty-five quid! So I was only being offered 275 quid a week to play in the First Division. I think it was Howard's way of clipping my wings and bringing me down to earth.

'QPR offered me 600 quid a week. I understand that Wednesday fans were upset and some may have held it against me, but I ask them: what would you have done?

'I wanted to stay, but Howard had made it clear that there were new players coming in and he wanted me gone.'

These sales offered Wilkinson crucial wriggle room in the transfer market, enabling him to give the squad an injection of fresh, hungry talent.

The manager opted to replace Megson with Andy Blair, a man who had played against Barcelona for Aston Villa and earned a reputation as one of the more cultured players in the league. It was a reputation he would burnish at Hillsborough, adding a touch of guile to the Wednesday midfield – despite his often crippling self-doubt.

'I had a great engine,' Blair recalls. 'In fact that was my nickname when I started out at Coventry, "Engine". People say I could pass the ball, too. But to be honest I never thought I had that much ability.

'Gospel truth – only when I left Sheffield Wednesday to rejoin Villa did I think "actually, maybe I can play." That was the first time I thought I could make it as a footballer.'

Fortunately Wednesday's two biggest signings that summer had self-confidence in spades – and they would go on to form a symbiotic relationship in the months ahead.

Brian Marwood and Lee Chapman were both out of the classic Wilkinson school. Both had been around a bit, both were hungry to succeed and both possessed a lively mind which would serve them well in later life (like Lawrie Madden before him, Chapman had been offered a place at Manchester University before settling on football).

At Wednesday, the pair complemented one another perfectly. Marwood was a prototype David Beckham, a winger whose lack of pace was compensated by his ability to bend crosses around his opponent. Chapman couldn't get enough of them.

Strong and smart, Lee Chapman fitted perfectly into Howard Wilkinson's system – and into the Wednesday family.

Off the pitch, one might have expected Chapman, who was already in a relationship with the actress Leslie Ash, to be a bit too refined for the rough-and-tumble of Wednesday's dressing room. But while Chapman was certainly a cut above the standard football fare – he would occasionally take team-mates on cocktail-tasting sessions, or on gastronomic tours of Sheffield's most exclusive restaurants – he was always right in the thick of it when the banter started flying.

'I was the son of a footballer,' says Chapman. 'I'd grown up in dressing rooms, had the initiations. You learn to attack first before getting it and learn how to bounce back.

'What I found at Wednesday was amazing. Sometimes dressing rooms aren't honest places. There are people there that you wouldn't like to be in a bunker with, but there was a lot of honesty in the Wednesday dressing room. Maybe not the greatest players in the world, but totally committed. We used to go on a night out and everyone would turn up. That would never happen now.'

There can be no more glowing testament to Chapman's character than his friendship with Lyons, who took the new signing under his wing as soon as he arrived. Within weeks the skipper had moved into the neo-Georgian pile Chapman had acquired in High Green (Wilkinson, incidentally, was 50 yards down the road) and would stay there for the rest of his Wednesday days.

'People might think Lee was a bit of a fashionista, but really nothing could be further from the truth,' says Lyons.

'We were kind of the odd couple, because Chappy was conscious of his weight and his image, so we ate different foods. And he was a bit fernickety about his clothes, too – he'd always have to have the right clothes on when we went training.

'But he wasn't really flash at all. He pretended to be a bit flash but really, he was just one of the lads. We had the same sort of humour. We loved winding people up.

'The only thing I'd say against Chappy is that he didn't bring Leslie Ash down to the training ground more!'

*   *   *

By the time the first game rolled round, Lyons, Chapman and their cohorts were more than ready. They knew they had a strong squad of players, and Wilkinson had well and truly beasted them during pre-season training.

'Howard changed when we went up, 100 per cent,' Sterland says now. 'Even more running, and even more detail!'

The curtain-raiser pitted Wednesday against Nottingham Forest on a beautiful late-summer's afternoon at Hillsborough. The visiting team featured Ian Bowyer, whose goals had sent Wednesday down all those years earlier. Gary Megson, however, was left out completely, the latest in a long line of players to suffer at Brian Clough's whim.

Wednesday were given the perfect start when Marwood was brought down in the area, allowing Sterland to score from the spot (although the kick had to be retaken after Gary Shelton encroached). Forest levelled, but then Varadi gave Wednesday the lead early in the second half with a classic individual goal.

Picking the ball up in his own half, Wednesday's number nine ran at the retreating defenders before smashing the ball home from the edge of the Forest penalty area, sending the entire ground into a paroxysm of joy. All the frustration and pessimism of the last 14 years was blown away in an instant; it must surely go down as one of the greatest goals in Wednesday's history.

The third goal, however, was dredged from the other end of the aesthetic scale. Forest goalkeeper Steve Sutton made a complete hash of a Marwood cross, enabling substitute John Pearson to bundle the ball home with his knee. Pearson had scored in front of the Kop thousands of times in his dreams but it had never been quite like this.

'It's funny,' Pearson says. 'Before that game Howard called me in and said, "Lee's starting today. I think he's going to score goals for us. I don't know how he does it, it hits him on his knee, it hits him on his bum and he just seems to get goals."

'I remember the ball hitting my knee and honestly I thought "oh no, it's going over." But in the end it just looped into the net. Looking back I should have run over to Howard Wilkinson and pointed at my knee!'

Despite that great start, Wednesday took time to really find their feet. They won their first three home games but hadn't won any of their four matches on the road when they faced their first big test at the end of September.

Liverpool, having sold Graeme Souness in the summer, were going through a sticky patch and had just been held to a 0-0 draw by Fourth Division Stockport in the League Cup. They were also missing Ian Rush, the most feared goalscorer of the age, to injury.

Nonetheless they were still able to field Dalglish, Hansen, Whelan and Lawrenson, a line-up that would have chewed up and spat out most teams in Europe.

But Wednesday were undaunted.

Blair recalls, 'Before we even got out of the gates at Hillsborough, Howard stopped the coach. He stood up and said, "If anyone doesn't think we can win this football match today, get off the coach now."

'I thought that was genius. The team talk was done. He was the only one who ever did that in my career. It was psychological, and he meant it for sure. He knew no one was going to get off that coach.'

Apart from that, Wilkinson's pre-match routine was no different to any other game. It didn't need to be. The coaching staff were obsessive about every game: when preparing for an away match, they would even train with the specific type of ball their hosts used. Their tactics – turn the opposition defence and keep pressing from first minute to last – didn't need to be tweaked either.

The approach worked perfectly. Unlike 99 per cent of sides who went to Anfield, Wednesday took the game to their illustrious visitors. Liverpool didn't know what hit them.

Madden, a substitute that day, says, 'It was great. It vindicated everything we were working towards at that time. We never parked the bus. Our attitude was that we could go anywhere and give anyone a game.

'The previous season we'd taken 12,000 to Anfield in that League Cup replay. We'd been outclassed, to be honest. But what I really remember from that game is the Wednesday fans chanting "we'll be back, we'll be back." Then we went back the next year and won and sang "we told you so!"'

For Lyons, who'd never won at Anfield during his 11 years at Everton, the result was doubly sweet.

'Yeah, winning at Liverpool was great for me. For as long as I can remember, I've been a mad Evertonian – and I had a season ticket at Goodison from the age of eight. My dad was a big blue and got me into Everton practically as soon as I could walk.

'That doesn't mean I hated Liverpool. I was big mates with Terry McDermott and I'd grown up playing schoolboy football with David Johnson, who also played for Liverpool during their glory years. I had mates on both sides of the fence.

'But beating Liverpool was still incredible. I'd been out of the team when Everton finally beat them at Goodison in 1978, when my best mate Andy King scored the winning goal. I always felt like I missed out a bit there, so it was great to finally beat them, particularly that great team they had.'

* * *

Now Wednesday really hit their straps. They briefly went second in the table with a 5-0 win over Leicester, including a Varadi hat-trick, and after a sticky pitch in November they hammered Southampton on 29 December, then won at Old Trafford on New Year's Day. The victory was achieved with a penalty save from Martin Hodge, who'd seen one of Gordon Strachan's previous penalties in the programme.

With each new scalp that Wednesday claimed, the criticism ratcheted up another notch. Their direct, aggressive style became the *bete noire* of the football chatterati. After the game at Old Trafford, Denis Law suggested the Yorkie upstarts should be thrown out of the league.

Outwardly, in front of the press, Wilkinson vehemently defended his players' honour. In the confines of the dressing room, however, he found a way to turn it to his advantage.

John Pearson remembers, 'Howard would bring the papers in on a Monday and say, "Ah, look at these. That's what they think of you, they all think you're just a bunch of long-ball merchants." He got that siege mentality going, that "everyone's against you" attitude.

'At the same time he'd show us a clip of Glenn Hoddle doing a long pass. "Look at Glenn Hoddle, when he plays that ball, it's a thing of beauty. When we do it, it's hoofball." He was very clever like that. He used every tool he could possibly find to get that extra five or ten per cent out of us. It made us even tighter.'

But when Chelsea visited Hillsborough for a League Cup fourth round replay at the end of January, not even the most snobbish of observers could complain about the fare on offer.

Wednesday flew out of the traps. Lyons and Chapman scored with headers and then a superb goal by Marwood gave the hosts what seemed like an impregnable half-time advantage. Chelsea were simply unable to cope with Wednesday's up-and-unders or their unremitting effort.

But the visitors, inspired by substitute Paul Canoville, somehow clawed their way back after half-time. To the horror of the crowd they pulled back the deficit, then went ahead. Wilkinson watched on in stunned apoplexy, unable to believe that his brilliantly orchestrated defence was melting like an ice lolly in a blast furnace.

But then, with time ebbing away, Sterland broke into the box only to be tripped by Chelsea defender Doug Rougvie. Zico picked himself up, spotted the ball down and stroked it into the back of the Leppings Lane net.

Wednesday eventually lost out in the second replay, this time at Stamford Bridge, and the season rather petered out – although they did manage another victory over United, thanks largely to more heroics from Hodge.

Despite the end-of-season slump, everyone involved could be happy with what they'd achieved. The new boys had dished out bloody noses up and down the land, and had established themselves in the top ten despite one of the tightest budgets in the division.

Yes, Wilkinson's men had ended up closer to the relegation zone than champions Everton in terms of points, but they had also finished above Forest and Aston Villa, two clubs who had won the European Cup in the recent past. And they'd garnered the third-best defensive record in the league, vindication of all those hours spent drilling on the training ground.

The manager wasn't satisfied though. Throughout his career, Wilkinson liked to refresh his squad every summer with new recruits who would buy into his ferocious training regime. Now, with a couple of quality signings, he felt he could take the final step towards major honours.

And so, after years of frugality, Wednesday's board finally flopped open their wallets. Wilkinson went out and spent £1m on two of Britain's most highly rated young players, Mark Chamberlain from Stoke and Garry Thompson from West Brom. To put that splurge into context, Gary Lineker, the First Division's most expensive signing that summer of 1985, cost only £925,000. Thompson's transfer fee, at £720,000, was over four times Wednesday's previous record.

The holder of that record, Imre Varadi, had already gone to West Brom by the time Thompson came the other way, sold to balance the books and to help persuade Albion to part with their crown jewel. At the time, fans were shocked – this was the hero of Anfield, a player who had clearly proved himself capable of succeeding on English football's highest stages. In the end, though, the decision didn't come back to haunt Wednesday: Varadi's subsequent career (and even his underwhelming brief return to Hillsborough) would vindicate the decision to part ways.

John Pearson's sale would also be vindicated in time. Honest grafter and top bloke though he was, Pearson struggled to find the net regularly throughout the rest of his career. But that didn't make the sale any less painful either for the player or for the fans who adored him.

'It was horrendous,' Pearson recalls now. 'Howard told me, "Lennie Lawrence [then the Charlton manager] is at a hotel in town and he wants to speak to you. I think you should go and see him." I said, "Well I don't want to go and see him," but Howard said, "Ah, it's a bit rude that, he's come all the way from London to see you."

'In the end I went to see Lennie and he made me an offer. I said I'd think about it, but I went back to Howard and he asked me what Lennie had offered. I told him and he said, "Oh crikey, I don't think I'll be able to offer you that." So I replied, "Well, I'm not bothered, I'm not going."

'So this went on for about three or four weeks. I remember going to a restaurant in London with Jimmy Hill, who was a director at Charlton, and him being really nice. In the end I told Lee Chapman what I was earning and he said, "You can't turn that down." They were almost doubling the first offer.

'Obviously I never wanted to leave Wednesday, but I left with some great memories. I played every single minute of every single game in the promotion year, and I'm really proud of that.'

As if Pearson's exit wasn't galling enough for the supporters, they also had to cope with the departure of their icon, the man who had done more than anyone to bring them back to the big time.

'I'd achieved all I wanted to achieve in football, and now I wanted to try management,' Mick Lyons says. 'I enquired about Stoke and then got the Grimsby job. I wanted to have a go. Howard knew I wanted to be a manager. He didn't stand in my way.

'There were plenty of tears when I finally decided to move on, though. I remember coming home one day and just started crying. Everyone was really fantastic. I just loved the place, loved the people, everyone at the club, the physio, everyone.

'The fans were great, too. When we lost games at Everton, you'd bump into someone after the game and it'd be "you didn't do this, you didn't do that". But at Wednesday it was always "we", not "you".

'I was desperate to succeed for Wednesday and it would have been great to keep playing for them. My time was up though. No regrets.'

Looking back on his career now, Lyons is modest. He describes himself as 'a limited player' who made up in effort what he lacked in skill. However his achievements and legacy bely this modesty. Lyons is immortalised in the Everton hall of fame; if Hillsborough had one, he would be among the first inductees.

In fact, when Wednesday fans pick their all-time XI, Lyons is routinely named as captain. The only shame is that they can't pick him 11 times.

*   *   *

Even without their talisman, Wednesday enjoyed an excellent season in 1985/86. This time they finished fifth, which would have been enough for a place in Europe had it not been for the horror of Heysel the previous year.

There were plenty of highlights along the way, too. Liverpool were held to two highly creditable draws. Even more impressive were the two victories over Manchester United, the first of which ended their 15-game unbeaten start to the season.

Perhaps it should have been even better. Perhaps Wednesday could have gone a step further and challenged the Merseyside duo at the top of the table.

But while Liverpool had Ian Rush and Everton had Gary Lineker, Wednesday's own big-name hotshots were firing blanks. Thompson and Chamberlain, bought to help the club push on, swiftly found themselves frozen on the fringes. Wilkinson regularly left them on the bench, unable to trust the talent he had paid so much to acquire.

Prior to arriving at Hillsborough, Thompson had been one of the most feared centre-forwards in England. Chamberlain had played *for* England, starring alongside John Barnes in that iconic win against Brazil in the Maracanã. Together they would manage only 15 goals between them while wearing the blue and white stripes.

Some will suggest Wilkinson never gave them a chance. To his detractors, those who think he was just a dour footballing luddite, the travails of his two biggest signings prove that the bluff old schoolmaster was incapable of understanding maverick talents (an argument later given substantial heft by his falling-out with Eric Cantona).

Chamberlain certainly appears to subscribe to this view. In the rare interviews he has given about his time at Wednesday, he has said that Wilkinson destroyed his confidence by refusing to back his ability, and he questioned why he was even brought to Wednesday if they had no idea how to play him.

Thompson, though, paints a far rosier picture. While he admits Wilkinson's initial refusal to pick him was a shock – 'I went from being the record signing to picking up sweaty jockstraps' – he has nothing but kind words for the man who took him to Hillsborough.

'I never wanted to go to Sheffield Wednesday, if I'm honest. There were loads of other clubs in for me, including Villa, my boyhood team. I was really keen to go there. But the Albion never sell players there, and Wednesday were offering so much money that they couldn't turn it down.

'In the end I went over to Hillsborough to talk with Howard, more out of courtesy than anything, and took my wife and son with me. At one point, Howard's gone out of the room, my missus has gone off house-hunting with his missus and I'm like, "Where's my son?"

'So I look out of the window and Howard's down there with my son on the pitch, showing him how to score at Hillsborough. I thought, "He'll do for me." If a man can spend time in all that hullabaloo, with agents and everything, to keep a child happy, I'll have him all day.

'We certainly had our differences. I remember after one early game he accused me of not trying and the other players had to drag me away from him. I came in the next day with a transfer request and he just threw it in the bin! I couldn't believe it. Just rolled it up, threw it away and asked me why I was still in the office.

'We had a proper stand-off after that. Chambo ended up coming round my house and begging me to back down. Thankfully I had the other players to help me get through that period, because Howard was breaking me.

'But yeah, we respected one another. And his attention to detail was frightening. He was 15 years ahead of everyone else.'

Thompson ended up getting his move to Villa just a year after signing for Wednesday. But he admits now, 'It was a massive mistake. I realised it within two weeks of moving.

'Wednesday were a proper, scientifically run, well-organised club. Villa were the opposite. It's like the old girlfriend, you see her with another geezer and she's looking a million dollars. That's what it was like for me when I saw Wednesday play.

'I just wish I'd scored more there. My goalscoring record was embarrassing and I hold my hands up. People used to talk about my hard work, as if that compensated for the lack of goals, but that pissed me off. Work rate should be a given when you're a professional footballer. Strikers are supposed to score goals.

'I never gave the Sheffield public what they'd seen at West Brom and they'd see at Villa. That's the Garry Thompson I wanted them to see and they didn't see it. To my dying day, that's the thing I will regret.'

But as the new hotshots struggled to justify their top billing in 1985/86, those on the undercard were providing star turns every week.

The craggy veteran Paul Hart, drafted in as a short-term replacement for Lyons, was certainly a downgrade but Wednesday's defence was so well organised that it didn't really matter.

'We were so well drilled as a defence,' Nigel Worthington says. 'Mick was an amazing leader, so it was a big blow when he left, but we just got on with it. Whoever came in, we just knew where each other would be, and what was expected of each one of us.'

To further stiffen that defence Wilkinson had brought in Glynn Snodin, who would make nearly 60 appearances over two seasons before going on to further success at Leeds. And, to add extra protection, he had managed to entice Gary Megson back to Hillsborough.

Even by Wilkinson's standards, this was a handy bit of business. Megson was snared for a fee of just £70,000, a little over a third of the fee Wednesday had received 12 months earlier. And while some may have thought him damaged goods, having failed to win a first-team place at either Forest or Newcastle, Megson would soon scotch this notion with his colossal presence both on the pitch and among the squad.

'Meggo was a real sharp bloke,' Thompson recalls. 'He had a nickname for everyone. I was "Fat Wallet" because I was apparently earning such a big salary.

'But my God he was a leader, too. If the team wasn't playing well, he'd just go round the whole lot of us and tell us what we were doing wrong. "Thommo, hold the ball up. Marwood, get those crosses in. Mel, start getting up that flank." And he was always right.

'Gary sometimes gets stick for his time as a manager, but I think perhaps he tried to be too much like Howard. If he'd just let people see the real him, and stuck to being himself, who knows what he would have achieved.'

With Megson leading the way and players like Sterland and Marwood blossoming, Wednesday flew out of the traps by winning four of their first five games. Champions Everton brought the upstarts down to earth by handing out a 5-1 walloping at Hillsborough, but it was the merest of blips.

The best result came at home to Manchester United in mid-November. Ron Atkinson's swaggering aristocrats arrived on the back of a three-month unbeaten run since the start of the season but Wednesday gave them a torrid evening, seizing on every loose ball and sending a ceaseless barrage of aerial missiles into the night sky. Chapman's late winner in front of the Kop was no more than his team deserved.

'I still remember that game,' Chapman recalls. 'We just pulverised them throughout. United were under the cosh all game.

'But that's just how we played. I'd never run so much as I did at Wednesday, all those runs up and down Ewden Reservoir, but it allowed us to play a pressing game. You see Liverpool and City doing it now – well we were doing exactly the same back then. We were able to bully teams throughout the game.'

As if to prove the point, Wednesday went to Old Trafford in April and won 2-0, a victory that showcased Wilkinson's ultra-aggressive style at its very best – set up by a player who exemplified his brilliance as a talent-spotter.

Just a few months before his goal at Old Trafford, Carl Shutt had been a mechanic playing for Spalding United. The rest of the football world had already turned its back, but Wilkinson, for the umpteenth time, saw something that had slipped everyone else by.

Players plucked from obscurity usually take time to adjust to their new surroundings, but Shutt adapted seamlessly. With Thompson misfiring, he and Chapman became Wednesday's most reliable source of goals. While Chapman would terrorise defences in the air, Shutt provided the sort of penalty-box prowess that had been missing since Bannister's departure.

It wasn't quite such a smooth transition off the pitch, though. Nicknamed 'Trigger' by his team-mates, Shutt's naivety made him a natural target for a dressing room full of razor-wire wits. Chapman was particularly keen to get one over on his new striking partner.

'I remember putting on a fake reporter's voice and ringing Shutty up, asking him for an interview to discuss his rags to riches story. We went on for a while, asking him loads of questions!

'Then we got a local photographer, who we knew, to go round and tell him to dress up in a mechanic's overalls. I think we even got him to jump up in the air with his tools at one point.

'He took it well when he found out though. Or at least I think he did!'

*　*　*

Even with Shutt's infusion of goals, Wednesday ultimately lacked the firepower and the consistency to mount a title push in the spring of 1986. They could beat the best teams in the land but they were also hamstrung by a series of silly defeats against teams they should have put away with ease.

However their dogged style, and their ability to rise to the occasion, were ideally suited to an FA Cup tilt. And so, after spluttering through the early rounds, Wednesday's push for Wembley gradually gathered momentum. Shutt scored twice to polish off Derby in a fifth-round replay and then blasted home an absolute barnburner to secure victory over West Ham at Hillsborough a week later.

That meant a semi-final at Villa Park against Everton, who at the time were still duking it out with Liverpool for control of English football. Howard Kendall's team may have flattened them earlier in the season but Wednesday knew they were fit, strong and tactically savvy enough to run anyone close in a one-off game.

Just as they had at Highbury three years previously, Wednesday fans packed into the home end to cheer their team on. At one stage the BBC cameras zoomed in on a group of supporters perched precariously against the wall of the stand, scrambling for any vantage point they could get.

In the end the tie became an unseemly arm-wrestle, one of terrific substance but precious little style. Everton went ahead when substitute Alan Harper lobbed Martin Hodge, but Shutt equalised almost instantly. For a few minutes the door to Wembley swung open – and then Graeme Sharp slammed it shut.

Looking back, the players are divided in their opinion of the game. Chapman, whose preparation was cruelly hampered by a bout of hepatitis, thinks certain key players were blighted by nerves on this grandest of stages. Others, however, believe Wednesday did everything they could.

'We were the better team against Everton for 90 minutes but then we ran out of gas,' Lawrie Madden says. 'Everton paced themselves better. All of a sudden we made one or two errors. They didn't win the game so much, we just made errors they took advantage of.

'All the pundits were getting excited about an all-Merseyside final, and I have to admit we'd have loved to spoil that. We had plenty of chances, and missed them. We outplayed Everton, really.

'Credit where credit's due, though. They dominated extra time. You've got to score when you're on top and we didn't do it.'

After matching one of the best teams in Europe over two hours, Wednesday ended up with nothing. There was no disgrace in losing to such a good side but they knew that the chance of glory had just slipped through their grasp.

For Martin Hodge, the defeat was particularly painful. Not only had he lost out to his former club; Everton's first goal might have been averted had he stayed on his line.

'Alan Harper is a good friend and we're both scouting now. He still gives me stick. Just a few months ago, I was at Scunthorpe and he came up to me and said, "Hodgie, what about that chip I did you with?!"

But as a goalkeeper, you have a millisecond to make a decision and I made the wrong one. Alan had a lot to do to score from there, but he did.'

It was the start of a miserable few months for Hodge. In the summer of 1986 he was informed he was in the England party to go to Mexico for the World Cup, only to be told on the day of the flight that he was no longer needed because Gary Bailey was going instead. He says the two disappointments rank side-by-side as the biggest blows he suffered in the game.

'I'd lost a semi-final for Everton against West Ham in a replay back in 1980, when Frank Lampard's dad scored in about the 119th minute. Then this. It was one of the toughest moments I had in football.'

A lot of his team-mates would say the same. For that Wednesday side of the mid-'80s, the shoot-out at Villa Park was the closest they would get to major honours. When they finally reached Wembley five years later, the squad would be almost completely different.

Could that particular bunch of players have pushed on to success? Madden feels that, in the end, the squad just liked that little bit of quality to go with all the graft.

'We didn't have a Kenny Dalglish – although who did? – and we didn't have a prolific goalscorer. In the end that might have stopped us taking that final step.'

Had Thompson or Chamberlain delivered then perhaps Wednesday would have gone on to greater things. Had Wilkinson possessed the sort of creative game-breakers he would later command at Leeds, maybe all that mud and sweat would have finally turned to gold.

In the end it wasn't to be. Wednesday's – and Wilkinson's – trip to wonderland would have to wait, for a few years at least.

7

BIG RON

It's Valentine's Day 1989. Britain is loved up, basking in Margaret Thatcher's free-market miracle which has birthed the world's most buoyant economy.

Up and down the land, couples are staring into each other's eyes and swooning to Marc Almond's 'Something's Gotten Hold of My Heart', reflecting the copacetic optimism floating like a plume of candyfloss across the nation.

And in Sheffield, a lifelong love affair is about to begin.

*   *   *

WHEN RON Atkinson swaggered in for his first day at Sheffield Wednesday, fans would have been forgiven for thinking this was a match made in hell.

Wednesday were sinking in the quagmire of the relegation zone and there appeared no chance of redemption. The squad was packed full of monochrome cloggers, a drizzly mishmash of bad decisions.

Atkinson, in contrast, was Mr Bojangles. He was champagne and sun beds, a Swiss Toni long before *The Fast Show* arrived on our screens.

Sure, Atkinson was a footballing romantic who could produce pretty teams and put smiles on people's faces. But the man to right a ship listing towards the Second Division? Atkinson seemed like the sort of bloke who, had he been stranded on the *Titanic*, would have been crooning with the band as the ship went down.

But the new relationship would set sparks flying. So much so, in fact, that 30 years on Atkinson is still being voted Wednesday's greatest manager. Like every relationship the combination had its ups and downs, but Atkinson infused Wednesday with an attacking brio not seen at Hillsborough for donkey's years. His teams still set the benchmark for how Wednesday should play.

Once again, though, we're getting a bit carried away. Before turning to Big Ron we need to consider the chain of events that brought him to the club.

*   *   *

For more than two years, Wednesday had been gently subsiding. Since those giddy highs in the spring of 1986 the club had slowly and inexorably slipped down the table. There'd been some great days, such as a 7-1 thrashing of Queen's Park Rangers, but also bleak ones like a 6-1 mauling at Leicester.

On the final day of 1988 Liverpool won 5-1 at Hillsborough. The 'Wilkinson out' chants were starting to rattle around the half-empty stands. Those halcyon days of giant-slayings and cup semi-finals suddenly seemed a long way away.

Bit by bit, the squad so painstakingly constructed by Wilkinson had fallen apart. A succession of key players were allowed to leave, and potential replacements such as Mark Wright baulked at the miserly terms put before them. The frugality of Wednesday's board was a constant source of frustration to players, manager and supporters.

Peter Shirtliff left Wednesday for Charlton in 1986. He'd been out of contract and thought a change of scenery would benefit his career. When he got to London, however, he was surprised by how much more cash was on offer.

'I was on £300 a week at Wednesday, maybe £350,' Shirtliff recalls. 'Charlton didn't even have their own ground, and they nearly doubled my money.

'Wednesday signed one lad for £250,000, another one for £450,000, another lad from non-league, and all that to replace one player! Then eventually I got signed back for £500,000. Crazy.

'At the time, I thought they [the board] disliked local players doing well. I think it was at boardroom level. It was like, "We want them to do well but we don't want them to do too well." It was almost a culture issue, that homegrown players weren't as well rewarded.

'It wasn't something that people talked about, but it definitely caused resentment.'

Many of the departees would go on to enjoy spectacular triumphs elsewhere. Brian Marwood won a league title within 12 months of arriving at Arsenal. Lee Chapman and Carl Shutt would repeat the feat at Leeds. Their success only made Wednesday's stinginess harder to fathom.

Eventually things came to a head. Wilkinson pleaded with the board for a fresh injection of funds to overhaul the squad. He got nowhere.

Perhaps the bean-counters were wary of sanctioning more big-money flops after Garry Thompson and Mark Chamberlain. If that was the case, however, Wilkinson could point to signings like Marwood, Shutt, Martin Hodge and

Nigel Worthington. His brilliance in the transfer market had not only ensured Wednesday's stability in the top division, it had boosted the Hillsborough coffers, too. In their first four years back in the First Division Wednesday had made a £1m profit on player trades.

So when Leeds came calling in early autumn 1988 they found a receptive audience. They were fourth from bottom of the Second Division and, for all his gripes over money, Wilkinson had a good relationship with Wednesday chairman Bert McGee. When he told his wife about the offer, she said he was crazy. But gradually Wilko came round to the idea.

Leeds were still one of the great names of English football. Their ground, while in need of renovation, was a match for Wednesday's. And, crucially, they were offering significant funds. As Wilkinson has since said, it was 'a chance to really fly'.

Even without Wednesday's parsimony, Wilkinson would have been forgiven for wanting a fresh start. He'd spent the previous five years turning his boyhood club into First Division regulars. All those lung-busting schleps through the wind and rain, all those analysis sessions when everyone else had gone home, had surely taken their toll.

In the end he'd achieved feats which would have seemed ludicrous back in 1983. He'd won at Anfield and Old Trafford. He'd created the league's fittest, most well-drilled team. And he'd groomed two international footballers in Worthington and Chris Morris (Mel Sterland would win an England cap just a month after his departure, becoming the first Wednesday player to wear the Three Lions since the 1960s).

Yes, his playing style certainly had its detractors. And his man-management could sometimes be a little brusque. Andy Blair recalls one particular incident with a squirm.

'One of the biggest disappointments in my football career was when Howard asked me if I thought I could be captain, early in my time at Wednesday. He even compared me to Graeme Souness – although he added that it was mainly for the way I strutted around the pitch!

'So the first game Mick Lyons was either suspended or injured, I thought, "I've got a chance." Then Gary Shelton was made captain. That tore me to pieces. I struggled to recover from that, mentally. He got into my brain and deep down, I've never told him, but that had a huge psychological effect on me.

'In fact I'd say that was the biggest psychological blow in my career. Worse than my knee injury. He led me up the garden path and closed the gate.'

Looking back, Blair says he found Wilkinson, 'a contradiction. He'd wear the suits with the handkerchief, an ex-schoolteacher, articulate, but I found him introverted also. The flamboyant stuff didn't fit his character.'

However he is at pains to stress that, for all their disagreements, he had huge respect for Wilkinson's tactical nous and his ability to motivate a team. 'Howard was fierce in his preparation. I loved his attention to detail. I really enjoyed his philosophy, his way of playing.

'His motivational talks could be great, too. The best meeting we ever had was when Howard compared us all to breeds of dog. I was a long-haired Afghan, only good for walking the streets with the rich women from London, because he thought I was a bit arrogant. He was unerringly accurate!

'The best dog he said to be a footballer was a Jack Russell. The only dog he said who was a Jack Russell was Gary Shelton. I remember just giggling for hours. Still remember it fondly.'

Others offer equally glowing tributes. Bannister, Blair's old mate and fellow iconoclast, recalls, 'Howard got the right people around him. The physio Alan Smith was amazing. Best physio I've ever worked with by a mile. He'd plan every exercise down to the last repetition. The diet was completely different, too. We were eating the sort of food that footballers eat today. Howard was amazing like that.'

Martin Hodge concurs. 'Howard's the best manager I ever played for. People say he was this, he was that, but really he was miles ahead. He was doing the vitamins, the rehab, the running – all the stuff that people were doing ten years later.

'At the time you hated him and you hated what he was doing, but you look back and think, "By God, he was the best." He's the last English manager to win the Premier League [Wilkinson guided Leeds United to the old First Division championship in 1992, the final season before the Premier League started], and that speaks for itself. You'd never think he was your friend but he brought the best out of so many people.'

Perhaps the most telling tribute comes from Mick Lyons, a man who knows a good manager when he sees one having previously played under Harry Catterick, Howard Kendall and Jack Charlton.

'Howard Wilkinson was a top manager, you won't find anyone better. And he was a top person, too, just like Jack was. If anyone had a go in the press, he'd defend us.

'To this day, when I'm taking kids training, I practise loads on set-pieces. That's what stands out most about Howard. His attention to detail.'

In the end, though, Wilkinson would provide the most vivid demonstration of his attributes elsewhere. At Elland Road he would win promotion with another hard-bitten team, built around the old Hillsborough icon Lee Chapman. Only this time, armed with sufficient funds to buy top-class players like Gary McAllister, Tony Dorigo and John Lukic, Wilkinson would take the final step, guiding Leeds to their first league title in 18 years.

It could, and perhaps should, have been Wednesday.

*   *   *

For all the manager's obvious frustrations, it appears few had any inkling that he would be moving on.

Ian Cranson, one of those who'd been brought in to plug the gaping hole in the squad left by Shirtliff (and another who would be held up as a Wilkinson mistake) recalls, 'I had no idea he was even thinking of leaving. I'd signed for him on deadline day earlier that year – he'd been very persuasive, telling me to commit to Wednesday when there were other clubs interested. Had I known he'd be off, I might have decided not to sign and reassessed my options in the summer.'

David Hodgson was another of those signed in the final few months of the Wilkinson regime. The two men went back a long way, having worked together with the England under-21s.

But Hodgson remembers that, 'it was a shock when he left. It just came out of the blue. You get whispers in changing rooms, but I don't think anyone saw it coming.

'I remember it being one of those times when you look on the news and it flashes up "Howard Wilkinson has left Sheffield Wednesday". It wasn't quite as big a shock as when Kenny Dalglish left Liverpool, for example, but no one saw him leaving his hometown club.'

Hodgson adds that, while some of the players 'were probably just starting to find the day-to-day training a little bit monotonous', there was no indication that Wilkinson had 'lost the dressing room' to coin that most hackneyed of football cliches.

'No one was tired of Howard as a person. Look at the number of players who went to play for him at Leeds. You don't do that if you've lost faith in a guy.

'I cannot recall an unhappy changing room. I can't recall any players criticising him from a coaching or man-management perspective. I actually thought he was a fantastic coach.'

Whether Wednesday's board were as surprised as the players by Wilkinson's departure is a question that will never be answered. What's clear, however, is that they had few real alternatives when it came to finding a replacement.

There were practically no foreign managers in those days, so the pool of potential hires was shallow indeed. Only a handful of managers in the country had a better record than Wilkinson and all of them were in stable jobs elsewhere.

So the Wednesday board decided to take a punt on Peter Eustace, a man who had served Wilkinson throughout his managerial reign and been a fine player for Wednesday in their sepia-tinged glory days. Eustace had no pedigree in the dugout, but promoting from within was still common practice back then: this was a time when Liverpool and their boot room were winning everything in sight. The players appeared happy with the appointment, too.

Eustace was formally confirmed as manager after overseeing two victories as caretaker, the latter a highly impressive 2-1 victory at Southampton. But almost as soon as the appointment was rubber-stamped, Wednesday's form collapsed. The next 12 games yielded only a single win, culminating in a 3-0 defeat at home to Nottingham Forest and then a 5-0 pasting at Coventry in the first game of 1989.

Things briefly improved with draws against Arsenal and Liverpool, the two clubs that would contest the First Division Title, but then twin cup humiliations at the hands of Blackpool and Blackburn forced the board to act.

Eustace's reign remains the shortest of all Wednesday managers; never has the fabled Peter Principle been so literally applied.

The players are adamant that they did everything they could to help the new boss. 'Peter Eustace had the respect of the players,' Mel Sterland says. 'We were the ones who got him the job. But I think the pressure got to him. You could see the nerves in him, and that transmits to the players as well.'

David Hodgson believes Eustace's lack of faith in his own principles hastened his downfall. 'Peter changed the whole philosophy from a training perspective, and tried to change the way we played too. He was right to stamp his own authority on the team but a lot of those players had been successful under the high-intensity, long-ball method of Howard. I'd been at Liverpool, played for John Neal [at Middlesbrough], so I was used to playing under managers who wanted to pass. But some of them found it difficult to adjust to it.

'Then when it wasn't working, Peter tried to revert back to what had worked for Howard, with the running and the physical work. But the players just weren't having it. I think that's what cost him.'

Hodgson also recalls one slightly farcical incident that is impossible to imagine happening on Wilkinson's watch. 'We played Spurs and I got taken off, which I was very unhappy about because I know for a fact I was playing really well. Peter brought me off, I went straight down the tunnel, I picked up the phone and rang my girlfriend and said, "I'll be home in ten minutes."

'Then I got in the car and drove home.'

*   *   *

By now, many Wednesday fans were starting to wonder whether history would repeat itself. Just like in the 1960s the team was falling apart and the board had started to appoint the wrong managers. The decline was starting to look irreversible.

Thankfully, one of Britain's most colourful bosses had become available.

Ron Atkinson had just been turfed out by Atlético Madrid after losing his battle of wills with the club's bombastic president Jesús Gil. Before moving to Spain, he'd taken West Brom to the brink of the league title and won two FA Cups with Manchester United, producing some gorgeous football along the way.

While his teams could be flaky, as Wednesday had demonstrated several times, his overall managerial record was still excellent and he had a powerful advocate in Chris Turner, who had returned to Hillsborough from United in the summer of 1988 as a replacement for Martin Hodge, who had decided to take on a new challenge at Leicester.

So, in the end, the Wednesday board agreed to take the plunge. They knew Atkinson would be a total departure from Wilkinson in both personality and playing style. They knew the formula of the previous five years would be tossed away. But they also knew there was no other option.

When Atkinson met his new charges, reactions were certainly mixed. David Hodgson took a shine to the new man straightaway. 'When he arrived he called us all together and he went round shaking everyone's hand, then he got to me and we had a chat in Spanish. We'd both been out in Spain, so we had that in common straightaway. It was great for a manager to know where you'd been and what you'd done.'

Mel Sterland, however, was less impressed by the bronzed bigmouth who was now holding court.

'Big Ron were a fucking different breed! When he came he got us all in the centre circle, started to tell us that he was going to do this and that, and then suddenly a gust of wind lifted his barnet up! Fucking hellfire. I burst out laughing, it was so funny. He had all this hairspray on and the wind sent it everywhere.'

Soon, however, it became apparent that the new gaffer, for all his brashness, knew what he was talking about. Ian Cranson, who would soon be on his way, says Atkinson 'came in, identified our problems and found the right solutions. He brought in Richie Barker, who was a good coach, and just got us to work hard, playing only slightly differently to how we'd played previously.'

After the toil of the Wilkinson regime, players naturally warmed to Atkinson's new, football-first approach.

'Under Howard – and it's something I've always been proud of – we worked very, very, very hard during the week on the fitness side,' Nigel Worthington says. 'But when Ron came in, everything was done with the ball, we had short-sided games, 11 against 11, different exercises around the ball.

'Ron really sold it to us, too. Sometimes he made you feel a bit better than you were, and that was one of his strengths as a coach.'

This appraisal is echoed by Lawrie Madden, who says that in contrast to Wilkinson, Atkinson did very little on the training ground. But that didn't matter; he had Barker to do all the drills for him. Atkinson was not a coach but a manager, and a brilliant one at that.

'Ron's skill was his man-management,' Madden recalls. 'He kept people happy, he kept people involved and he was genuinely committed. People think he was topping up his tan in a sun bed at the training ground but that's a complete media fabrication. Ron was nothing like that. His sole focus was Sheffield Wednesday.'

Another common perception is that Atkinson was too loose with players and allowed a bacchanalian culture to develop on his watch. His United teams were famous for playing teams off the park but then drinking one another under the table. The Wednesday lads soon found out this depiction wasn't accurate either.

'Ron didn't actually like champagne,' Madden continues. 'Sure, he'd have a glass, but he didn't really like that. He'd prefer a beer or a glass of wine.

'Yes he would go out with the lads a lot more than Howard would, but it had a purpose. It was part of his man-management, talking to the players and building team spirit. He certainly wasn't giving us carte blanche to go out on the booze every night of the week.

'But he got this image as Champagne Charlie and it stuck. To be fair, he didn't exactly try to disown it, did he?!'

Another of Atkinson's key strengths, cited by Madden and other players, was his judgement of players (an attribute which would serve him well as a commentator until the use of a racial epithet cost him his ITV contract). It was an attribute that he would demonstrate within weeks of his arrival.

Backed by a desperate Wednesday board, Atkinson returned to West Brom – where he'd enjoyed a brief second spell before moving to Spain – to sign Carlton Palmer, a raw-boned young grafter who'd only recently been converted from a centre-half into a box-to-box midfielder.

Palmer was practically an unknown and plying his trade in the middle of the Second Division. But his hard-running style, embellished by Atkinson's subtle promptings, would make him one of the most effective players in the country.

'There were a few clubs interested at the time,' Palmer remembers. 'Chelsea were in for me too, and they were putting together a very strong team. I wasn't fussed about London, I'd turned down London before, but Wednesday looked like they might be relegated so it was a difficult decision.

'I had a long chat with Nobby Stiles, who was coaching at West Brom and had played a major role in my early career. He said, "You're not signing for the club, you're signing for the person." That's something I've always taken with me and it's always been true: the people who know you best get the best out of you.

'To this day, I remember driving along the road coming off the motorway into Hillsborough and it just felt right. And I never look back. I work in Shanghai now, but we still have a family home there and I never left even when I signed for Southampton. And we won't leave. I love the city.'

However, in true Wednesday fashion, the books had to be balanced. So after 10 years of flying up and down the Hillsborough flanks, Mel Sterland was sold to Rangers. The player was open to a new challenge and a fee of around £1m was too good to turn down.

Carlton Palmer was box office, on and off the pitch. The midfielder was bold, brash and outspoken – but had the talent to back it up.

Nonetheless, the manner of Sterland's exit would leave a lasting mark on the player. In fact he is the only man interviewed for this book to have anything bad to say about Atkinson.

'It was gutting [to leave]. I had my best days there. I didn't go for the money, I wanted to play in Europe.

'Anyway a few months later, he [Atkinson] tried to sign me back. Graeme Souness had told me to buy a house, he asked me if my wife and kids were happy, then he told me he didn't want me and I'd probably be in the reserves if I didn't go!

'So I was up in my house in Bridge of Allan, and the phone rang. The caller said he was Ron Atkinson. I said "stop fucking about" and put the phone down. Gospel truth. The guy rang back again and said, "Mel, it's Ron Atkinson, how do you feel about coming back to Sheffield Wednesday?" I said, "I'm not for sale." He said "yeah you are." I said I'd signed a four-year contract and he said he'd heard different.

'He offered me £500 a week, the same money I'd been on when I left, with a sponsored car. I said no thanks. When I went to Leeds I was on £2,000 a week with £1,000 appearance money! If Ron had offered more money, I'd have gone back to Wednesday.

'It hurt me when Ron offered me that derisory amount, to be honest. And when my testimonial came round, Ron wouldn't let me have it at Hillsborough. I had to have it at Elland Road. It was my club, I supported them, I'd given everything to them, and he did that to me. I was absolutely gutted. It hurt me so much.'

*   *   *

The departure of such an iconic player, and totemic personality, could easily have knocked Atkinson's rebuild off-course before it started. Instead things began to fall into place.

Wednesday picked up crucial victories over Luton and Charlton and began to inch away from the bottom. Then they faced a crucial double-header against two fellow strugglers: a home match against QPR followed by a visit to Newcastle.

With tension ratcheting up, Atkinson decided to let his men off the leash, as Chris Turner recalls. 'We played QPR on the Saturday. Trevor Francis was manager, Ray Wilkins was in midfield. We lost 2-0. There was a lot of doom and gloom that Saturday night. We knew we'd blown a big chance to pick up points.

'I went home, but a lot of players we had from Birmingham, Carlton Palmer, Steve Whitton, they went out on the Saturday night. Then they carried on on the Sunday lunchtime.

'When we got on the bus in the early afternoon to go up to St James' Park, half the lads were still pissed. If you'd lit a match on that bus the whole thing would have gone up. Dave Bennett missed the bus and had to catch a taxi.

'So we played Newcastle the next day, big game, 30,000 people, and we won 3-1!

'Ron knew what was happening. He didn't turn a blind eye but he knew how to manage it all. He knew how to handle players and get the best out of them.'

Wednesday's opener at St James' Park was scored by Dean Barrick, a 19-year-old making his debut. But the headlines were written in the second half with a spectacular strike from a man who would become famous for them.

With Newcastle straining to get back into the game, David Hirst picked up a loose ball on the right-hand touchline. Socks rolled down to his ankles, Hirst set off in the manner of a jinking wing wizard from yesteryear, drifting this way and that as he slalomed towards the penalty area. Then, like a magician dipping into his box of tricks and pulling out a trench mortar, he unleashed a left-footed shot which flew into the top right-hand corner, crashing in off the post for good measure.

In that one moment of brilliance a star was born.

*   *   *

Some players, like Mick Lyons, chisel their names into club folklore with their heroic bravery. Others, like Terry Curran or Chris Waddle, light up gloomy winters' afternoons with their outrageous skill. And then there are those who connect with the fans on a fundamental level and come to embody something deeper about what their club represents.

David Hirst was one of those players. Born in Cudworth, just a short drive up the M1 from Hillsborough, he became a Sheffield everyman: a blue-collar guy who liked a pint and was as honest as the day is long. The crowd would have warmed to him even if he hadn't been good. But boy, was he good.

Like Curran, Hirst was a maverick from mining stock, a talent that flowered in the sooty soil. He spent his formative years in the booze-soaked school of Sunday League football, then rose through the youth ranks at Barnsley. By the time he made his debut, aged only 17, he was already a man; all those battles on boggy pitches against grizzly centre-halves had equipped him with courage as well as talent.

However, Hirst only signed for Barnsley after going for trials at several other Yorkshire and north-east clubs. The most shambolic trial, of course, came at Wednesday.

'I was there for three days at the training ground,' Hirst recalls. 'We had three or four games in the morning, then more in the afternoon. I played in all the morning games, scored goals, did really well. Before every game, they'd called my name out to let me know which team I'd be on.

'Anyway we were due to go back to Hillsborough for some soup and sandwiches before the afternoon session, and as I went into the changing room to put my trainers back on, one of the scouts came up to me and asked for my name. When I said "David Hirst", he said "ah, we didn't know you'd arrived!"

'So I went back inside, picked up my belongings and went out to my dad, who'd come down with me. "What are you doing?" he asked. "Going home," I replied. "If I've played in all the games, scored goals, had my name read out every time and they hadn't even realised I'd turned up, I'm not staying."'

That one mistake would cost Wednesday £300,000. Hirst made such an impression in his debut season, 1985/86, that Wilkinson felt compelled to take a punt.

'Alan Clarke, the Barnsley manager, just called me into his office and said, "I've sold you, go home and get a suit on and go over to Hillsborough," Hirst recalls. "As an 18-year-old lad who's only played a few games, you do what you're told to do! And they were a First Division club, which was a big step up.'

The fee was huge for a teenager at the time but Hirst began repaying it almost instantly, scoring with the second touch of his home debut against Everton. Thereafter his progress was slower as Wilkinson sought to ease the new signing in gently and polish his rough edges.

Even in March 1989, after nearly three years at Hillsborough, Hirst remained a work in progress. He had all the tools of a top-class striker but had yet to find the knack of scoring regularly – prior to the Newcastle game he'd scored only 17 times for Wednesday. The fact that he was still wearing the number ten shirt, rather than nine, illustrates the fact that he had yet to truly establish himself as a bona fide centre-forward.

Under Atkinson's careful tutelage, however, Hirst would make the final leap. His manager's constant praise and positivity would give him the confidence to transform from promising youngster to national superstar.

'I'd had a really good relationship with Howard,' Hirst says. 'He was a great man-manager, with his own ideas. Peter Eustace was good, too. But I became really close to Ron. I got him and he got me. In fact we often call each other even now, just to have a chat and a laugh.

'He was a manager that believed in me when I wasn't scoring goals, and he saw what potential I had. He'd tell me not to worry – "Yes, you're missing the chances, but you're getting the chances, the goals will come." Strikers thrive on confidence and if you've got a manager who believes in you, you can feel more comfortable in the game.'

The Newcastle missile marked a turning point, the first real 'wow' moment of Hirst's career. But, as he recalls now with a grin, the goal occurred almost by accident.

'I was actually on my way off the pitch! Big Ron had shouted to me, "Hirsty, come over this side, you're coming off next time the ball goes out." I guess I was looking a bit leggy. Then when I was out on the right wing, Greg slipped me the ball, I cut inside and put it in the top corner.' Simple then, really.

Over the next four years Hirst would score a further 83 goals, many of them as good as that wonder strike at St James' Park. In that golden period between 1989 and 1993 he would pillage defences up and down the land with his power and pace. As the old saying goes, he wasn't just a scorer of great goals; he was a genuinely great goalscorer.

But for all his achievements, Hirst never lost touch with who he was. He remained a happy-go-lucky Yorkshire lad who had time for everybody. No matter where his football career took him, he was happiest having a pint at his local in the company of his mates.

'I'm from a mining background. My dad went down the mine, all my friends went down there, my mum and sisters worked in a bakery. I'm just a run-of-the-mill sort of person.

'Yes I liked a drink, not at the wrong time, but when it was appropriate – on a Sunday if we'd got a result the day before, we might go out for a couple of pints. That was how it was where I came from – you went to work and you went for a pint with your friends.'

Talent, charisma and a complete lack of airs and graces. Never has a man fitted the term 'local hero' more snugly.

* * *

Buoyed by that victory at Newcastle, Wednesday produced a timely spate of form. Liverpool dished out another walloping in early April but that was one of only three defeats in the final nine games.

In the end it came down to a shoot-out with Middlesbrough on the penultimate day of the season. Whoever lost would almost certainly go down, but in the end Wednesday ground out a win thanks to a second-half header from Steve Whitton. Atkinson strode on to the Hillsborough turf, celebrating with all and sundry.

The football hadn't been great, certainly compared to what would come later, but that didn't matter. Having looked like certainties for relegation only three months earlier, Wednesday had somehow got themselves out of it.

Ordinarily, thoughts would now drift to the following season and the chance of a rebuild. A time to bring in fresh players and look forward with renewed optimism.

But something far, far more serious than football had taken precedence.

8
DISASTER

'A tumult surrounding a tiny tunnel, a filthy, evil plughole sucking all life towards it and extinguishing the breath of all who were pulled into it. And it was dragging us towards it. We knew what was coming but could not break the crushing, malignant force.'

Tony Evans, Liverpool supporter and journalist, writing about his experience at Hillsborough in 1989.

*　*　*

WHEN WRITING about sport, hyperbole is never far from the tip of the quill. We use words like disaster, tragedy or catastrophe, but we don't really mean them. When men or women gather to knock a ball around, or run around a track, such words are just empty vessels used to elevate an event to a status it doesn't really merit.

But in 1989, an event took place at Hillsborough that justified every one of those words. The deaths of 96 people at the FA Cup semi-final between Liverpool and Nottingham Forest remains Britain's worst sporting disaster. It became a national scandal and continues to cause uproar more than 30 years on.

It is not the purpose of this book to rake up the mistakes made that day or try to throw fresh light on the tragedy in the hope of fingering a new guilty party. Thousands of people have already dedicated themselves to that particular task.

But to ignore the disaster would be to overlook something that has shaped Wednesday's entire history. They weren't playing in the match itself but the chaos that unfolded in their own stadium left an indelible mark on every single Wednesdayite.

No matter what glories are played out on the Hillsborough turf in the future, the stadium will always be known for that black day back in 1989. It is an event the club can never, and should never, forget.

*　*　*

When the World Cup came to England in 1966, Hillsborough was ahead of its time. The ribbon had just been cut on a £150,000 cantilever stand while the lower tier of the South Stand had been filled with row upon row of gleaming new seats.

The Leppings Lane End, meanwhile, had been transformed into a two-tiered stand, with seating for nearly 4,500 spectators and terracing below. At the time it was the acme of footballing sophistication: most of England's big grounds were ramshackle collections of wooden sheds and open concrete terracing with little or no protection afforded to those who used them.

But then the ground entered a kind of stasis. Although the authorities continued to award Wednesday their blue-riband fixtures – a total of 14 FA Cup semi-finals and a League Cup Final replay were hosted at Hillsborough between 1966 and 1989 – Wednesday's board allowed the ground to become dilapidated.

In 1979 the directors sanctioned a series of alterations worth around £120,000 to comply with the recently introduced Safety of Sports Grounds Act; the club received a certificate in recognition of the improvements. In 1986 the Kop was extended and covered at a cost of £850,000, giving spectators some long-awaited shelter from the elements.

But at the Leppings Lane End – the away end, let's not forget – the money was channelled into control rather than comfort. Perimeter fencing was added in 1977 and then the board decided to divide the terrace into a series of pens in 1981. But the surrounding infrastructure remained unchanged.

Instead of creating dedicated entrances for each of the new pens, the club left the narrow old row of turnstiles hemmed in on the banks of the River Don. The only means of accessing the central pens was a sloping tunnel, with a vertiginous one-in-six gradient, and the side pens were poorly advertised to those entering the concourse. Even the crush barriers were starting to crumble (in the aftermath of the disaster, investigators would open up one of the collapsed barriers and find a rolled-up newspaper from 1931).

There is a certain amount of context to bear in mind here. Wednesday were strapped for cash throughout this period, as a series of frustrated managers could testify. In the mid-1970s the club nearly went bust – in 1974 alone, they recorded losses of over £100,000 – and even after securing promotion in 1984, finances remained precarious.

Many other clubs were in similarly dire straits. This was a time before Gazza's tears, Skinner and Baddiel, and Sky's glossy marketing makeovers. The national sport had become a social leper, abandoned by the very society that had given it to the world. In 1988 ITV secured television rights to the entire Football League for a fee of just £44m – roughly one per cent of the amount received by the Premier League alone in 2018.

Hooliganism, which had first reared its misshapen head in the 1960s, had forced millions of match-goers away. Wednesday's own average attendance in 1989 was just 19,000, little more than a third of Hillsborough's capacity. In such a barren commercial environment it is perhaps easy to understand why directors became complacent about ground upgrades. Why spend a fortune for the safety of people who never turn up?

But even with all those caveats, Wednesday's failure to upgrade their crumbling facilities remains damning. Their willingness to operate without a valid safety certificate, or to upgrade the capacity of the Leppings Lane terraces following their segregation, can never be excused. The decision not to heed the advice of experts, like the engineer who suggested the Leppings Lane entrance be demolished and rebuilt, smacks of pig-headed penny-pinching.

There were plenty of warnings too. A semi-final in 1981 nearly ended in tragedy when Spurs fans were caught up in a crush at the Leppings Lane End just after the start of their match with Wolves. This resulted in 38 injuries and would likely have brought fatalities had the gates in the perimeter fence not been opened.

The FA responded by withholding all semi-finals from Wednesday for five years, but then bizarrely decided to allocate the 1987 semi between Leeds and Coventry to Hillsborough. That match, too, brought problems; Leeds fans who stood on the Leppings Lane that day recall seeing people fainting and trying to scale the fences.

In 1988 the FA again invited Wednesday to host its marquee play-off, this time contested by Liverpool and Nottingham Forest. That match passed without incident, so when the '89 semi rolled round with the same clubs involved, no one expected any problems.

Fatefully, however, South Yorkshire Police had removed its highly experienced chief superintendent Brian Mole, a veteran who had commanded several big games at Hillsborough, and replaced him with David Duckinfield, a greenhorn who had never supervised any event of this kind.

The train of disaster had now been set in motion.

* * *

The players of Liverpool and Nottingham Forest knew nothing about the removal of Mole, the appointment of Duckinfield or any of the myriad blunders which had turned Hillsborough into a deathtrap waiting to spring.

For them it was another chance to reach the FA Cup Final, a match then regarded as the most prestigious club match anywhere in the world. And no one was more excited than Lee Chapman.

Less than 12 months earlier, Chapman had decided to leave Wednesday for French club Chamois Niortais. However the move had proved a miserable failure. 'The club went bankrupt soon after I joined,' Chapman recalls. 'I was promised money they simply didn't have.'

Thankfully Brian Clough was on hand to bring him another shot at the big time. Just a week before the FA Cup semi-final, Chapman had helped Forest win the League Cup at Wembley. This game, against Kenny Dalglish's all-conquering league champions, was even bigger. 'Liverpool were the benchmark for everyone at the time,' Chapman says. 'It was a game the whole of Nottingham was buzzing about.

'I'd lost semi-finals in 1983 [with Arsenal] and 1986, so I was desperate to win. This was probably the hardest match of the three on paper – we were playing Liverpool after all – but we had a good group of players so we thought we had a chance.'

The people of Sheffield were excited about the game, too. By a quirk of the fixture list, Wednesday had been given the afternoon off. They were scheduled to play Norwich but the East Anglian club were involved in the other semi-final.

For Chris Turner, it was a chance to take his young son to one of his first big matches. Turner had returned to Sheffield the previous summer and now he could savour one of English football's biggest occasions in his own backyard.

'Semi-final day was huge then,' he recalls. 'And it looked like the game was going to be a classic.

'Liverpool were the best team in the country but Forest were cup specialists. We couldn't wait for the game.'

As the day itself began to unfold, all seemed normal at first. But then a huge bottleneck began to develop outside the Leppings Lane entrance, exacerbated by Duckinfield's decision not to stagger the entry of supporters. Liverpool fans became jammed in the tiny enclosure, putting enormous pressure on those trying to get through the grinding old turnstiles.

With kick-off approaching and the congestion getting ever more dangerous, Duckinfield decided to open the huge perimeter gate and let everyone in. With no proper directions, this teeming swathe of humanity flooded into the central tunnel, straight into the already-packed central pens. Duckinfield had simply pushed the crush inside the ground. Now there was nothing anyone could do to stop it.

Not that anyone knew it elsewhere in the stadium. Yes, those central pens looked pretty packed, but it was semi-final day. The prime spots behind the goal were bound to be rammed.

David Hodgson was sat in the North Stand with a couple of lads he knew from his time at Anfield in the early '80s. His mates' kids had tickets for the Leppings Lane end.

'Before the game a kid came on the pitch and his arm was completely distorted,' Hodgson recalls. 'I remember people shouting at him, typical Scouse humour. "Hey la, you're going to miss the game."

'But then a few minutes later it started to escalate. We were watching people try and get over the fencing right in front of our eyes.

'In my mind's eye, I can still see people climbing up and not being able to get over the fence, people trying to pull them up into the stand. I can see people trying to pull the fencing down as if it was yesterday.'

*   *   *

As implausible as it seems 30 years on, the match was not broadcast live by the BBC (it would take another year for the authorities to shift the semi-finals to a Sunday for live television coverage). However the match *was* beamed out by Irish broadcaster RTE.

Looking back at the film, one can see the mounting chaos whenever the action reaches the Leppings Lane End. More and more spectators are seen gathered on the track behind Bruce Grobbelaar's goal; screams can even be heard coming from the terracing.

However the commentators continue to call the match as if nothing were happening. And it appears that, as events unfolded, those down on the pitch were equally oblivious to the unfolding horror.

Chapman recalls that 'you could see the end was packed when we came out, but it was a big game. At the time you're just focused on the match itself, trying to get off to a good start.' With a place at Wembley at stake, the players' attentions were laser-focused.

Matters came to a head in the sixth minute. Liverpool's Peter Beardsley hit the Forest crossbar, an incident which some believe led to the collapse of a crush barrier in one of the Leppings Lane pens.

Within seconds, referee Ray Lewis was calling the players off. The ball was at Chapman's feet when the whistle went.

'I remember having the ball down by the corner flag at Leppings Lane. Then the referee blew, a policeman ran on and they told us to come off. That was the first inkling we had that something was badly wrong.'

As injured spectators flooded down from the terracing, the Hillsborough pitch began to resemble a battlefield, with police officers running around like shell-shocked lieutenants trying to get a grip on the situation. Fans in other parts of the ground looked on aghast, with no information about what was happening.

Eventually, David Hodgson decided to go and find out what was going on. 'As a Wednesday player, I thought I could speak to someone. So I went up the stand and down the back, past where the gym was.

'The game must have been stopped about five minutes earlier. I climbed over at least 30 bodies, all covered in black bags. I thought "bloody hell, they're dead." They say a lot of the people died a long time afterwards, but I can tell you there were people dead five minutes after the game was stopped.

'I wanted to have a word with Kenny so I walked round the pitch, towards the tunnel where he was standing. The security guards knew me so they let me walk over.

'I said to Kenny "this can't go ahead" and he said "no, it's getting called off." So I walked back to the stand and I said to my mates, "Lads, this is getting cancelled."

'By now the Leppings Lane End was carnage. My mates' sons were in there and there were no mobile phones. It was impossible to even get close to the pitch to find the kids. The lads were panicking. All they could do was go to the pub, where we'd agreed to meet afterwards, and hope the kids turned up.'

As the scale of the problem began to emerge, the two sets of players remained sealed away in the bowels of the stadium, unsure whether they would be asked to restart the game.

'We were in the dressing room for ages and no one came to tell us what was going on,' Chapman says. 'Eventually, I decided to go out and find someone who could give us some information – I'd only just left Wednesday so I knew a lot of people.

'Then I saw Bob Gorrell, the marketing manager, and he was in tears. He just told me that people were dying, they were carrying bodies off on stretchers. I couldn't believe it.'

An announcement came over the tannoy advising spectators to go home. The stands emptied in near-silence as people took in the enormity of what had happened.

'I was devastated,' Chris Turner recalls now. 'I remember seeing the bodies lined up outside the stadium as we left. You were stunned at what you'd just seen.'

Eventually, Turner and his son made it home to their relieved family. David Hodgson's mates managed to find their sons at the rendezvous point. Across Sheffield, fans queued for hours to get on payphones and local people threw open their homes to allow the traumatised match-goers to call home.

Meanwhile millions of people across Britain sat glued to their TVs and radios as the death toll kept rising. By the time the BBC broadcast its evening news bulletin, the number had reached 74. When ITN went live, it had reached 93, and it would soon rise to 95 (a 96th victim, Tony Bland, would remain in a vegetative state until his life support machine was turned off in 1993).

No one was quite sure what had caused the crush. When *Match of the Day* went out that night, Peter Wright, chief constable of South Yorkshire Police, said a gate had been opened outside the Leppings Lane terraces but he did not know who had opened it. What was abundantly clear, however, was that something had gone terribly wrong.

For the people of Sheffield, the sense of shame and bewilderment was particularly acute. How could their beloved sporting temple have become a slaughterhouse? How had the people in charge of their club allowed this to happen?

John Pearson was still living on Oakland Road, just a mile from Hillsborough. He'd been playing for Leeds that day so the news didn't reach him until he arrived home.

'I just remember bursting into tears when I saw the ground. I couldn't believe it,' he says. 'People had actually died at Wednesday.

'Crowd safety was always an issue at that time. I'd made my debut because of the riots at Oldham, where Jack went on the pitch to ask the fans to calm down. 'But for this to happen to all those innocent people? I was still a young bloke and I often went out into town after games. But I wasn't out that night, no way. I just remember getting home and not believing it. Has this seriously, really happened?'

* * *

In the days after the disaster, players from both clubs would visit injured supporters in hospital in the hope of providing a small token of solace. Chapman recalls, 'Me, Nigel Clough and a few of the other lads went to visit victims in hospital near Sheffield. We saw one of the guys in a coma, we were all by his bedside. He was in a coma for two years and sadly didn't make it. Those are the sort of things you don't forget.

'It really affected me for a good while afterwards.'

David Hodgson, who still had many friends on Merseyside, decided to make his own trip at the suggestion of Wednesday physio Alan Smith. Together they went to the Royal Hallamshire Hospital where many fans were clinging to life.

'I don't regret going, but I saw things, things that stayed with me. I saw youngsters whose heads had expanded because of crushing… horrific, just horrific. Even to this day it's in my mind.'

The disaster continued to dominate the news agenda for months afterwards. The Conservative Government commissioned the Taylor Report and its findings would mark a before-and-after in the way English football treated its fans. Never again would supporters be forced to risk their own safety in such shambolic conditions.

For Wednesday, the disaster meant that the Leppings Lane terrace would be closed forever. But the effect was really far deeper than that. A black pall continued to hang over Hillsborough for years afterwards and the players had no option but to try to play their way through it, as Lawrie Madden recalls.

'We just got on with it. We carried on as best we could. Obviously we were aware of what was going on but we needed to put it to the back of our minds. It was all we could do.'

Seven months after the disaster, Liverpool returned to Hillsborough for a league game at Wednesday.

'It was eerie,' Peter Shirtliff says. 'We had to line up at the Leppings Lane End for a minute's silence with the Liverpool players. They were all in tears more or less, they were in no fit state to play the game.

'One thing that always sticks in my mind is that when it was all quiet, an owl flew across and screeched. I'll never forget that.

'It was difficult to play in that game, to get yourself right from the kick-off. Once the game started and you could concentrate, things got easier. It was really hard for the Liverpool lads.'

In the 30 years that have passed since then, the Hillsborough disaster has been the subject of several enquiries, a string of books and innumerable newspaper articles, not to mention a full government inquiry. 'The Truth', to coin *The Sun*'s infamous headline from 1989, has finally won out.

While South Yorkshire Police have received the bulk of the blame for their appalling actions leading up to the disaster, Sheffield Wednesday remains associated with negligence and mismanagement. For those who were present, the images remain burned into the retina of their mind.

'I remember it like it was yesterday,' Chris Turner says. 'Even now, when I go back to Hillsborough, I look back at Leppings Lane and remember the scenes that I saw.

'Even today, I think the hangover's still there.'

9
DOWN, SOMEHOW

Rarely has there been a more turbulent time in modern British history than the end of March 1990. Protests in London against the so-called Poll Tax, Mrs Thatcher's last and most toxic major decision as Prime Minister, were about to escalate into a full-scale skirmish with police remembered as 'The Second Battle of Trafalgar.' Meanwhile, in Manchester, inmates at Strangeways Prison were gearing up for a riot that would last 25 days.

But in Sheffield, at least, Wednesdayites could relax in the knowledge that their team's First Division status was secure for another year.

With six games of the season to go, Wednesday had reached the magical 40-point mark. They'd won four of their previous six matches, including 1-0 victories over both Arsenal and Manchester United and a 4-1 hammering of Coventry, the best display of the whole campaign. They weren't quite mathematically safe but a couple more results would do the trick.

So Ron Atkinson decided to give his lads some RnR. The players went away on three separate occasions, flying to Guernsey and the Isle of Wight and playing exhibition kickabouts – the sort of thing that would normally be left until the end of the season.

At the time, the move probably made sense. Atkinson's players had fought clear of the relegation zone with a mixture of grit and inspiration so he probably thought they deserved to let their hair down a bit. The money raised from the friendlies would help alleviate the club's financial worries, too.

But whatever the motivation for these jollies, they betrayed a sense of confidence that would prove spectacularly misplaced.

In the space of six agonising weeks, Wednesday imploded. Those final six games, against teams with little or nothing to play for, yielded only five goals and three points. Even then they would have got away with it were it not for a freak result elsewhere.

There have been more dramatic relegations in football history, but none has been as unexpected. Or, indeed, as unnecessary.

* * *

AS FOOTBALL pundits have been telling us since time immemorial, the First Division is a marathon and not a sprint. And while Wednesday's late stumble may have sealed their fate, their descent owed just as much to the false start they made the previous autumn.

While the Liverpools, the Arsenals and (yes, even) the Millwalls seared out of the blocks at the end of that long, hot summer of 1989, Wednesday found their shoelaces tied together. In the first 11 games of that 1989/90 season Atkinson's men accrued just six points, a run that left them marooned at the bottom of the table.

The heaviest blows were wielded in London. Wednesday were hammered by Arsenal, Spurs and Chelsea, and even fellow strugglers Luton beat them with ease at Kenilworth Road, a result which would be crucial in the final analysis.

Much of the blame for that appalling run fell on the defence, which was about as robust as the communist regimes collapsing all over Eastern Europe at the time. But the attack was equally culpable. By the start of October, Wednesday's strikers had mustered just two goals.

The shocking start had pundits everywhere scratching their heads. Wednesday looked a solid team: the ever-reliable Chris Turner had made the goalkeeping slot his own again, and Atkinson had brought Peter Shirtliff back from Charlton to give the defence some much-needed aerial prowess. Alongside him was Nigel Pearson, a man who rivalled Bryan Robson and Tony Adams as the most inspirational leader in the country – and had no peer when it came to sheer hardness.

'Boy, the lads respected Big Nige,' David Hodgson recalls. 'He was tough as nails.

'I remember my very first day. I was going round, introducing myself to the lads as you do, and I didn't know Nige from Adam. Anyway he came up and smashed me at the top of the arm, just below the shoulder, it gave me a dead arm! That was just the way the big plank greeted people.

'But yeah, he had total respect from everyone. The players would go anywhere with him.'

Hodgson himself had decided to move on by this point, lured away by the riches on offer in Japan (Atkinson had promised to sanction the move as long as the player didn't tell his team-mates his new salary, lest they be tempted to follow him).

But Wednesday still had David Hirst, and the manager had finally added his namesake, Dalian Atkinson, after months of unsuccessful bids. Carlton Palmer, rapidly establishing himself as one of the most promising midfielders in the division, was always on hand to support the talented frontmen.

So what was going wrong? Well for all Atkinson's improvements, there were still gaps in the squad. Wednesday were weak down both flanks and they lacked a dash of flair in midfield, having sold Gary Megson to Manchester City over the summer. Atkinson had tried to lure his old mate Gordon Strachan, only for the ginger schemer to choose Howard Wilkinson and Leeds United instead.

But perhaps the biggest problem was mental. Players' heads could easily drop when they went behind, a point amply demonstrated by the maulings they took at the big grounds down south.

Atkinson certainly picked up on this. Lawrie Madden recalls a conversation in the autumn during which the manager laid out his intention to add some more devil to the squad.

'I remember Ron told me Howard's team were too nice. He said we had some good players, but he wanted some scallywags in the team. He didn't mind players having a stand-up row, he didn't mind arguing with players, but he wanted big personalities, like himself. That's the Scouser in him I guess!'

In fact, the gaffer already knew the jack-the-lads he wanted. And, by the time they left S6, these two cheeky chappies had become Hillsborough royalty.

*   *   *

John Sheridan and Phil King came from opposite sides of the tracks. Sheridan had been born on a Manchester council estate within spitting distance of Old Trafford, a place where scallywags scowled on every corner; King had been brought up in the rustic confines of the West Country. He had honed his craft at Exeter and Torquay before becoming a cornerstone of Swindon's impressive side under Ossie Ardiles, while Sheridan had been signed by Brian Clough only to suffer the same fate as Gary Megson (after making his debut, Clough had told Sheridan, 'Young man, I'm giving you a rest,' only to apparently never speak to him again).

They were very different personalities too. King's team-mates remember him as a clown prince, a purveyor of japes and bonhomie. Sheridan was more guarded and could occasionally tear colleagues to ribbons with his acidic tongue on the field.

'Jesus, he could be a horrible man,' Hirst says, wryly. 'He would have a go at anything out on the pitch. If I mis-controlled a ball he would call me every name under the sun… my family, my friends, whatever came into his head. They'd be harsh words. And after the game he'd come over and say, "Sorry about that earlier, Hirsty, it just comes in and comes out mate. Don't take any of it to heart." You knew that if he did that, he cared about you.'

It was a quality that Atkinson saw in both men. He knew they could both play, and, even more importantly, they were just the sort of firebrands who would energise his side. Indeed, the two would become firm friends almost as soon as they were thrown together that autumn.

'We were very different,' King says now. 'Shez was quite an aggressive character on and off the pitch. There'd be situations where you'd have to talk him down, he'd be getting into bits and pieces, whereas I was a joker in the pack, cutting the top of people's socks off.

'But we started rooming together at Wednesday, and he and his wife are still best friends with me and my wife. He was a top player too. For me, there was no better midfielder around than John Sheridan when I played with him.'

King and Sheridan signed on 2 November, a Thursday, and were immediately thrown into the team for their debuts on the Saturday. The opposition? The team Sheridan had just left.

Forest came into the game on the back of a seven-match unbeaten run and had thrashed Crystal Palace 5-0 in the League Cup a few days earlier. Wednesday's last match had been a thoroughly depressing 1-0 home loss to Wimbledon.

But the unfancied visitors dug in and eventually got a bizarre reward when defender Terry Wilson hacked into his own net. For a team that had been finding it impossible to score, Wilson's brain fade was manna from football heaven.

Buoyed by this shock victory, Wednesday slowly and painfully improved. Charlton and Queens Park Rangers were dispatched, and there was even a delightful victory over Sheffield United in the Zenith Data Systems Cup. But the best performance was saved for a sombre late-November night at Hillsborough.

Liverpool arrived in Sheffield for their first visit since that awful day seven months earlier. By a macabre quirk of the fixtures computer, the match had originally been scheduled to be played on Easter Monday, 16 April – a day after the first anniversary of the tragedy.

It was a night that demanded attacking football and something to distract everyone's attention from the concrete void at one end of the ground. And it was Wednesday who roused themselves, with a display so full of zest and vigour that their storied opponents would have been proud of it themselves.

It was a night when Dalian Atkinson's brilliance, which had flickered all season like a fire flailing on a damp winter's day, finally burst into flame. The Wednesday number ten tormented the Liverpool defence all evening before sealing victory with a 20-yard curler in the last minute. As he ran off to celebrate, Atkinson wagged his finger to the Kop as if to admonish anyone who had dared doubt his talent.

In the end, Atkinson's time at Hillsborough would be all too fleeting – just like his manager's, in fact. The two men shared more than a surname: both were huge characters who enjoyed the nightlife and brought extravagant gifts to their lines of work. Dalian's explosive style was ideally suited to Ron's buccaneering football philosophy, too. But in the summer of 1990 Atko the Elder received an offer that was too good to turn down.

So all Wednesday got from Atkinson was 38 games and ten goals. But still, what a player. He could be inconsistent, he could be frustrating, but of all the star names who donned the blue and white stripes during this period – Waddle, Hirst, Bright – none of them had the combination of power, pace and skill that Atkinson possessed.

Tragically, Atkinson is not around to tell us about his brief time at Wednesday. Knowing the exuberance and zeal with which he lived his life, the stories would no doubt have been belters. But instead, we have the memories of a truly unique talent, one that every Wednesday fan who was there at the time was privileged to witness.

*   *   *

As the season entered its midway point, Atkinson's partnership with the more predatory Hirst was just one of several double-acts in what was becoming a well-balanced team.

Shirtliff and Pearson were building an understanding at the back, and cutting out some of those silly errors that had dogged Wednesday earlier in the season. In midfield, Sheridan and Palmer were beginning to pick up one another's frequencies.

And out on the left King and Nigel Worthington were shuttling up and down the flank, covering one another's backs and accentuating their respective strengths.

'Ron bought Phil because he was so good going forward,' Worthington recalls of their partnership. 'I was by no means a left-winger, but I could work hard up and down.

'So Ron came up with this system where we would alternate positions. I was there to do a job out on that left-hand side, be neat and tidy and get crosses in if and when. Then when Kingy got ahead of me and bombed on, I would just drop into my natural position. It worked really well.'

Now all that was needed was someone to come in on the other side, where a Mel Sterland-sized hole still needed to be filled. As always, the boss was one step ahead.

'I didn't know much about Wednesday when Ron got in touch,' Roland Nilsson says. 'It was a club that had great followers, the ground was big, and I knew about the tragedy that had happened. I knew the team was okay, although they weren't doing well in the table when Ron asked me to come over.

'A few clubs had been interested, but it was more difficult to move then because of all the rules around having too many foreign players, and they had to be playing in the national team. Moving abroad didn't happen that often then. There was a Greek club and a Spanish club, but nothing concrete.

'But I saw that I could make a difference. They were struggling with the right-back, they'd tried a few, and I saw my chance to come over and play in the English league. Ron told me, "We've got a good side going, we're not going too well but with you in the team we'll start to make progress and young players will grow. If you join you'll enjoy it."'

Even now, it's hard to fathom how Atkinson managed to spirit Nilsson over to Sheffield. After all, he was a key player for the Swedish national team and had appeared in the semi-final of the European Cup (in fact it was during that semi, against Barcelona, that he'd made the switch from the right wing to right-back to cover for an ill Glenn Hysen).

In the end Wednesday got their man for a fee of just £375,000, which must rank as the grandest act of larceny since Ronnie Biggs and his cohorts hatched a plot to flag down a mail train. Nilsson established himself as the best right-back in the country, and probably beyond. 'He was one hell of a player and one hell of an athlete,' Nigel Worthington recalls. 'He was a bit like Kyle Walker today, but maybe a little more refined.'

Roland Nilsson was the perfect right-back. Wednesday have never made a better signing.

But Nilsson wasn't just a great player. In an era when hardly any foreigners made it to these shores – on the first Premier League weekend in August 1992, there were only 13 non-British or Irish players – Nilsson was a pioneer, helping chart the course to today's polyglot jamboree. This middle-class kid, who played the piano and had trained for a role in business before turning pro, proved that urbane continentals could adapt to the testosterone-fuelled maelstrom of an English dressing room.

'It wasn't actually that big a shock,' Nilsson says. 'Yes there were big characters. Carlton was always shouting, Dalian wanted to have a good laugh, David Hirst and John Sheridan were always taking the piss. But we'd had a team full of stars at Gothenburg and it was the same. A lot of laughs, a lot of shouting when that was needed.

'The biggest thing was the focus on football. In Sweden people enjoy football but in England people live for it, and not just during the weekend. They follow it all week.'

In Nilsson, the Wednesday fans found a player who matched their devotion, a man who was as committed to the blue and white stripes as they were. In their all-time Wednesday dream teams most fans would probably have him at right-back, even ahead of Mel Sterland.

There can be no greater compliment than that.

*   *   *

Nilsson made his debut against Luton just 24 hours after arriving at Hillsborough. The new signing had a stormer but even though Luton gifted Wednesday the lead with a freak own goal which ballooned into the net off defender John Dreyer's face, the home side were unable to cling on to victory. Again, it would prove extremely costly in the end.

However Wednesday then produced a brilliant display to beat QPR in the final league game before Christmas, and then they pushed Liverpool all the way at Anfield on Boxing Day. A creditable draw at Southampton was followed by a New Year's Day victory over Manchester City, which remains the last top-flight game not to be filmed.

It's a pity, really. Had the camera crew bothered to turn up they'd have captured a cracking Wednesday display, illuminated by goals from Hirst and Pearson. And viewers would also have witnessed Hirst going in goal after an injury to Kevin Pressman forced an emergency reshuffle in the second half.

The fact that Hirst kept a clean sheet is impressive enough. When you consider his 'preparation' for the game, it's positively miraculous.

'We'd stayed in the Hallam Towers the night before,' Hirst recalls wistfully. 'Ron had given us a 9pm curfew, no phone calls through reception, because we had a 12 o'clock kick-off the next day.

'Everyone was up for breakfast at seven or eight o'clock, and when we got to reception he'd laid a bottle of pink champagne on every table. To this day I thank Ron for getting me into that!

'It was just a toast to welcome in the new year because we couldn't do it the night before. But some of the players didn't like pink champagne, so I took it upon myself to do a bit of minesweeping for them. I'm not sure exactly how many glasses I had – people who were there tell me it was quite a few, but after the first couple I kind of lost track!

'So we kicked off, I opened the scoring in the first half and then after half-time Kevin came out for a ball against David Oldfield and damaged his cruciate ligament in the collision. As all this happened, I was standing up top – I wouldn't say worse for wear, but I was probably a bit more tired than I would be normally – and I could see Carlton being called over to go in goal.

'So I went over to speak to Ron and asked what was happening, and he told me Carlton was going in net. So I joked, "I'm not being funny gaffer, but Carlton struggles to control it with his feet! What's he going to be like with his hands?" I volunteered, took Kevin's shirt off him and played the remainder of the game in goal. I broke my finger, but apart from that it went perfectly!'

The whole situation sounds more Dog and Duck than First Division: the star striker going between the sticks after sinking a few glasses of bubbly before the game. But Dave the Cat and his half-cut heroics appear to have galvanised the entire squad. Between New Year's Day and the end of March Wednesday picked up 19 points from ten games, a run of form that wouldn't disgrace a championship contender.

Arsenal, the *actual* champions, were beaten 1-0 at Hillsborough thanks to another comical own goal, this time from Steve Bould after 14 seconds. Manchester United were then seen off by the same score, with that emphatic win at Coventry sandwiched in between. The draw at Wimbledon marked six weeks without defeat (and that run-ending loss against Aston Villa was one of the great 0-1s of all time).

Wednesday still weren't scoring floods of goals but they were at least stopping them. And the attack was now looking significantly more fertile thanks to another opportunistic Atkinson signing, a man who would have a lasting impact on Wednesday's fortunes.

*   *   *

Trevor Francis was out of a job when Big Ron came knocking. He'd been sacked as manager of QPR a couple of months earlier and was facing a career crossroads. The path into management, which had seemed so obvious for such a bright young man, had suddenly reached a dead end.

But Francis could still play. Although he was about to turn 36, he hadn't lost the magic that had earned 52 England caps and won a European Cup for Nottingham Forest. Atkinson told him to stop moping about the QPR dismissal and get back to the job at which he'd always been peerless.

When Francis arrived in Sheffield and began working with his new team-mates, his ability shone like a beacon on the misty winter's mornings. All the players interviewed for this book remember the brilliance he routinely displayed, both in matches and on the training ground. He had lost his searing pace, but that didn't matter. With barely a swish of his regal right boot he could float the ball into precisely the spot where Hirst was waiting.

Not only was Francis a brilliant crosser of the ball, he was also a genuine winner who had tested himself on the biggest stages and had the medals to prove it. And even though he was only brought in to play a bit-part role, his arrival gave the players another major lift.

Sheridan began to rival Paul Gascoigne as the best creative midfielder in the country, scoring superb goals against Derby and Coventry. Worthington rampaged down the wing, giving Wednesday a cutting edge they'd lacked all season. And on the other side Franz Carr, on loan from Nottingham Forest, was producing some of the best football of his career. Now Wednesday weren't just a pretty side; they looked like one of the most dangerous teams in the division.

Then the whole thing fell apart.

*   *   *

The rot started against Tottenham, when Wednesday threw away a second-half lead in the spring sunshine. At the time, no one was particularly worried.

Wednesday had produced two excellent goals and been undone by the brilliance of Gary Lineker, a player so good he could make any team look stupid. All they needed was a couple of results.

But the results wouldn't come. There was another slip-up at Hillsborough, this time against Southampton, and then the flukiest of own goals cost them a point at Manchester City. When QPR took the points at Loftus Road, alarm bells began to ring.

But then Charlton were vanquished by a classic double from Hirst, meaning that survival was all but secure. Safety would be reached with merely a point at home to Nottingham Forest, who were in tenth place and still coming down from their recent victory in the League Cup Final. Even if Wednesday lost they would still stay up if Luton, who had only won once away from home all season, failed to claim three points at Derby.

Suffice to say, things didn't go according to plan.

At the worst possible moment, Wednesday reverted to the wretched form they had displayed at the start of the season. Meanwhile Luton pulled a performance from the nether regions of nowhere to win 3-2 at the Baseball Ground.

Even those who weren't at Hillsborough that day will have seen the footage of the players fluffing unmissable opportunities and then being gut-punched on the break. Of Ron Atkinson slumped against the dugout, resting his head on his forearm in bewilderment.

The players, of course, have their own memories of that agonising day. Lawrie Madden says, 'When we were chasing the game and it came through that Luton were winning, I remember some people in the crowd turning on us. As a player, when you hear the fans doing that, it's a horrible feeling.

'Then there was a roar around the ground because people thought Derby had scored. But I was near Ron and he turned round and told us it wasn't true. There was a guy nearby on the radio and he knew what was actually going on.'

Of course, the guy with the radio was right. A goal had arrived at Derby, but it had gone the wrong way. A daisy-cutter from Kingsley Black had somehow bamboozled Derby's Peter Shilton, arguably the greatest English goalkeeper of the modern era, and Luton's route-one football had somehow guided them to First Division salvation. For Wednesday and their gifted squad the only road was down, towards the rutted dirt tracks of Plymouth, Port Vale and Bristol Rovers.

* * *

When looking back at the reasons for that crazy implosion, several players interviewed for this book pointed to those island getaways in early spring. Peter Shirtliff, for example, says, 'I enjoyed playing under Ron. But I think if you asked him about the end of the season he might say he relaxed too much.

'I remember we played a game on the Isle of Wight. I have no idea why, I don't get it at all. At the time I didn't resent it, but you look back after the season's finished and think, "Why on Earth did we do that?"'

Lawrie Madden agrees that the trips offered little value from a footballing perspective. 'We played the local teams over there. They were never serious tests. We were used to playing in the top league and then suddenly we were playing the local island teams. They were barely better than pub teams, really.'

However Madden is quick to add that it wasn't arrogance or carelessness on the manager's part. Instead, he says, 'Ron was trying to come up with ways to change things. It was a long season and, rather than stick with the same old routine, he was trying to break things up and refresh the players, give them a change of scenery. He was always looking to keep the lads happy.

'The club had always organised trips during the season. I remember under Howard we played games in Kuwait, to bring some money in. We'd play the Saturday in Sheffield, travel down to Heathrow Saturday night, fly out Sunday, play the match Monday and fly back on the Tuesday. They were not nice trips, and we'd often be a bit lackadaisical on the following Saturday. Ron's trips were nothing like that.'

Instead of blaming the manager, Madden suggests the players themselves were lulled into a false sense of security by their great run of form in February and March, 'I think being honest, we probably thought we had enough points and maybe took our eye off the ball because we thought we were safe.'

It's also true to say that Wednesday suffered some outrageous luck in those final games. Peter Shirtliff's own goal at Maine Road was a sickener but the sheer number of times they hit the post and bar in those closing weeks without actually scoring must surely be some kind of record.

'In the matches we played, it wasn't that we were putting in bad performances,' says Roland Nilsson. 'In some games we were playing really well but we couldn't score. I felt we just didn't get the points we deserved.'

Worthington echoes these comments, and believes Wednesday perhaps became victims of their own footballing principles. 'Maybe we focused on the style of football, which was great, and forgot how to win ugly,' he concludes ruefully.

But whatever the reason for the relegation, it left the entire club reeling. After playing host to an unspeakable tragedy the previous year, now Wednesday's footballing pride had been stripped from them too.

Worthington recalls 'a total silence' in the dressing room after the game as the players came to terms with what had happened. Chris Turner concurs. 'We were gutted, just stunned. People barely spoke afterwards.'

Little did anyone know what the next 12 months would have in store.

10
DREAMLAND

Buried in the dark recesses of YouTube, beneath the millions of fitness videos, make-up tutorials and skateboarding cats, lies a fascinating time capsule for Wednesday fans.

The video is called A Will to Win *and was originally released as a VHS for supporters in the autumn of 1990, one of those homespun attempts to monetise fan culture in the days before Sky and the Premier League. Footage from the training ground, including an unusually large amount of close-ups of players getting their legs massaged, is interspersed with interviews from players and staff.*

Most of the interviews are banal stuff, filled with the monosyllabic soundbites that any football fan will be familiar with. But there are also two little titbits that seem uncannily prescient in light of what came later.

Ron Atkinson, bullish despite the recent relegation, tells his interviewer, 'I like my teams to play the way that I like to watch a game played. I don't mean that I want us to turn into amusement arcades… I want us to be winners.'

Chairman Dave Richards, meanwhile, gushes in his praise of the manager, lauding his professionalism and attention to detail. At the end of his segment, the Wednesday chairman decides to sign off on a grandiose note.

'Given the opportunity, he [Atkinson] could make Sheffield Wednesday better than Manchester United.'

* * *

WHEN ATKINSON and Richards gave those interviews, they weren't talking about the short-term. Of course not. Wednesday had only just gone down and it would be a long time before the nation would consider them 'winners'. And it would be even longer before they would be considered better than Manchester United, who had just won the FA Cup.

But, incredibly, both men would be vindicated within a matter of months. Atkinson masterminded one of the greatest seasons in Wednesday's history, one in which the team didn't just win but did so with verve and vigour, in keeping with the very best of the club's traditions.

And Richards's claim was proved, quite literally, correct.

* * *

Most triumphant seasons end on a beach with the players celebrating their league or cup glory with sun, sea and sangria. But for the Sheffield Wednesday team of 1990/91, the beach was where it *started*.

The players had just endured one of the most agonising relegations imaginable, losing their top-flight status after a series of bizarre results. The players had ended the campaign slumped in the dressing room, locked together in a state of stunned silence.

Most managers would have sent them home to mope, but Ron Atkinson was not most managers. He decided to take them away for a few days in Marbella where they could have a few beers and forget about what had just befallen them. It was the first in a series of masterstrokes he would pull off over the next 12 months.

It is a trip Carlton Palmer recalls well. 'The lads were stunned after the relegation. To go down with the points we had, it was fucking unheard of. And then Luton, who had been losing every game away from home, went and won at Derby… unreal. But then – and by the way, who does this? – Ron took us away the next day.

When the Wednesday players gathered for pre-season before the 1990/91 campaign, few could have imagined what they would go on to achieve.

'When we arrived, he called a meeting on the front lawn of the hotel by the pool. He's got his briefcase with him. He says, "Listen, I know we're all disappointed, and it's unlucky that we've gone down. But we're going to piss the league next season, no doubt about it. We're going to come back early, we're going to be the fittest team, and we're going to play the best football."

'So he opened his briefcase, got out a bunch of passports and said – and bear in mind, we've got internationals in the side who would have been wanted by other clubs – "anybody who wants to go, anybody who's not up for it, anybody who doesn't want to do what I'm going to ask you to do, take your passport and fuck off." So obviously nobody moved, and then he said, "Right, we're all in this together then. Have a great week and if you get locked up, you're on your own!"'

To the swarthy Spanish locals, it must have been quite the sight: a rotund English *guiri,* his mahogany skin turning a glistening red beneath the Iberian sun, brandishing the sort of briefcase usually held aloft by chancellors on freezing mornings outside Downing Street. But the message hit home.

When they eventually headed back to England the players proved as good as their word. Instead of abandoning Atkinson's salvage operation and finding a First Division club, Wednesday's star names decided to stay and fight.

It's inconceivable to imagine that happening now. Today, players like David Hirst, Roland Nilsson and John Sheridan would have jumped long before the first parachute payment arrived. The moneyed elite would have gleefully carved up the squad and Wednesday would have been condemned to years, possibly decades, of purgatory in the one-horse towns of the Second Division.

But times were different then. Back at the start of the 1990s, relegation didn't carry such a massive financial penalty and venal agents had yet to slither into the lives of top players. And, crucially, Wednesday were ambitious. Richards had taken over as chairman in April, intent on adding a glint of glamour to the old Sheffield steel. On his watch Wednesday would stop letting their best players slip away.

Lawrie Madden says, 'The masterstroke was keeping the team. I remember talking to Ron afterwards and him saying he thought [Manchester] United were going to come in for Ronald Nilsson. They didn't have an established right-back then and word on the grapevine was they were looking for one [Nilsson says he heard the rumours, but doesn't know if they were true]. Had they come in, Wednesday would have been powerless to stop him leaving. And he'd have been a snip.

'But Roland went up to Ron and said, "I was part of the team that got relegated, I want to be part of the team that get promoted." I'm not sure you'd get that loyalty in this day and age.

'It was also a different time then, financially. These days if you get relegated, there's no way you can keep the players. But then the financial gap wasn't as great.'

The one big fish who did slip the net was Dalian Atkinson, who would earn the affectionate nickname 'El Txipiron', or 'The Squid', at his new employers Real Sociedad. The Basque club were among Spain's biggest spenders at the time (they had lured John Aldridge from Liverpool the previous year), and the fee of £1.7m represented an amazing return on Wednesday's investment the year before.

Of course, this rampaging bull of a centre-forward would leave a major hole in the Wednesday attack. But his managerial namesake now had the funds he needed to tinker with his squad and complete the overhaul he had begun so impressively the previous winter.

To fill the gap in the forward line, Atkinson's gaze fell on Paul Williams, who had also just been relegated with Charlton and was recommended by Shirtliff. Having played for England's under-21s, Williams could easily have held out for a First Division club and avoided the hassle of moving his young family out of London. He'd already turned down a move to QPR, when a certain Trevor Francis was manager. But upon meeting Atkinson he was wooed instantly.

'I came back off holiday and Lennie Lawrence [then managing Charlton] told me Wednesday had made an offer,' Williams recalls. 'I'd played with Carlton Palmer for England under-21s and I knew a bit about them. I knew they'd been relegated, of course. But wherever you're from in the country, you know Wednesday are a big club with a massive fanbase.

'I met Ron at his house, which marked him out straightaway. When I'd talked to other clubs it might be at a hotel or at a motorway service station, which is where a lot of football deals are done. He allowed me to meet his partner and see where he lived. That was a good impression.

'I'd spoken to QPR, I'd spoken to David Pleat at Spurs, I'd spoken to Ray Harford at Fulham; everything seemed to be more formal and clinical. But Ron was very jovial, very down to earth, very nurturing in a strange way. He was a big man and he just made me feel very comfortable.'

Williams wasn't as flashy or as skilful as the man he was replacing. But his background had equipped him with a burning desire to succeed, ideal for Wednesday's current circumstances.

'Growing up, there'd been 100 families on the street and we were the only black family. People wouldn't talk to us. On occasion my brothers and sisters would come home and say they'd been spat at, cars would drive past and people would shout all kinds of things. I'd be chased by skinheads when I took my girlfriend to the train station, that was a regular occurrence. We weren't even allowed out after dark.

'I was cocky, looking back, but I was never one who crossed the line. I'd been raised in a single-parent family, a very strict upbringing. And when I played football, I was a hard worker. I'd make runs all the time and set up goals for my team-mates.'

This relentless work ethic and constant willingness to stretch defences made Williams the ideal foil for David Hirst. Now, centre-backs had to drop deeper to prevent the ball over the top, which would leave Hirst more space to pick up possession and run at them.

'He [Williams] was probably my favourite strike partner,' Hirst says now. 'I'm close friends with Mark Bright and we played a few games together. Chappy [Lee Chapman] was good too, in the early days, how he played – do nothing for 88 minutes, run around for a couple for minutes and score the winner! But Willo was great for me. We used to joke that we had a deal going – I'd score the goals and he'd do the running!'

Williams, for his part, says he is 'honoured' by Hirst's praise. 'The two of us weren't bosom buddies. We didn't go out much – I didn't drink and I didn't socialise with the players that much – but I idolised him as a player. At that time he was fantastic. And the respect was mutual.

'On the field he did what I couldn't do and I did what he couldn't do. Maybe he and Dalian had been a bit similar – both liked the ball to feet, both of them were very tricky – whereas I think he and I complemented one another a lot better. And Ron spent a lot of time trying to get the team to acclimatise to our strengths.'

After King and Worthington, and Palmer and Sheridan, Atkinson the alchemist had found another set of elements that bonded perfectly.

* * *

But, as he put together his promotion jigsaw, Big Ron knew he still needed to find a piece that would slot into the hole in front of Roland Nilsson. Ever since he'd tried and failed to sign his old mate Gordon Strachan, Atkinson had struggled to fill that void on the right-hand side. For all Trevor Francis's elegance and the tenacity of Franz Carr, no one had truly clicked into place.

In the end Atkinson decided to sign not one player, but two.

Danny Wilson and John Harkes are another of those classic odd couples who were thrown together at Wednesday during this period. Wilson had been brought up in Wigan, a mill town famous for meat pies and rugby league, and had already turned out for seven Football League clubs. Harkes, by contrast, had been raised just a few miles from New York City and had never even set foot in the English game. While Wilson looked every inch the nuggety English terrier, Harkes would go on to be named among *People* magazine's 50 most beautiful people on Earth.

What they had in common, though, was a boundless desire to succeed which would make them folk heroes on the Wednesday terraces.

Wilson had recently displayed that desire by helping to keep Luton in the First Division – at Wednesday's expense. Just a few days after that feat of escapology, in fact, he and his Luton team-mates had been to Marbella on their own piss-up, and bumped into the Wednesday lads in a bar. 'They were absolutely shattered,' Wilson recalls now (perhaps Ron had yet to give them their spending money).

Nonetheless, after being introduced to Atkinson via his Northern Ireland team-mate Nigel Worthington, Wilson was happy to make the move.

'Luton had aged together. A lot of players were leaving and Wednesday were a bigger opportunity. Plus my wife's family were from Chesterfield and we had two young kids. We wanted them settled, so Sheffield was perfect.'

While Wilson was completing his move to Hillsborough, Harkes was playing in Italia '90, part of the first US team to make the World Cup finals in 40 years.

Wednesday were initially reticent about signing him and would only sanction the deal after Harkes completed a lengthy trial in the reserve team. Other internationals might have scoffed at the idea of auditioning for a Second Division side. Not Harkes, though.

'It was massive for me to make it in England,' he says. 'I'd grown up in a football-mad area – my hometown, Kearny, is featured in the documentary

John Harkes became a vital cog in the Wednesday team, first under Ron Atkinson and then Trevor Francis.

Soccer Town USA, and other US players like Tony Meola and Tab Ramos came from there. My dad had been a footballer in Dundee, he'd been in the British Army and come to the US, where he met my mum at the Scots-American club.

'I'd actually been over to Wednesday before the World Cup. The owner of the Albany Capitals [a team Harkes had played for], knew someone in Sheffield. I'd gone over with Tony Meola in January, I'd done well and Ron had asked me to stay until May. But given we'd just qualified for our first World Cup and had loads of warm-up games, I said I preferred to stay with the national team.

'I went back on trial after the World Cup, it went on through August and September and my agent, Ian St John, told me Blackburn and Celtic were interested too. I went and had a trial at both of them but my heart was with Wednesday, so I went back.'

Harkes finally convinced Atkinson of his worth and a contract was agreed. The new signing threw himself into the Yorkshire life, thrilled to be given a chance on the English stage.

'It wasn't a culture shock to move to Sheffield. My family was all over the UK, I'd been back and forth as a kid, growing up with the banter. Sheffield was a blue-collar town and I had a hard work ethic. It was a great fit.'

Harkes does admit, however, that he found his teammates' drinking a bit of a surprise at first. And it was after one of the squad's beery nights that the season almost unravelled before it even got started.

Not content with the jaunt to Marbella at the start of the summer, Atkinson decided to take the squad on another foreign excursion during pre-season. This time it would be a training camp rather than a booze cruise, and the destination would be Sardinia, which had played host to England during the World Cup. In fact, it had been specifically chosen to host England because its pine-scented tranquility would deter the fans from getting into any scrapes.

So a group of finely tuned, highly motivated professional athletes wouldn't cause any trouble, right?

Paul Williams sets the scene. 'We'd all been out to a restaurant and I think I'd gone back early. Then one of the lads came up to my room and said, "You need to come downstairs, there's some people there who want some autographs." So I reluctantly went down with a couple of the other lads, and Shez [John Sheridan] was there too.

'In the end Ron came in through the hotel foyer and saw us. "Willo, get yourself off to bed," he told me. He knew I'd left the restaurant early and I was in my shorts, so it was obvious I'd come from my room.

'Anyway the next thing I hear is Ron and Shez having a proper argument. Ron is calling Shez a disgrace, Shez is having a go back. Then I heard the sound of fighting. I came out and they were scrapping on the floor, with players trying to break it up.'

Other players remember the fracas too, although their accounts of the severity vary. Some say it was nothing more than a shouting match. Peter Shirtliff, for example, remembers, 'It wasn't a fight, just a bit of an altercation that was done and dusted quickly.' Nonetheless, it represented a major distraction and a clear challenge to Atkinson's authority, coming from such a key player.

Plenty of other managers – plenty of other Wednesday managers, indeed – would have sent Sheridan home the next day and probably alienated him for good. Atkinson, though, took a more subtle route.

The following day, the manager got his squad together, apart from Sheridan. 'He asked us what we'd like him to do,' Palmer remembers. 'We said, "Gaffer, he was out of order, do what you've got to do, but we don't agree with you selling him." So he called Shez in and said, "You can stay, and you've got them to thank."'

All the players interviewed for this book agree that Atkinson's handling of the spat was perfect. Rather than losing respect, he emerged with his standing enhanced. The players knew he was a fair man who would treat them like adults and not overreact if they crossed the line.

'It was a masterstroke from Ron,' Williams says. 'He made a situation that was quite detrimental into a positive, and gave players the freedom to manage it. That was a big step forward for the whole squad.'

* * *

And so to the first game, away to Ipswich Town. For the thousands of Wednesdayites who flooded the M1, their team had a surprise in store – a brand-new away kit of canary-yellow shirts and blue shorts, the same colours worn by Brazil.

Atkinson had actually unveiled it to the players the day before, one of those laser-focused ploys which served both to relax his charges and inspire them. 'Ron said, "Well if we want to look like Brazil, we might as well play like them,"' Nigel Worthington remembers. 'So we went out and the whole team played some fantastic stuff. We were running on air from what he said.'

Wednesday won 2-0 that day and over the next few weeks they produced football that would have had even Zico and Socrates drooling. The first ten games yielded eight wins, two draws and 25 goals.

'It was brilliant, it was banging,' Danny Wilson says of that opening run. 'We were playing in front of 30-plus thousand every week. The fans really got behind us.'

Whereas previously Wednesday had struggled to generate goals from midfield, now they were flying in from everywhere; whereas previously everything had gone through Sheridan, now everyone was busting out the flicks and tricks (even Shirtliff pulled off a nutmeg in the mauling of Plymouth).

The most eye-catching part of the team was up front, where Hirst was blossoming into an elite centre-forward. In those opening ten games he plundered eight goals, including four in the first home league match of the season against Hull, in which he also hit the post. With Williams alongside him, Hirst was about to enter the most prolific spell of his entire career.

But the most symbiotic part of the team was the midfield, which was now perfectly balanced. Palmer provided the team's heart and lungs and Sheridan added the eyes and ears. It was an engine room that would fire the Wednesday team to the top of English football over the next four years.

Under a different manager, both men would have been out of the door before the season had even started. Sheridan, of course, had had that altercation with Atkinson in Sardinia, but Palmer had tested his patience too. Towards the end of the previous season, in the days before a game at Crystal Palace, Palmer had smoked a spliff – only to then be called for a routine drug test. To avert a ban, a member of the Wednesday backroom staff had had to pee in Palmer's bottle and pass it off as the player's sample.

Rather than banish these two mavericks, Atkinson had given them their head. Now they were rewarding him.

'People got it wrong when they played us,' Palmer says. 'They always thought I would take the runner, but I never did, and that's where the problem came in for them. Shez would take the runner, because he sat deep – and people forget how fit he was. So therefore, whoever their other midfielder was, the one who didn't have the legs, had to try and run with me.'

The pair could scarcely have been more different in their approach to matches. Before every game, to settle his nerves, Palmer would run up to the Wednesday sponsors' lounge and grab a tot of brandy from Bob Gorrell. 'I told him and the girls that I'd be back at 4.45 for the man of the match award,' Palmer beams now. Sheridan, meanwhile, would be collected in his thoughts, often watching the racing on the dressing room TV.

Nonetheless, the pair could read each other's games with almost telepathic accuracy. While other players needed instruction, Palmer and Sheridan had excellent football brains and were confident in their ability to interpret what was happening in front of them. They could work things out for themselves.

'Shez and I were very close, but we didn't even talk about what our jobs were,' Palmer says. 'We just adapted. And Ron let us adapt.'

* * *

However, no amount of talent could stop the Second Division pitches turning to glue, or opponents using knees and elbows to make up for their lack of skill and elegance. So, inevitably, Wednesday came back into the pack as those golden summer days began to fade.

Infuriatingly the unbeaten start to the season finally ended at Millwall, a team whose kick-and-rush philosophy was the antithesis of Wednesday's. The visitors roared into a 2-0 lead at The Den, playing some of the best football seen in the division for many a year, only to be pegged back in the second half as injuries to Nilsson and Pearson took their toll.

Phil King remembers, 'Bonuses started at 400 quid a win that season, and they kept going up 100 quid every game we went unbeaten. Going into that Millwall game, we were 12 unbeaten and we stood to get 1,300 quid.

'So we were 2-0 up at half-time and everyone's thinking "kerching!" Then Roland does his cruciate, Nigel gets carried off and it all goes wrong.'

That loss was one of five games without a win, and a further trickle of five draws followed in December. Although Wednesday recovered their mojo at the start of 1991 they could never quite recapture that early-season form.

But even when the wins wouldn't come, Atkinson found a way to keep the players pressing forward.

'Ron worked the bollocks off you,' Danny Wilson says. 'He knew fitness was a prerequisite. But it was varied, too. It wasn't just one-dimensional. If Ron thought we needed that physicality in the training, we'd do a lot of hard running and fitness. But other weeks it would be five-a-sides and team play.

'Ron knew the game. He'd been a player as well. If he could see players were pissed off, he might ease off. And he always had a trick up his sleeve.

'He would boast to other players about you, just tell them, "Wow, we've got a real player here haven't we?" when you did something good in training for example. It was great for your confidence and he knew exactly what he was doing.'

The day-to-day routines were organised by Richie Barker, who commanded the universal respect of the players – even when his fitness routines left them gasping for breath.

'It was very much good cop-bad cop,' says Hirst. 'Richie would put the cones out to do the running, and Ron would come out and do the five-a-sides when he fancied a game.

'On a number of occasions I saw Richie put dozens of cones out for the running drills from eight to ten o'clock, then Ron came out at quarter past ten and said, "Come on, Richie, put them away, we're having a five-a-side." That's a manager who knows how to get his players on his side!'

But Atkinson knew how to employ stick as well as carrot, and the baton was very much in evidence when Oldham came to town at the start of November, hot on the heels of that Millwall defeat. It was one of the few home games that season that didn't yield three points, but it was arguably the most memorable match of the entire league campaign.

Oldham were an excellent side, having reached the League Cup Final and FA Cup semi-final the previous season, and they stunned the home crowd with two expertly taken goals, both of them set up by a marauding right-back called Paul Warhurst. Wednesday were as wasteful in attack as they were sloppy in defence.

At half-time, with players laying into one another, Atkinson suddenly let rip.

'It was hilarious,' says Palmer. 'I'd been away with England, think we had a training camp that week, and I'd been out on the lash. A few others had been away, and we were fucking lacklustre in that first half. At half-time we were all tearing into one another – Big Nige had me by the throat.

'Then Ron came into the room, as angry as I'd ever seen him. He was so angry that he could hardly speak. Then he just went ballistic – he got these tea cups and was hurling them against the wall!

'Finally he just turned round and said, "You got us into this fucking mess, now you go out and get yourselves out of it." And he went out and slammed the door so hard you thought it was going to crash off its hinges!'

Others remember the incident too, although their version of events is slightly different. Williams says the manager didn't spray his ire around the team; instead, he directed it solely at Palmer. 'Ron was almost nicknamed Carlton's dad because he and Carlton had such a close relationship. But that day they just went at it. I'm not sure who made the first comment but before we knew it the two of them were in this verbal argument and then all of a sudden Ron threw a flask of tea and went to fight him.'

Whatever the truth, the meltdown had the desired effect. Wednesday roared back in the second half, led by Palmer, who galloped around the field like Shergar on speed. It was one of those afternoons when the team and crowd were joined in a pulsating circuit of emotion, feeding off one another.

Halfway through the second half, Wednesday were awarded a penalty. Then, with time ticking away, they got another. Sheridan, a man so cool that he probably used ice baths to warm himself up, converted them both. Cue bedlam on the terraces.

It wasn't a perfect performance but no one cared. Wednesday had faced a tough test from a quality side and pulled through. The half-time bust-up was soon forgotten in the comeback's warm glow, and it was a happy bunch of lads who trooped off to the pub that night.

'It was brilliant,' says Palmer now, roaring with laughter. 'We were all in the Devonshire Arms, and there's Ron on the ITV highlights programme, giving them chapter and verse on what he did tactically, what he told us at half-time and all the rest of it. And we're just pissing ourselves. "You did fuck all, you just slammed the door and told us to go and sort it out!"'

Oldham were just one of three teams vying with Wednesday for promotion that season. West Ham, putting together an attractive side under Billy Bonds, and Middlesbrough, who had assembled a fine crop of young players including Stuart Ripley, Colin Cooper and Robbie Mustoe, would prove equally redoubtable opponents. Crucially, Wednesday beat both teams on their own turf.

On New Year's Day Ron's boys went to Middlesbrough and came back with a 2-0 win. Then, in March, they visited West Ham, who had taken their place at the top of the division, and claimed a superb 3-1 victory, sealed by Paul Williams, returning to the club that had rejected him as a teenager.

'I actually got us to the ground that day!' Williams remembers with a chuckle. 'I remember us getting stuck on the North Circular. I had to direct the driver through a couple of shortcuts near the ground.

'I got tickets for my parents and my close family. I remember scoring the first goal and looking up to where they were with a sense of achievement.

'West Ham were my club. I'd sent letters to have trials there, I'd spoken to some of the agents and some of the scouts from West Ham, I'd made clear that I'd play there for nothing and I got nothing back. Not even a "sorry, but..."

'So yeah, there was some vindication.'

Despite those victories, in the end Wednesday finished well short of the Second Division title. A run of just six wins from their final 14 games left them six points adrift of Oldham, who beat them 3-2 on the final day. However by that stage Wednesday had already clinched promotion. With three teams going up automatically that season (the First Division was expanding from 20 teams to 22) it was never really in doubt.

Ordinarily, the failure to win a trophy that was so obviously there for the taking would have been a disappointment. Wednesday had been the bookies' favourites before the season kicked off and their squad was clearly superior to any other in the division.

Atkinson had certainly told the players he wanted to win the league. 'He wanted us to win it for the fans,' Williams says. 'He had a real respect for the fans. He would tell us to go and clap them after every game.'

But those same fans weren't particularly bothered. Because, by the time that final match at Oldham rolled round, they had far more reason to celebrate.

*   *   *

Up until 1991, Wednesday and the League Cup had mixed like lager and Lambrini. The only time the club had been involved in the final had been when it hosted the replay back in 1977. Not even the great side of the 1960s had come close to actually playing in it.

So when Wednesday won at Brentford in a second-round tie in early October, few would have imagined that their journey through the competition would end just nine miles up the road, at the most famous English sporting venue of all. A replay victory at Swindon in the next round didn't exactly set the pulses racing either.

But then Wednesday were paired with Derby in the round of 16, a tie that finally caught the Sheffield public's imagination. Derby could call on Mark

Wright, Dean Saunders and Peter Shilton but they were sliding down the First Division. This was a chance to put down a marker and show the football world where Wednesday belonged.

In the end the tie went to a replay at the Baseball Ground, where Wednesday had been knocked out the previous season. For the fans, however, it was a most welcome treat; a trip to a top-flight ground, a short hop down the M1, and only a couple of weeks before Christmas.

Thousands took up the opportunity, flooding the away end and shaking the old ground to its crumbling foundations (in fact it was one of the earliest known appearances of the supporter famously known as Tango, whose comely physique was picked up by the ITV camera crew). Those baying hordes were treated to a marvellous display from their heroes, inspired by one of the best goals any Wednesday player has ever scored.

After 32 minutes the ball was switched to John Harkes, filling in for Nilsson at right-back, 40 yards from goal. Instead of pressing the American rookie Derby decided to back off, presumably thinking that a goalkeeper of Shilton's class was never going to be beaten from that far out.

'It was a great switch from Nigel Worthington,' Harkes says. 'Ron and Richie had been encouraging me to get forward and no-one seemed to put any pressure on the ball, which was surprising. By the time I took my second touch I'd made my mind up that I was going to hit it.'

The ball seared the net with such force that it cannoned into the stanchion and bounced back out again. Shilton, who'd thwarted some of the world's best strikers at Italia '90 just six months earlier, never stood a chance. The veteran goalkeeper was left on his haunches, looking around in bewilderment at what had just happened.

The thunderbolt would win the goal of the season award, one of those strikes that will be replayed for as long as people watch football. For Harkes, and the American footballing community, it was a coming-of-age moment.

'That was a big platform for me as an American player. There'd been some in the lower leagues but I was the first in the top league. We were trying to get back to top level. That helped to put us on the map.'

In the second half, Wednesday simply overwhelmed Derby. The beleaguered hosts simply couldn't live with the Second Division side's guile and spirit. Williams put the game beyond Derby's reach and in the end 0-2 flattered them.

That victory set up a quarter-final tie with Coventry, who had beaten holders Nottingham Forest 5-4 in the previous round (after being 4-0 up in the first half). With Nilsson still injured, Wednesday had a problem at right-back. Atkinson had just signed Viv Anderson – coincidentally as it would turn out, from Manchester United – but the former England defender was cup-tied. Coventry's left-winger, David Smith, was one of the trickiest players in the league and would need some experienced handling.

In the end Atkinson opted to shunt Phil King over to right-back, which meant Nigel Worthington had to drag himself off his sick bed to play on the other side.

'I had food poisoning before that game, and was feeling really rough,' Worthington recalls. 'The big man came to me and asked me, "How are you feeling?" I said, "Well I'll give it a go, and stay on as long as I can." I remember thinking, "Little Micky Gynn, he's sharp, he's got quick feet. This is going to be tough."

'I lasted the 90 minutes but I don't know how. I felt so rough, I was walking about in a daze. But you have to dig in. You're not just doing it for your team-mates, you're doing it for the team and the club.'

In the end Wednesday won 1-0 with captain Nigel Pearson scoring a beautiful goal on the turn, then later clearing a shot from Cyrille Regis off the line. It wasn't as convincing as the Derby demolition, but it was enough.

Of the three potential opponents Wednesday could have pulled in the semi-finals, Chelsea were probably the least threatening. The other semi-finalists, Manchester United and Leeds, would both go on to finish in the top six that season, while the west Londoners would limp home in 11th spot. This was still a long way from the days of Zola, Mourinho and Abramovich, when Stamford Bridge was still a bear pit of far-right skinheads rather than a haven for cappuccino-swilling cognoscenti.

But Chelsea were still dangerous. They'd beaten champions-elect Arsenal a couple of weeks before the first leg of the semi (the only defeat sustained by George Graham's team all season) and would scalp Liverpool before the campaign was out, too.

In the end, however, Wednesday simply battered them. This wasn't one of those plucky acts of backs-to-the-wall heroism by a lower-division side, digging in and nicking a goal on the break. This was a sustained performance of tactical and technical superiority.

The tie was effectively settled in the first leg at Stamford Bridge. Instead of cow-towing to their opponents, who'd beaten them 4-0 in the league the previous season, Wednesday simply went for them. Second-half goals from Shirtliff and Hirst barely reflected the gulf between the sides.

'That was all about the mentality of Ron,' Palmer says. 'I remember Ron turning around on the coach, and telling us "there's not two fucking legs here, there's only one leg." Normally in a two-legged semi-final, the team that plays away first is cagey. But Ron just said, "Fuck it, let's get it won." That was our mentality. And I think it took them by surprise. But that was how we played.

'We had good players. No, we had great players! All over the pitch. And with Hirsty we had a striker who was just unplayable at that time. In fact, in the dressing room afterwards, we weren't overjoyed or anything. We were disappointed we hadn't done more of a job on them.'

The second leg at Hillsborough turned into one of the great nights. Since those glory days of the 1960s, only the Boxing Day Massacre of 1979 can rival it for sheer elation.

After Pearson opened the scoring with a trademark header, Danny Wilson treated the home fans to another goal that would become the stuff of legend in S6. Palmer won a header on the edge of the Chelsea box and the ball dropped to the little dynamo, who volleyed into the top-left corner of the Kop net. 'That's that,' said commentator Alan Parry. It certainly was.

'When that goal went in, that was us at Wembley,' Wilson recalls. 'We were in a great position prior to that goal, but that sealed it. As players we knew we were in the final. You could feel the relief all around the ground – there was no need to bite the nails.'

Chelsea pulled one back in the second half, but the coup de grace was applied in the closing minutes by Williams, outpacing Ken Monkou and lifting the ball over Dave Beasant. Cue bedlam.

'Within 30 seconds, everybody was on the pitch,' the scorer recalls. 'You couldn't move. It was packed. I wasn't scared at all by the crowd though. it was just a sense of euphoria.'

Typically, Atkinson had foreseen the mayhem that greeted the final whistle. He'd told the players to expect a pitch invasion and even advised them to park their cars around the back of the stadium, rather than the main car park, so they would be able to get away more easily. As it turned out, though, no one was in the mood to drive home.

After champagne in the dressing room, the players decided to head out, first to Hanrahan's and then Josephine's. Williams, a teetotaler with a young family, says he decided not to go out on the tiles, but few others showed such restraint.

Peter Shirtliff, who'd set things off with that goal at Stamford Bridge, remembers being out until two in the morning as players mingled with supporters and gladly accepted the free beer and bubbly that was sent their way. Wilson even recalls Atkinson popping in for a drink. 'He didn't buy us one though!' he adds with a smile.

The next day, the players had to drag themselves in for a warm-down. Shirtliff recalls that 'everyone was hanging' but no one really cared. Twenty-five years after their last major final, a quarter-century of disappointment and recrimination, Wednesday were back at Wembley.

11
GLORY AT LAST

'It's a free kick now to Sheffield Wednesday.

'They've brought Shirtliff forward as well as Pearson, and Pearson has certainly scored some important goals this season, he's got 12. There's Shirtliff.

'Now what we might well find is Worthington ducking over it, or rather playing it down the byline for Harkes who might well make a little run down that right-hand side.

'There he goes, there goes Harkes. Now will Worthington play it? No he plays a long one this time, and it might come...

'A TERRIFIC GOAL! BY SHERIDAN! A TERRIFIC GOAL FOR SHEFFIELD WEDNESDAY!

'That really rattled off the post and into the back of the net beyond Les Sealey, and the Second Division side are in the lead!'

*   *   *

THERE HAVE been more memorable bits of commentary, certainly from the great Brian Moore. But it's a monologue that has gone down in the annals of Sheffield football history, replayed millions of times in living rooms around the city.

In those few seconds, Wednesday clinched the biggest honour of their modern history. John Sheridan's cannonburst secured victory over one of the most famous clubs in English football, a team that would beat the great Barcelona just a month later.

But this wasn't a case of plucky underdog defeating a complacent opponent. The very idea implies that Wednesday were somehow inferior to Manchester United. In fact they were every bit the equal of Alex Ferguson's team, as they'd proved throughout their march to Wembley. And in the final itself they were comfortably the better team. The match was won not with odds-defying, backs-to-the-wall spirit but with control and quality. This was a team that knew it was as good as United, or anyone else in the country, and revelled in the chance to prove it.

This wasn't a giant-killing. This was a giant-*awakening*.

* * *

If you're a Wednesday fan reading this and need a shot of pride right now, consider this: the Owls are the only team from outside the top division to win either the FA Cup or League Cup since 1980. That's over 40 years and more than 80 finals.

That they achieved the feat at all is impressive enough. That they did it against United, who'd thrashed Arsenal and Liverpool en route to Wembley and were about to take down Barca in the European Cup Winners' Cup Final, makes it a victory for the ages.

Wednesday didn't even have a full-strength team available for selection. While Alex Ferguson had all his star players to choose from, Ron Atkinson was denied the services of Carlton Palmer who had been sent off in a defeat at Portsmouth a couple of weeks before the final. Thirty years on, it remains a source of regret to Palmer himself.

'Ron had warned us before that game to be careful,' he remembers. 'But we were going for the league title. I wasn't thinking of the cup final, I was just thinking about winning that fucking league game. In the end it was a reckless challenge. I deserved the red card, no argument.

'Ron went mad after the game. "Fucking hell, you daft bastard! You don't realise what you've just fucking done! You're out of the cup final now." He was more bothered about that than about losing the game!'

Faced with the loss of such a key player, 99 per cent of managers would have abandoned any idea of attacking United in the final. They would have packed the defence and hunkered down, hoping that the football fates would take pity on them.

But Atkinson knew his team still had more than enough to win. And, crucially, he knew that he still had the tactical nous to out-smart any manager in the game.

* * *

They talk a lot about big-game players. Those who can occasionally cruise through games and drift off during run-of-the-mill assignments but then pull out a big performance just when it matters most.

But there are big-game *managers*, too. And no manager has ever fitted this description more neatly than Ron Atkinson.

Atkinson's career was predicated on his ability to win big games. During his time at Manchester United he'd masterminded victories over Liverpool time and again, and guided his time to an FA Cup Final victory over champions Everton despite having a man sent off. Even in Wednesday's relegation year he'd conjured triumphs over Liverpool and Arsenal.

If you wanted a manager for a routine league fixture on a freezing Tuesday night, Atkinson wasn't your man. The conventional matches could occasionally catch him underprepared, perhaps because he thought his players were so good he didn't need to prepare for the opposition. Throughout his career, Atkinson never won a league title; his Wednesday team didn't even win the Second Division despite having the most talented squad by a distance.

But give him a glamour cup tie or the chance to topple a more fashionable opponent and he would come alive. The old 'let them worry about us' mantra, which could occasionally drift into complacency, would be replaced by a tactical masterplan that would stifle the opposition while at the same time accentuating his own team's strengths. The bigger the opponent, the better he became.

The United game was perhaps Atkinson's dream scenario. Not only did he have the chance to lift a major trophy, there was the prospect of embarrassing one of the most fashionable teams in the land – and sticking a finger in the eye of his former employers. With Wednesday odds-on to get promoted, he could afford to spend weeks plotting for the opportunity.

On the face of it, the threat from United was obvious. Lee Sharpe had spent the entire season tearing opponents a new one down the left wing and he'd saved his most destructive work for the League Cup. His hat-trick at Highbury in the fourth round had evoked comparisons with George Best, and he'd settled the semi against Leeds with an outrageous finish from practically the byline. For Roland Nilsson, just returning after a five-month lay-off, the young flyer represented a huge test.

But while Sharpe was so quick he might have left scorch marks on the pitch, United's right-sided midfielders sputtered up and down like rusty lawnmowers. Ryan Giggs had yet to become a first-team regular and Andrei Kanchelskis was still trapped behind the Iron Curtain. Ferguson's team would come to be defined by its deployment of two wingers but in early 1991 he was still shoving midfielders into that crucial right-wing berth.

Atkinson knew that, if he could throttle the supply line to Sharpe, it would force United to go to their dysfunctional right flank. So that's what the Wednesday players worked on as they prepped for Wembley: cutting off the ball to Sharpe and forcing United down a cul-de-sac.

'Roland and I worked for 30 minutes, five days in a row on planning how to stop Lee Sharpe,' Harkes recalls. 'Just doubling up, me closing the passing lane.' Nilsson remembers spending hours 'watching videos to see how Sharpe played, studying his movement and tricks. I spoke to John as well, so we had a clear plan. You need support to play against Lee Sharpe and we needed to be sure the left-back was dealt with too. Harkesy did a great job.'

United's lop-sidedness may have limited their attacking options but it also gave them extra muscle in the centre of the pitch. As well as Bryan Robson, they had future England captain Paul Ince and Neil Webb, who would have won many more caps but for injury. The absence of Palmer, with his long legs and bottomless lungs, made this overload even more daunting.

To counter this threat, Atkinson came up with a strategy that would take United's all-star midfield out of the equation altogether. Wednesday would stretch their opponents' defence with balls over the top, using Williams's pace against Steve Bruce and Gary Pallister, a pair of centre-backs who were superb in the air but not quite so comfortable on the turn.

When asked about his role, Williams remembers, 'I brought mobility and pace and an ability to run consistently for 90 minutes. I think that was an important strategy for Ron – we could stop them getting into a rhythm and their full-backs wouldn't be able to join in. Their full-backs usually helped start attacks, but they would leave spaces that I could exploit.'

When the ball was knocked over the top, Wednesday's midfielders would squeeze the space. But, as Williams says, they wouldn't over-commit.

'We knew we would be under pressure for large parts of the game, so part of the tactic defensively was to remain compact in the midfield. When we had the ball our midfield didn't always go forward as quickly as they could. Ron never wanted to be in a position where they could counter-attack.'

Atkinson knew that this game plan, while slightly more conservative than his preferred approach, would trouble Ferguson's team. But he also knew that tactics and formations on their own wouldn't be enough. He needed to get inside the heads of his players and enable them to play with the same freedom they displayed every week in the Second Division.

Here, again, he proved himself a master.

* * *

Like Brian Clough, Big Ron was a devout believer in the power of relaxation. He would happily allow his lads to have a drink on a Friday night if it would help them sleep. Lawrie Madden recalls that he even gave the players a tot of brandy in the dressing room before one freezing-cold midweek game at Hillsborough.

When a big match loomed, Atkinson would take any opportunity to bring some levity to the camp. His rationale was that the players were under enough pressure as it was: his job was to turn the dial down, not up.

Wednesday's squad wasn't laden with trophy winners. Although Trevor Francis had won (and scored in) a European Cup Final, and Roland Nilsson had reached the semi-final of the same competition, only three players – Chris Turner, Danny Wilson and the cup-tied Viv Anderson – had played in a Wembley final before.

But rather than trying to compensate for this dearth of big-game experience, Atkinson used it to his advantage. He turned the Wembley trip into a busman's holiday for his players, allowing them to enjoy their big weekend rather than thinking too much about the upcoming game.

Instead of billeting the Wednesday squad in a secluded spot on the outskirts of London where they could happily drive themselves potty, Atkinson booked them into the Royal Lancaster Hotel, just across the road from Hyde Park. Well, if you're going to do London you might as well do it properly, right?

'Howard [Wilkinson] was frugal when we went away, we'd stay in dormitories of three and four,' Lawrie Madden says. 'But Ron wanted to make it an experience. He wanted people to remember it. We made it into a three-day stay. Ron was brilliant at that.'

The squad travelled down to London on Friday morning, just hours after returning from a midweek defeat at Newcastle that Atkinson described as the worst performance of the season. Hirst recalls, 'The promotion challenge was going well and although we put 100 per cent in, no one wanted to get injured in that game. We were actually trying out things that we'd rehearsed on the training ground to beat Man United!

'I remember their goal, it was a cross which came back off the post and hit Chris Turner in the face. He even shouted "it's going over" as it came down. Honestly, no word of a lie, lads were laughing about it on the pitch.'

The trips to Tyneside and London meant Wednesday had to cover 300 miles in the space of three days. It was an itinerary that would test the resolve of a long-distance lorry driver, let alone a group of athletes who'd been playing twice a week for the last eight months.

So when the squad arrived in the capital the manager decided to give them a nice gentle workout to get the journey out of their legs, somewhere nearby that wouldn't require another gruelling trip through the central London traffic. Even by Atkinson's standards, however, the location of the 'training ground' was an unusual choice.

'We drove down on the Friday – players in one bus, wives, kids and partners in another,' Nigel Worthington remembers. 'Then when we arrived, Big Ron said, "Right, we're out training in 30 minutes." So we went up to our rooms, got ready, came down to reception and Ron took us over the road to Hyde Park!

'He made Chris Turner stand between these two trees, and said, "Shez, you go over there, and don't stop till I say." He made John Sheridan walk about 40 yards! As Shez was walking, the Big Man turned to us and said, "What is he doing?!"

'Anyway Shez eventually got far enough away and Ron told us, "Right, it's an attacking corner, get lined up." You should have seen the players' faces – you've got joggers and dog-walkers going past! But we just worked for an hour, practising all the set pieces with these 75-foot trees as goals.'

That night, the squad gathered for a meal with wives and partners to celebrate Trevor Francis's birthday. Atkinson chose an Italian restaurant, a decision which no doubt went down well with Francis, who'd spent several years in Serie A and was besotted with the culture. But this wasn't a night for rocket risotto and mineral water; in fact the evening was so bacchanalian it was like a scene from the last days of Rome.

The occasion is remembered particularly fondly by Gordon Watson, a man who wouldn't even play in the final. Watson had only just joined from Charlton and had been brought along for the experience. However, by sheer coincidence, he found himself centre stage.

'Ron booked the Tiberio, a restaurant in Mayfair, and it turned out that my friend's parents ran it,' recalls the man universally known as 'Flash'. 'When we got there they gave me extra food and made a big fuss of me. It was amazing – I was still only 20 and had only moved out of south London two months earlier, and now I was being treated like one of the stars.

'I remember us all turning up, there must have been about 50 of us, and it was an amazing night. I remember Trevor getting a telegram from Giorgio Armani – that was a different level of fame from the rest of us!

'Honestly, people staggered onto the coach back home. We took over the restaurant and people were absolutely smashed on wine. You didn't know people were smashed until they got up and tried to walk! People were trying to show how sober they were. Red wine, white wine, cigars flying around... everything.'

In today's micro-managed world of ice baths and protein shakes, it's impossible to imagine any coach giving their players such a long leash before a big game. But the players believe that boozy night was exactly what they needed.

'That was the cleverness of Ron,' Hirst says. 'If he felt the pressure was building on the players he'd look for a way to try and take it off them.

'We'd done all the work in Sheffield, we'd prepared properly for the game and we knew what each of us had to do. There was no point in us staying in our rooms, being in bed by a certain time. That would only have increased the nerves.

'So Ron said, "No, we'll go out for a bite to eat. If you want a beer, have a beer, if you want a glass of wine, have a glass of wine." We were all grown men and he trusted us.

'It may have gone a bit pear-shaped when the flaming Sambucas came out though!'

At some point in the evening, the Wednesday lads vividly recall Martin Edwards, the chairman of Manchester United and the man who had terminated Atkinson's contract at Old Trafford five years earlier, striding into the room with a couple of his entourage.

Again, it's easy to imagine the cogs in Atkinson's mind whirring away furiously as he planned the invitation. He'd have known that Edwards would return to the United camp with gleeful tales of Wednesday's debauchery, telling Ferguson and his players that their opponents were only in London for a good time and had given up on the match before it had even kicked off.

Of course, nothing could have been further from the truth.

*   *   *

The serious business resumed the next day. Atkinson took the players off to Bisham Abbey, the hotel that England used at the time, to shake off their hangovers and go over the final preparations.

'I remember we spent ages going over set-pieces,' Lawrie Madden says. 'I can't ever remember Ron doing a set-piece session, but he did on that occasion.' Given what would happen the next day, it would prove a very wise decision.

But even as the hours ticked down the mood remained relaxed. Turner vividly remembers he and Hirst, who were rooming together, taking a beer from the minibar before they tucked in for the night. There were no strict limits placed on the players, but then again, there never were. As Wilson says, 'He [Atkinson] treated us like adults. You knew when you could have a drink and when you couldn't.'

When the players rose on the morning of the game they found that their gregarious gaffer had one final trick up his sleeve.

Stan Boardman, then one of Britain's most recognisable comedians, was waiting for them in the buffet hall. Boardman, who had once been on Liverpool's books, had been close pals with Atkinson ever since they met in a Spanish bar in the 1980s. His brief was simple: accompany the players on their journey to Wembley and give them one final dose of tomfoolery before they entered the fray.

As the coach pulled out of Berkshire and began wending its way back towards London, Boardman rose to give them a little turn. Now even Boardman's biggest fans would admit his comedy was more Blackpool Pier than Edinburgh Fringe; his most famous joke was about German warplanes bombing his local chippy, not the sort of material you can imagine Stephen Fry or Stewart Lee resorting to.

But for a group of young men who'd spent their entire working lives in a football dressing room, Boardman's earthy banter was perfect. By the time they reached the capital, Madden says, the players 'were probably the most relaxed we'd ever been'.

Then the coach pulled into the stadium, the final turn on the road to Wembley. A sea of Wednesday scarves and stripes parted to let them pass, greeting their heroes with a collective roar of delight. The United fans, who'd been to the Twin Towers three times in the previous 12 months, had left it late in arriving; their less privileged rivals had come to soak up every second. For that afternoon at least, Wembley Way had become Wednesday Way.

In his final team talk Atkinson opted to keep things simple, as was his wont. Churchillian rallying cries weren't the manager's thing; Shirtliff recalls that he preferred to go to players individually in the minutes before games, giving them little words of encouragement and trying to ensure they took to the field in as good a frame a mind as possible. Having already scalped some of the best teams in the country, his players needed little geeing up on this occasion.

'We were doing as well as anybody,' says Hirst. 'Yes, we were in a lower division but we were challenging for promotion, we were scoring goals on a regular basis. We knew Roland and Harkesy were going to double-team Sharpe. We knew Shirty and Nige were going to look after Hughes. We didn't need any last-minute instructions.

'It was just about telling the players to go out and be ourselves. Make sure you win your battles and we'll see how it all unfolds.'

*   *   *

When you watch the game back, what's noticeable is how often United look for Sharpe early on. Every time Robson gets the ball he swivels and pops the ball over the top of Nilsson's head. But time and again, the wily Swede snuffs out the danger.

According to the players, those perfectly timed interventions sent confidence coursing through their veins. Wilson says, 'I can remember one particular tackle on Lee Sharpe, who was clearly a threat to us, and it really quietened things down. We'd practised that all week, and it worked.'

Wednesday had scored a crucial tactical victory in the opening exchanges and forced United to rip up the plan that had served them so well all season.

In truth neither side really hit their straps in that first half. On commentary, Jimmy Greaves described it as more like a 'pre-season preamble' than a cup final. Wednesday played like a side who were waiting for their chance. United played like a side who had pulled out their joker and found that the big guy in the shades sitting opposite them had been waiting for it.

Then, on 37 minutes, Wednesday got a free kick down the right. It was Sharpe, of all people, who gave it away, sticking out a hand and knocking down Nilsson's inside pass. With Pearson and Shirtliff in the side this was a major opportunity.

Worthington was the man charged with delivering the ball into the mixer. 'Nine times out of ten, Harkesy would run down the side of the wall, I'd feint to cross but then at the last minute, cut it back down the line. Harkesy would be in round the back, and he could float it in or drill it hard and low. We scored lots of goals that way.

'But on this occasion we thought United had probably done their homework. They'd have sent a scout and watched us on video. So we thought we'd do something different.'

So instead Worthington played a long, floated ball into the box. Ordinarily Gary Pallister would simply have headed the ball away, but Pearson's powerful challenge muscled him off-balance and prevented him from making firm contact. As the ball dribbled towards the edge of the box, United still had the chance to clear. But again Wednesday wanted it more.

Suddenly everything happened in a flash. Sheridan erupting on to the ball; the laser-focused missile fizzing through a crowd of bodies; the beautiful clunk of ball against post; the roar from 40,000 Sheffielders; the sight of Les Sealey hunched on the ground, incredulous; the goalscorer sprinting half the length of the pitch to reach the Wednesday fans, team-mates trailing in his wake.

As John Sheridan, the Mancunian who had adored United and been ignored, raced towards the people who had taken him to their hearts, his manager remained impassive on the touchline. One might have expected Atkinson, who had experienced his own share of Old Trafford heartache, to be dancing a jig of delight. But he knew the job was nowhere near done.

'Ron was so focussed,' says Lawrie Madden, who was sitting on the bench along with Trevor Francis. 'I remember walking off at half-time and him telling me and Trevor, "If it stays 1-0, Lawrie, you're going on. If they equalise, Trevor, you're going on." He'd already worked out what was going to happen.'

In the second half the magnitude of the occasion finally started to catch up with Wednesday. 'Trevor had told us before the game, "Don't get caught up in the day," Phil King says. "Don't get caught up waving to your fans, waving to your mum and dad." But we just said, "Shut up Trevor, We've never been to Wembley before!" He was right though. I remember getting cramp after 35 minutes! Emotionally we'd given everything.'

The intensity of Wednesday's pressing gradually began to relent. United's urgency increased, forcing corners and free kicks around the Wednesday box. Their fans, so quiet during the first half, began to finally find their voice.

Then with eight minutes to go United finally got their opportunity. The ball was sent wide to Irwin out on the right, and King was too knackered to get to him. United's Irish full-back sent in a perfect cross to McClair, totally unmarked. Thankfully his header was straight at Turner, who tipped it over the bar.

'That's what stands out most from the game,' says King. 'Not being able to cut out that cross. It could have changed the whole complexion of the game. Who knows what would have happened. It could have been my error that cost us. Thank God Chris made the save.'

Perhaps United knew then that their chance had gone. For all their huffing and puffing they were unable to fashion another clear opening in the closing moments. In fact, Wednesday looked just as likely to score as their illustrious opponents. With a little more composure, Hirst and Williams could easily have doubled the lead.

To shore things up, Atkinson brought on Lawrie Madden and told him to play on the right wing, add some extra defensive prowess and stop the ball reaching Sharpe. But even this was a calculated, pre-planned move.

'I'd actually been brought on in advanced positions a couple of times that season,' Madden says. 'When we went to Brighton and won 4-0, Ron brought me on and put me on the right wing. Then in the very next game, when we went to Bristol Rovers, he put me on up front! I guess he thought I would add a defensive quality and break things up.'

'It's funny what sticks in your mind,' Hirst says. 'I can recall a tackle by Willo on Sealey, which gave him a gash on the knee. The United physio came on and tried to get Les to go off but he was screaming and bawling to stay on. And I can remember Lawrie coming on on the right wing and going on a couple of jinky runs! We had a little giggle about that one afterwards.

'But we never stopped believing in ourselves. We knew we had pace, we knew we had an engine room, we knew we had creativity and we were never going to park the bus.'

Fittingly, the final move of the match was a Wednesday attack, which very nearly created another opening for Williams. When the whistle blew the ball was nestled in Sealey's arms, 100 metres from the Wednesday goal.

With that one wonderful peep from referee Ray Lewis, 25 years of anguish were unleashed in an instant. A collective wave of joy swept over the Wednesday end of the ground as players slumped to the turf and embraced one another.

But in the hour of triumph, Ron Atkinson remained calm. ITV's pitchside interviewer tried to tempt him into a lazy soundbite about how this victory avenged his sacking by United, but the architect of the victory wasn't falling for it. He knew that this was about Wednesday, not their opponents.

'We don't think we're a Second Division team,' Atkinson said. 'We think in the big matches, we're a good side. We haven't looked out of our depth today, have we?' When asked about United's late pressure, he pointed out that Wednesday had had three chances of their own. Just as he'd been all day, Big Ron was in total control.

*   *   *

Really, the man of the match award could have gone to anyone in blue and white. Turner had kept goal immaculately. Nilsson had shut down Sharpe. Wilson and Williams had covered more ground in one game than most players do in three. Sheridan had scored the goal. Phil King says that after the game, Atkinson suggested the award should have gone to him, so impressive was his display down the left-hand side.

In the end, the ITV commentary team gave the award to Nigel Pearson for the way he galvanised his team and nullified the threat of Mark Hughes, who was then the most feared – and fearless – centre-forward in the country. Hughes was a wonderful striker who would go on to score both of United's goals against Barcelona. Against Pearson, he barely got a kick.

Of course, this was nothing out of the ordinary: Pearson produced this kind of dominant display every week. Ever since he'd arrived at Wednesday in 1987 he'd been wrestling with ogreish centre-forwards and throwing himself in the way of loose balls with no regard for his personal safety. Like Mick Lyons before him, Pearson's selfless bravery was a source of constant amazement to his team-mates.

'He was great, Nige,' says Shirtliff, who played so many games alongside him. 'Honest player, knew what you were going to get from him every week. He was strong in the air and better on the ground than many gave him credit for. And what a leader. Not just on the pitch, but off it, too – he'd be the one organising nights out, booking restaurants for the team and their wives and making everyone feel involved.

'He was a different character to Mick. He was less vocal, preferred to lead with actions. But a brilliant guy.'

So it was fitting that Pearson got to lift the cup at the head of his exhausted team. Even then he excelled himself: rather than simply raising the battered old trophy to the heavens and then passing it down the line, he stopped at the top of the steps and held it still, so the Wednesday fans around the ground could get a good look. After so long in the shadows, looking on enviously as other clubs got to bask in the glory, they deserved to savour this moment.

As every Wednesdayite knows, Yorkshire TV thought this was a good time to cut the broadcast. Rather than staying with their victorious team and celebrating the region's first major football honour since the 1970s they felt it was more appropriate to broadcast a monster truck derby instead. It's hard to believe they'd have made the same decision had it been Leeds United climbing the Wembley steps that day.

But the hordes of Wednesday fans were oblivious to this act of broadcasting lunacy, as they danced in the aisles and embraced one another. And so, of course, were the players, as they got stuck into the champagne in the bowels of the stadium.

Practically everyone who'd ever set foot in Sheffield was in the dressing room, or at least that's how the players tell it. A galaxy of local celebrities thronged the winner's enclosure, trying to hive off a piece of the glory for themselves. But the players didn't care; they'd been through everything together over the previous 12 months and were just happy to share this moment.

'That victory was all about the team,' says Phil King. 'They were such a great bunch of lads.

'Steve McCall had played in all the previous rounds but Ron left him out of the final because he wanted to put Trevor and Lawrie Madden on the bench. So when we got our bonuses, we all chipped in so Steve could get his share. That's the sort of group we were, and that's what made it so special.'

The celebrations cranked up a notch when the squad got back to the Royal Lancaster, where a gala banquet had been laid on for them and their families. Some of the lads even claim that a cousin of Whitney Houston attended that night, although they can't remember the name.

Ron Atkinson, in his inimitable style, took to the stage to belt out a rendition of Frank Sinatra's 'My Way', but even the great man had to accept second billing this night. Paul Carrack, the Sheffield-born musician who had earned global fame through his work with Supertramp, Roxy Music and Mike + The Mechanics, treated the assembled throng to a special rendition of his cup final record, 'It's A Praise For Sheffield Wednesday'. The song had already gone viral among the Hillsborough fans and remains a classic 30 years on, with its perfect fusion of blue-eyed soul and working-class Steel City humour.

Naturally, a group of pie-eyed players decided to join him on stage, led by Phil King, the dressing room's jester-in-chief.

'I can still remember that line – "John Sherry, different class, Big Carlton covers every blade of grass",' King says. 'We had the song on tape in the car and my daughter used to play it over and over. So when Paul Carrack shouted "come up and sing" I didn't need much encouragement. None of us did to be fair, we were that pissed!'

Paul Williams, meanwhile, treated the crowd to a rendition of his dance moves, showing off the fleet-footed audacity that had driven Bruce and Pallister to distraction all afternoon.

'That's how I expressed myself, I guess,' he says with a smile. 'It reflected my heritage. I was quite a reserved character, but any inhibitions would have been gone that night. It was relief, enjoyment, achievement. Not many of us had played at Wembley, let alone won there. It was a night to remember for all of us.'

Others, however, were more reserved, happy to let their louder team-mates steal the show.

'To be honest the party wasn't the high-point of the day,' Hirst says. 'The game took so much out of the lads. I was absolutely shattered. I'm not sure if it was the game, the euphoria of winning or whatever.

'I remember going on stage but I wasn't singing. Then I remember getting down to my table, got a crate and never left my chair! That was perfect for me.

'It was a late one though. I sat up in the ballroom at the Lancaster with a couple of the lads, Big Ron, Stan Boardman and another comedian, Mick Miller, the bloke who did a sketch about Noddy with a drink problem. I got Mick to do that on a stepladder at about 5am.

'Ron had a couple of glasses, but in no way did he overstep the mark or get out of control. I've been on functions with him since and he never does. He just enjoyed being there with the lads, enjoying the moment.'

For King, Williams and the other ten men who took to the field that day [Francis was an unused substitute], the victory over United remains the pinnacle of their careers. None of that squad ever won another major trophy, a staggering fact when one considers the collective talent they possessed.

Their manager would taste success again, however. In 1994 he beat United in the League Cup Final a second time, this time with Aston Villa. If anything United were even firmer favourites in that game but Villa's victory was even more convincing, achieved with a margin of two clear goals.

But which of the two wins was more impressive? Well there's no comparison really. Atkinson took a Second Division team to Wembley, a team shorn of one of its most important players, and still managed to pull it off.

It remains the finest hour in Wednesday's modern history. And surely it is Ron Atkinson's masterpiece, too.

12
LIFE AFTER GOD

It's a beautiful August afternoon in South Yorkshire. The first day of the football season, that perfect moment when everyone is still unbeaten and dreams have yet to be punctured by reality's wintry chill.

The sky is a blissfully untroubled shade of blue with barely even the wrinkle of a cloud. The pitch is a flawless carpet of emerald green with no hint of the boggy morass it will soon become.

Hillsborough should be in party mode, ready to welcome its team back to the First Division. But instead the ground is tense. The buzz and banter of the new campaign is tinged with the sort of moodiness you normally get in a pub, just before a fight breaks out.

Then, suddenly, Ron Atkinson, the returning hero, the man who has restored Wednesday to their rightful place in the top flight, strides towards the dugout.

But it's the wrong dugout. Atkinson heads right, towards the visitors' bench rather than the one he's occupied for the past two years. Instead of the cheers of an adoring public, the stadium reverberates with the sort of boos and whistles usually reserved for a Saturday-afternoon wrestler. Chants of 'Judas, Judas' poison the summer air.

Just four months ago Atkinson was their God. And now this.

*   *   *

EVEN THREE decades on, it's hard to overstate the shock that rippled through Sheffield when Ron Atkinson walked out on Wednesday in the summer of 1991. His fearless team, the one he'd spent two years painstakingly constructing, had just won the League Cup and appeared ready for further honours on its return to the First Division.

The Wednesday fans had idolised players like Mick Lyons and Terry Curran, and deeply respected Howard Wilkinson. But this was different. They worshipped Atkinson like some kind of orange deity, a man whose managerial genius could turn water into wine (or, in his case, champagne).

But this was no unrequited obsession. Atkinson loved Wednesday: the people, the stadium, and the band of scallywags and streetfighters he'd moulded into a team. When speculation began to mount about his future in the early summer months, he told reporters he would be mad to leave.

And then, of course, he did.

The decision thrust Atkinson's apprentice, Trevor Francis, into the spotlight. And by most yardsticks the young man did extremely well. In his first season Wednesday would beat Chelsea, Tottenham and Manchester United and eventually finish third, the best performance by a newly promoted club since Brian Clough's champion Nottingham Forest team of 1978.

But there were stumbling blocks along the way. Wednesday would suffer a series of humiliating defeats and Francis's managerial style would cause friction with a number of senior players.

In fact, the 1991/92 season would set the pattern for the rest of Francis's time at Hillsborough. His teams would continue to produce excellent football but his regime would be continually undermined by squabbles between the manager and his senior players – often the ones that Atkinson had signed.

Some players claim that these issues arose from Francis's intransigence. They believe his nagging insecurity and his often clumsy approach to man-management sowed the seeds of his ultimate downfall.

But perhaps his biggest problem was that, in the end, he just wasn't Ron Atkinson.

*   *   *

Few clubs have ever entered the First Division with a stronger squad than the one Wednesday possessed in August 1991. The core of the side that had gone down a year earlier – Hirst, Palmer, Pearson, Nilsson, Sheridan and Worthington – were all still around, and that group had been given extra ballast by the additions of Harkes, Wilson and Williams.

In the weeks before the big kick-off, Wednesday broke their transfer record to sign Paul Warhurst, one of the country's most promising young players, for a fee of £945,000 from Oldham. It would be just the first in a spate of big-money signings as chairman Dave Richards and the board flexed their new-found financial muscle. Wednesday finally had the cash to match their ambition.

But they no longer had their manager.

Today, the players are philosophical about Atkinson's departure. Nigel Worthington says, 'If a player wants to go to another club, it's hard to hold them back, and likewise for managers. Ron was travelling two or three hours each way most days, so if his home was half an hour from Villa it made sense.'

At the time, however, it plunged the squad into turmoil. Danny Wilson says he 'didn't see it coming. We'd done so well. I understand it now, given his links with Villa, but at the time… I was on holiday when I found out, and yeah it definitely knocked the wind out of me.'

David Hirst, meanwhile, was away in Australasia, on his first tour with the England national team. He had been as close to Ron as any player in the squad but even he had no idea of what his boss was thinking.

'I heard when I was in the lift going down to breakfast. One of the England staff said, "Ron's left." So I was like, "Oh, okay!" I just thought that I couldn't do anything about it. I was 11,000 miles away and even if I'd been in Sheffield I probably wouldn't have changed his mind. You just have to get on with it.'

With so little time to react, it's easy to see why the Wednesday board went for Francis. Yes, he'd been bombed out of his only previous managerial job, at Queens Park Rangers. But he'd been a brilliant player, had spent time in Italy (then the acme of footballing sophistication) and been Atkinson's most trusted lieutenant for the past 18 months.

Plus there weren't many alternatives. Wednesday were unlikely to poach Graham Taylor, Terry Venables or Howard Kendall from more glamorous gigs elsewhere. Kenny Dalglish was available but he'd only just left Liverpool, broken by the stress of that awful day on Wednesday's own turf.

To replace Dalglish, Liverpool had gone for Graeme Souness, a man of similar age and experience to Francis. If the best club in England could take a punt on a rookie, then why not Wednesday?

The Souness parallel is a particularly interesting one. He and Francis were best mates and football had led them down remarkably similar paths. They'd scaled Europe's greatest peaks at the turn of the 1980s, winning four European Cups in a row between them, before joining forces at Sampdoria, where they both fell in love with *La Dolce Vita*. Then they'd reunited at Rangers (Francis had even advised Souness on players to sign) before deciding to try their luck in Sassanach country.

Both men were intelligent and urbane, driven by an intellectual curiosity rare among footballers of their era. They would both make great pundits when television came calling and they were doubtless excellent company at dinner parties.

But perhaps they both lacked one thing: the ability to compromise with those they disagreed with. It would prove to be a major factor in their managerial careers.

Initially, Francis's singularity provoked nothing more than benign amusement. Lawrie Madden says that while Francis was a terrific professional and highly respected, he was 'marmite' among his peers, a bloke who could rub people up the wrong way and didn't always help himself.

As an example, Madden recalls the end-of-season trip to Marbella in 1990 when the players were desperately trying to regroup after their shattering relegation. Instead of going out with the team and bonding after an evening meal, Francis opted to go straight back to the hotel. In such a tightly knit group of players, that sort of thing mattered.

Chris Turner gives a similar impression. 'I used to sit next to Trevor on the bus and have a chat, but some of the lads used to take the piss out of him because he was a bit flash.

'He'd have his pink Italian newspaper, and when he'd go training he'd put his wallet in the club safe because it was full of cash! When you've got characters like Nigel Pearson and Carlton Palmer, they're always going to seize on stuff like that.'

As a manager, this same streak of pride and refusal to bend to the norms of football culture would cause problems. The players paint a common picture: while Francis was a good man and a decent manager, he was often let down by his people skills.

'Trevor was a brilliant player, for sure, but his man-management skills weren't as good as Ron's,' says Phil King. Peter Shirtliff concurs. 'I found him all right, but he'd pick you one week, then he'd drop you without telling you why. He didn't think he had to tell you. He was a bit aloof.'

These communication problems would dog Francis throughout his regime. And his old mate Chris Turner was one of the first to feel the consequences.

After an enjoyable trip to the US where Wednesday played a showpiece friendly against the national team designed to capitalise on the popularity of John Harkes, who played a half for both sides, the new manager took his team to Portsmouth for one of their final pre-season games.

Turner remembers, 'Trevor called me and Kevin Pressman into an annex of the dressing room. He just said "heads or tails?" I asked "what for?" and he said, "To decide who plays first half." He couldn't decide who to go with, so he was giving us half each.

'So I just said, "Look, I don't mind. Kev can have first half, I'll have second half." In the end it didn't matter, because Trevor went and signed Chris Woods just before the new season, and I was out.'

Woods was a marvellous goalkeeper. He'd required another record outlay from the Wednesday board but, as the fans would remind their rivals approximately 567,358 times during his spell at Hillsborough, he was England's number one. What's more, his spell at Rangers had given him more medals than practically the entire Wednesday squad put together.

However, for Wednesday's incumbent goalkeepers, that was little consolation.

'I took it much better than Kevin did,' Turner says now. 'He went mad. He was shoving transfer requests into Trevor every day. It was a horrible time for Kevin because he knew he'd be the number two for a while.

'It was a massive disappointment, for sure. Trevor never intimated anything to us about bringing a new keeper in, and I'd been close to him.'

Turner and Pressman would have been forgiven a little schadenfreude during that opening-day match, another of those quirks of the fixtures computer which brought Ron Atkinson straight back to the team he'd walked out on.

Wednesday started superbly. Hirst bent a mind-boggling banana shot into the Kop End goal and set up Wilson for the second. But Woods let Villa back into the game with a feeble flap late in the first half and Atkinson's new team never relinquished the momentum. Steve Staunton slammed home the winner five minutes from time.

But those opening-day jitters were soon forgotten as Francis's team produced a string of performances that had Big Ron stamped all over them.

On the second weekend of the season, Wednesday went to Elland Road for a showdown with another former manager and would have taken the points against Howard Wilkinson's Leeds had it not been for the scrappiest of late equalisers. Then they beat Everton, hammered QPR and got a draw at Anfield, a result which was still a monumental achievement given that Liverpool had won ten of the last 16 league titles and hadn't finished outside the top two for a decade.

'We had top players,' Carlton Palmer says when talking about that early-season run. 'There was a great balance in that squad. It was full of lads who could mix it and who could play. In the Second Division we'd had a team that could dig out results, so if teams wanted to fight us, we'd fight them and then find a bit of quality to do them.

'But then if you go up to the First Division and you've got quality players, it's easier. Because you've suddenly got more time on the ball and it's less frenetic. The First Division actually suited us more.'

Francis, at that stage, was happy to let things carry on as they had under his predecessor. 'Trevor didn't really change much,' John Harkes says. 'At that time, he was still a young manager and was happy to take on what had been successful before.'

While training was tightened up (the Thursday afternoon kickabouts, designed partly to sharpen Atkinson's own fitness, became noticeably less frequent), the basic drills remained unchanged. Francis was still registered as a player so had to delegate much of the planning to Richie Barker, whose attention to detail was unsurpassed. All Francis really had to do was pick the team. And by this stage the team practically picked itself.

'It was still Ron's team, and Ron's mentality,' says Hirst. 'The players that we had were capable of doing the job and we'd proved that over a few years. Trevor inherited those players and we pretty much played the same way.

'We had a good core of players who, if things weren't going right, were capable of sorting it out between ourselves. It was a very honest, demanding culture. If there was a fall-out, there'd be a fight. Then we'd shake hands and go for a beer.'

Even when Nigel Pearson was injured, as he often was that season, the armband could be seamlessly passed on to another senior player, such as Danny Wilson or Viv Anderson. In fact, every single one of Wednesday's regular starters was a leader, a man who would stand up and take charge when things were falling apart around them.

'I'm a big character, but that dressing room was full of characters,' Palmer says proudly. 'Seven of that team went on to be managers, which tells you everything about the strength of mind that was in the dressing room. Roland Nilsson, Viv Anderson, Nigel Worthington, John Sheridan, Danny Wilson; there must have been four or five lads in there who captained their country.

'It was a very, very strong dressing room and everyone played their part. I loved playing football and I wanted to win, and that was a big thing that went through the dressing room. That's why we had stand-up rows with each other in the dressing room and on the training pitch, and that's why that team did so well. Everyone was held to account, not just by the manager, but by each other.'

*　*　*

As the final embers of summer fizzled out, it was clear that Wednesday were now a serious team. Chelsea, Southampton and Crystal Palace were all swatted aside at home; Manchester City, West Ham and Everton were all bested on the road. When champions Arsenal visited Hillsborough, Wednesday should really have beaten them, and even in their disappointment the fans could revel in a precocious display by Chris Bart-Williams, an unknown teenager who looked totally at ease against Paul Merson, David Rocastle and Ian Wright.

But the undoubted highlight of that first few months back in the top flight came at the end of October with a rematch against those gobby upstarts from the wrong side of the Snake Pass.

Just as they had in 1985, Manchester United arrived at Hillsborough top of the league and unbeaten. Their team was greatly improved from the one that had fallen flat at Wembley; Ryan Giggs and Andrei Kanchelskis were now in harness down the wings, and Peter Schmeichel was bestriding the goalmouth like a Viking colossus.

In one of those topsy-turvy games typical of the period, Wednesday took an early lead (through Hirst, of course), then let it slip with two defensive howlers from Paul Warhurst. With time ebbing away like the autumn daylight, the hosts were heading for an undeserved defeat.

In desperation, Francis threw on Nigel Jemson, a young striker he had only just signed from Nottingham Forest. The impact was remarkable. First, Jemson trapped a hopeful shot from Nilsson and slotted the ball over Schmeichel with the assurance of a man who had played 300 games. Then, with seconds remaining, he headed in a corner in front of the stunned United fans.

For the scorer, it was particularly sweet. Jemson, a Lancashire lad, had grown up vehemently disliking United. He'd even cut short a trial at Old Trafford to sign for Brian Clough at Forest. The chance to celebrate in front of the visiting supporters on Leppings Lane was too good to miss.

'Where I grew up, you either like United or you don't, and I was definitely in the "don't" camp,' he says now with a chuckle.

'Later, I was playing for Bury [in the suburbs of Manchester] and my wife was pregnant. She went into labour, and I drove her to Macclesfield, about an hour away, so I wouldn't have a kid born in Manchester. That's what I felt about them.

'So yeah, it was good to score those goals.'

That match should have been the springboard for a brilliant spell at Hillsborough. But Jemson's career at Wednesday was thrown off course, quite literally, when he suffered a car accident in the new year and never quite hit his straps again.

Given that Jemson was once described by Brian Clough as the only person in the world with a bigger head than himself (the manager even punched his young prodigy for defying his instructions after one reserve game), one might assume he was a disruptive figure at Wednesday. But not a bit of it.

Jemson meshed instantly into the Owlerton fold. He recalls that the atmosphere was so good that players would arrive early to training so they could muck around with their team-mates or go for a natter at Lily's, the nearby cafe which provided a welcome bacon butty.

Most of the lads would go to an Italian restaurant on a Friday afternoon, where they would talk about the forthcoming game over a soft drink. Like West Ham's fabled salt-and-pepper sessions of the 1960s, those meals created a melting pot of ideas where the players could talk tactics and build the team spirit that would pull them through the following day.

It was an environment in which everyone was welcome, provided they were willing to put a shift in when they pulled on a striped shirt and take the banter when it came their way. John Harkes, as an American, received more than his fair share.

'Oh my God, they wouldn't stop taking the mickey out of my accent,' Harkes recalls. 'Hirsty, Nigel Pearson, Shez, Kingy, all took turns in their own way. I loved it though, it was quite funny to hear their different takes.

'They all seemed to think every American either spoke super-fast, or slowed it down as if they were in a Western movie like John Wayne! I tried to correct them at times, but all in all, I enjoyed it and it was great fun. It brought us closer together.'

Hirst himself says, 'We used to dig each other out over everything – what you drank, what you drove, what you wore. If you didn't have what it takes, you had to come in with a big hat on! Whatever shoes you were wearing, whatever jacket you were wearing... and me as much as anyone.

'I was a jeans man, still am, and I have to admit I was caught out with the double denim on more than one occasion. The old Texas Tuxedo! You can imagine how that went down.'

Hirst and Palmer vied for the role of smart-arse supreme and revelled in one another's company. Two straight-talking men with sharp mouths and a sardonic sense of humour, they were always fighting to get the last word in.

'Me and Carlton were the best of mates, the worst of enemies, everything,' Hirst continues. 'We both liked a drink and a bite to eat and we filled a lot of time doing so. He'd dig me out, I'd dig him out, and that was how it was. You'd say your bit, they'd say theirs and everyone took it in the right spirit.'

The banter and the bonhomie, the togetherness and the no-holds-barred accountability all added up to what Phil King remembers as 'the best dressing room I was ever part of.' King, no slouch himself when it came to the wisecracks, recalls, 'You had the groups in the club that you knew would go on to be managers. You had the lads like Nigel Worthington, Nigel Pearson, Danny Wilson – the ones who were looking long-term, the ones you could see were going to stay in football.

'But then there were the single lads who wanted to win Saturday, go out and get pissed up, and try and pull a bird or two. Hirsty was the city stud in those days! God, he used to get mobbed everywhere.

'It was so good that you'd almost rather spend time with the lads at times than go home to your family. Sometimes, when we were coming back from away games, when we got to a service station I'd ring up the wife. "Bloody traffic on this M6, it's a nightmare! Not sure what time we'll be back, probably be late though." So I'd get a couple of hours with the lads in Josephine's. Result!'

Like King, most of the squad were experienced pros who'd been around a bit and earned their standing in the game. But among all those hard-bitten warriors, a young Cockney urchin was having the time of his life.

Gordon Watson had endured a tough upbringing, flitting between children's homes and throwing himself into football for salvation. But as time went on and his talent took him towards a career in football, Watson says he became less disciplined; by the time he arrived from Charlton in 1991, treading that well-worn path between The Valley and the Peaks, he had morphed into a bona fide man about town. Sheffield's raucous nightlife suited him perfectly.

'When I got to Sheffield I could have gone out eight nights a week,' he says with typical enthusiasm. 'To be honest my main mates weren't footballers. I was into

Hotpants, Trash, Occasions, all the trendy places. I'd go out with the supporters to places like the Leadmill on a Thursday night, although I wouldn't be drinking before a Saturday game.

'But I was happy to mix with the players, too. If we went out, we all went out together. And wow, we had some fun together!

'I even used to take some of the other lads to the gay night on a Wednesday night because one of my friends was a promoter. All the women wore was negligee, knickers and high heels, and I was 21 years old! I used to rave about it to the boys, but as you can imagine, I got some funny looks at first.

'I remember I eventually dragged the lads along one night, and I had to practically force them in. Then, the next week, they were the ones dragging me!'

As time went on, Wednesday's *esprit de corps* became legendary. Players from other clubs would join them after games in Sheffield – including the most famous English name of the era.

Paul Gascoigne had just embarked on his sojourn in Italy but would regularly come back to England to play for the national team or recover from injuries. He was good mates with players such as Hirst and Palmer, and the Sheffield public were happy to give him space to let his hair down.

Gazza was still a superstar, untainted by the problems that would blight him in later life, and publicans were delighted to welcome this national treasure. Requests for lock-ins usually received a favourable hearing, nowhere more so than at the Devonshire Arms in Dore, where many of the players lived.

Hirst vividly recalls he and Gazza once starting an impromptu game of Play Your Cards Right with the starstruck punters, while Watson harks back to a crazy night at the back of the pub, 'Can't remember why Gazza was there, but it was great. They ended up throwing pizza around at half two in the morning!'

It's just a shame that the Wednesday lads couldn't persuade Gazza to ditch the glamour of Serie A and move to South Yorkshire. Although, with John Sheridan around, he might have struggled to break into the team.

* * *

As he usually did in big games, Sheridan scored in Wednesday's first televised match of 1992. But it was Watson who made the headlines. In fact, he briefly became football's public enemy number one.

The occasion saw Howard Wikinson return to Hillsborough for the first time since leaving three and a half years earlier. Unlike Atkinson, he was never going to be greeted with boos and 'Judas' chants from the home crowd, but ITV still booked the match for its prime Sunday afternoon slot. It duly attracted one of their biggest audiences of the season.

Halfway through the first half, with Leeds winning 2-0, Watson nipped in behind the dozing Leeds defender Chris Whyte and nicked the ball away from him. Watson fell to the ground and won a penalty, to the obvious disgust of the entire Leeds team and millions watching on the box.

Looking back on the incident now, the footage is damning: Watson pushes the ball away from Whyte, takes a step, then falls over with no one anywhere near him before writhing on the ground, holding his leg. Even today, when diving is as commonplace as Alice bands and tattoo sleeves, that sort of theatrical pirouette would draw criticism. Back in 1992 it was considered a stain on the soul of the game.

The footage went viral... well, as viral as it could go in an age when most people got their football news from Ceefax. Pundits up and down the land joined the condemnation. Even *Saint and Greavsie* piled in, suggesting Watson was a cheat. But all these years on, the man himself is unrepentant.

'I was only 20 years old and learning my trade. One of the first players to get booked for diving was Trevor Francis. In fact he used to dive on the training ground, just leave a leg! He'd got that from Italy. He used to say to us "if you get touched, go down." So that's what I did.

'I remember getting round Chris Whyte and he scraped my ankle. I can swear to you a million times that there was contact. Watch the footage back – my right foot never touches the ground again, I take another step with my left and I flip over.

'But when I got home and watched it on the video I'd taped, it caused uproar. People talk about *Saint and Greavsie*, but you should have seen the stick my own family gave me. My father in law said I must be ashamed. He was so annoyed about it that he went home, leaving his son in law at the house!'

For the rest of the match, Leeds took their frustration out on Wednesday's beleaguered back four. Lee Chapman helped himself to a hat-trick, seizing on another unconvincing display from Woods. Mel Sterland, meanwhile, had a storming game, although he admits that 'it hurt a little bit, seeing everyone leaving on the Kop before the end.'

To get mullered once might be deemed an accident, one of those madcap days that can happen in football. But then it happened again a month later when Wednesday shipped six goals in the last 20 minutes to lose 7-1 at Arsenal. It was a match that exposed the first real cracks in the Francis regime and set him on a collision course with two of his players, both of whom were largely blameless in the defeat.

Paul Williams was a substitute that day. 'Carlton was getting a bit riled up, so Trevor told me to go on,' he recalls. 'It was the last few minutes, and we were already 7-1 down. I told him, "No gaffer, we're gone. What are you throwing me on for? If you want to make a real statement, take Carlton off and play with ten men."'

For Williams, it would soon be the end of the road at Hillsborough. Within a few months he would be sent back to London, the first in a long line of players who were binned before their shelf life had come to an end. Today, while he refers to Ron Atkinson as a 'man's man… I've got as much respect for him as I have for any man' he is cooler about his successor.

'I was in awe of him [Francis] growing up, and he was a great manager and coach, but I don't think I revere him in the same way I do some other managers. My relationship with him was somewhat tarnished.'

A couple of days after the Arsenal game, Phil King faced his own backlash.

'I looked at the *Green 'Un* after the game and it said "Phil King, star man: 5",' he says. 'So then I walk in on the Monday and Trevor goes through the whole team. "Okay, Woodsy, unlucky with a couple of goals. Hirsty, shame about those missed chances. Roland, hard lines for this or that."

'Then he gets to me. "Kingy, what the fucking hell were you doing?!" I couldn't believe it. So we had a proper ding-dong, and he told me to fuck off indoors. So I was like, "Yeah, right, I will."

'We had a game the next night, but when I reported in Richie Barker pulled me over. "Boss wants a word with you." So I went to see him in his office and he said, "You told me you didn't want to play tonight, and I've accepted that." I told him I'd never said that, but his mind was made up. It got in the papers as well.

'But then, before the game on the Saturday, Trevor called me in again and said, "Right, you're in tomorrow, let's move on."'

Despite Francis's attempt at reconciliation, the spat left a scar in his relationship with King and a contract dispute between the pair ensured that it continued to weep for months afterward.

'In training, we'd be playing these piggy in the middle games and I'd be flying in, trying to leave one on people – Trevor as much as anyone,' King continues. 'In the end I snapped my cruciate going in too hard at the start of the next season. I ended up missing six months.'

* * *

For all the shock and anger of those two defeats, perhaps the most grievous blow was inflicted by the ne'er-do-wells from across town. Sheffield United sidled over in mid-March and claimed a comfortable victory, the second time they'd beaten Wednesday that season.

Wednesday had created most of the chances in that first meeting at Bramall Lane back in November. Palmer had hit the underside of the bar, Anderson had had a goal disallowed, and Wilson had missed with the net gaping.

But in the return match at Hillsborough, on the filthiest of Yorkshire nights, Wednesday were simply outfought. Two of the goals came from the sort of slapstick defending last witnessed during the relegation year, and the third was coughed up by Woods, who made a horribly limp attempt to smother a punt downfield. Like Leeds and Arsenal, United had exposed Wednesday's underbelly with a simple aerial bombardment.

To Wednesday's credit, they rallied from that trio of high-profile defeats. The wheels may have wobbled disconcertingly but they were soon screwed back into place.

After that rotten display in the derby, they lost only once in their final ten games and picked up impressive wins at Tottenham and Nottingham Forest. It was enough for a third-placed finish, seven points off top spot.

In light of what transpired later in Francis's regime, the lofty league placing achieved in 1991/92 has been somewhat forgotten. But it was a superb achievement: Wednesday had finished above Arsenal, Liverpool and Spurs. They'd proved that the League Cup Final win was no fluke and they'd done so playing some of the best football in the country.

But could they have done even more? With Hirst, Palmer and Sheridan all at their peak, bolstered by brilliant youngsters such as Harkes and Warhurst, perhaps Wednesday could have pushed for the title that season.

After all, that edition of the First Division, the final season before it morphed into the Premier League, was almost uniquely open. Liverpool were slowly spiralling into their 30-year tailspin and Arsenal didn't have enough squad depth to take their place. Chelsea, Tottenham and Everton were all kicking around in mid-table; Manchester City were still wandering in the desert, looking for their saviour. The perch, as Alex Ferguson was later to describe it, was up for grabs.

In the end, of course, it was Howard Wilkinson and his own recently promoted team who scrambled up it, albeit temporarily. And they did so with help from a man who could have joined Wednesday.

In January 1992, Eric Cantona had pitched up at Hillsborough, ostensibly on trial. He'd been forced to quit the French game after kicking a ball at a referee and then going round the disciplinary panel and calling all the assembled delegates 'shitbags.' Due to freezing weather around Sheffield, Cantona was only able to play once for Wednesday – an indoor six-a-side game against touring American side Baltimore Blast, which the Owls lost 8-3. The story goes that Francis asked Cantona to stay at Hillsborough for outdoor training, Cantona refused, and Wilkinson nipped in to sign him for Leeds.

Looking back now, Francis insists Cantona was never actually on trial. He claims he was simply doing a favour to French national team manager Michel Platini as Cantona needed some practice. However, this begs the rather obvious question: why would Cantona have come all the way to South Yorkshire? News footage of the time, which shows Cantona's interpreter saying the player 'wanted to play in England' and Francis saying 'it's up to him' would certainly suggest a deal was in the offing.

Some players suggest the transfer was never really on. They say it was impossible to judge Cantona in those indoor sessions and no one in the squad was particularly shocked when the player went on his way. Two accounts, however, paint an altogether different picture.

David Hirst was injured at the time but he clearly recalls witnessing Cantona's brilliance from afar.

'I remember we trained at Aurora, the old indoor centre near Meadowhall, because we'd had snow' Hirst says. 'I was running around the pitch with the physio Alan Smith and I remember watching the game. Cantona was superb. He was chipping the keeper from 35 yards, everything.

'I heard that Trevor wanted him to stay an extra week, so he could see him on grass, but I never got the full story. He went to Leeds and they won the title, he went to Man United and they started winning titles. There's got to be some kind of correlation there hasn't there?'

An even more striking account comes from Chris Bart-Williams, who was still living in a hotel when Cantona pitched up.

'Eric came to stay in the same hotel as me, and he was a class guy. I didn't speak any French and he didn't speak any English, but we had dinner together, with a glass of wine in his case. He was a fun guy but very polite and courteous with it.

'And boy, could he play! He had what people in the game call happy feet. The ball just seemed to stick to him. His awareness of others, the way he used his body. In that indoor game you could see he was just class.

'So when he turned up at Leeds, it was a shock.'

It's easy to be overcritical of Francis here. Signing Cantona represented far more of a gamble at the time than it appears in the rear view mirror. As discussed earlier in this book, this was a time when foreigners were still an exotic, often misunderstood species in the English game.

Yes, Wednesday had enjoyed success in bringing Roland Nilsson from Sweden, but Scandies were a relatively known quantity. A Frenchman, however? The British game had only really known Didier Six and he'd hopped back over the Channel after one solitary season with Aston Villa.

Plus Cantona was no ordinary Frenchman. He'd effectively been expelled from France, so wild that even his fellow Gauls couldn't tame him. Francis already had plenty of sulphur in his ranks with players like Palmer and Sheridan. Did he need another combustible element in the mix?

The facts are, however, that Cantona won a championship in five of his six seasons after leaving Sheffield. Not only did he help Leeds drag themselves over the line in his first season, he then provided the catalyst for Manchester United's era of dominance.

Yes, Cantona wouldn't have been able to protect Woods and his defence from high balls into the box. His lack of English may not have helped him mesh with Wednesday's alpha males. But the thought of him playing little give-and-gos with Sheridan, and feeding the ball through to Hirst, remains one of the great 'what-ifs' of Wednesday's history. And there'd be plenty more of those over the season to come.

13

THREE TIMES UNLUCKY

It was a goal that didn't deserve to settle a kickabout on Endcliffe Park, let alone an FA Cup Final. A blunderbuss header from a lumbering centre-half which ballooned up off the goalkeeper and didn't even wrinkle the back of the net.

But with that one witless, charmless goal, in injury time of extra time of a replay, Wednesday's season had come to naught. At the same end of Wembley that witnessed Sheridan's rocket, players now sat slumped on the turf, beaten. In the stands behind them, fans stood open-mouthed, unable to comprehend what had just happened.

Wednesday had deserved to win one cup, and possibly two. Over five hours of football they had outplayed Arsenal only to lose through a pair of defensive mistakes. Had they taken their chances, those errors wouldn't even have mattered.

But at least the supporters could look forward to brighter times as they made for the exits. Their team had proven itself as good as any in England. All they had to do was stay together and honours would surely come by the bucketload...

* * *

THEY SAY the darkest hour comes just before dawn. But sometimes the reverse is true, too.

In the early months of 1993, Sheffield Wednesday dazzled with megawatt brilliance. The fact that they reached two cup finals was amazing enough, but what was even more impressive was the way they did it. The demolition job on Blackburn Rovers in one semi-final was followed by the clinical dismantling of their cross-town rivals in the other.

That team had it all: the youthful thrust of Paul Warhurst and Chris Bart-Williams tempered by wise old heads such as Viv Anderson and Nigel Worthington. The power of Carlton Palmer and the elan of David Hirst. Trevor Francis had taken the machine left by Ron Atkinson and bolted on the brilliance of Chris Waddle, a player who enraptured the entire league. All the cogs whirred away in perfect harmony, their gears gliding into place with the velvet synchronicity of a Swiss watch.

And then, suddenly, the light was switched off. That team of all the talents, which had been so carefully constructed between 1989 and 1993, was crudely dismantled for reasons that have never been adequately explained, its stars replaced by players who were barely half as good.

But if 1993 was a finale for that great side, what a tour de force they gave. Fans who were around at the time will always have the memories of the team that could outplay anyone in the country and outfight most of them too.

If Wednesday fans ever see a better team than that, they'll be even more fortunate than Arsenal in those two cup finals.

*   *   *

The 1992/93 season was the first of the Premier League. The year when football's prehistoric age gave way to modernity. When the grim old days of long balls, tight shorts and freezing terraces were swept aside to create The Best League In The World(™).

In reality, the changes for which Sky so readily claims credit took years to materialise, and were catalysed by several factors – including, of course, the tragedy that took place at Hillsborough. Nonetheless, looking back, it's clear that 1992/93 was a watershed of sorts. Before it, the league had been dominated by hard-bitten British players with military haircuts, who bullied opponents with power and aggression. After it, the power would pass to silky pin-up boys and quixotic foreigners (most of them, unfortunately, playing for Manchester United).

The Wednesday team that approached this formative season straddled both eras. They had nuggety enforcers like Nigel Pearson and Danny Wilson, men who would go toe to toe with anyone in the league. But they also had gifted playmakers like John Sheridan, whose skills were perfect for Sky's glitzy new jamboree. And in John Harkes and David Hirst, they had two lads who looked like they'd stepped straight out of a *Just 17* poster.

'That was a great side,' says Carlton Palmer now. 'If teams wanted to play football, that was fine by us, we had players who could run rings round them. And if they wanted a scrap, that was fine too – as Wimbledon found out once or twice when they tried it on.'

It was a team with no obvious weaknesses. But just a few weeks before the big kick-off, Trevor Francis went out and made it even better.

On 17 July Wednesday signed England superstar Chris Waddle from Marseille for a fee of £1m. The transfer caused a minor sensation in English football, not least because of how clandestine it was. Francis did such a good job of keeping the deal under wraps that even his own players knew nothing about it until they turned up for pre-season training at Middlewood Road, then in the middle of renovation work, and found Waddle sat in the portakabin waiting for them.

Just a couple of years earlier, Waddle had become the third-most expensive player in football history when he went to France. Twelve months before that, he'd made the shortlist for the Ballon D'or. Signing such an illustrious name would have been beyond Wednesday in the past but, once again, chairman Dave Richards had pulled out all the stops to show the world that his club could now lure the biggest talents in the game.

Francis, a man who enjoyed the finer things in life, readily brought into his boss's vision. Waddle wasn't even the first Geordie genius on his hit-list that summer; the manager had already tried to get Alan Shearer, only to find the price too high for even Wednesday's ambitious board (in desperation, Francis had at one stage suggested to his business partner that they bid from their own pocket). But, in Waddle, he landed a player who fitted his team even more perfectly than Shearer would have done.

Waddle gave Wednesday the creativity they had previously lacked in wide areas and his magnetic skills sucked defenders towards him, creating space for his midfielders to pile into. And as well as being a top player, he was a top bloke, who would happily work with his team-mates to help them unlock their talents.

For players such as John Harkes, Waddle became both a role model and a close mate, someone who was always happy to share little nuggets of advice about the intricacies of wing play.

'He was a massive influence on me. Not just on the field but off it. It's still a strong friendship now. My wife and his wife Lorna got along extremely well.

'From a training perspective, I'd go up to him and ask if we could do some extra work afterwards. He'd do it with me. How you receive the ball, how you manipulate the ball, how you cut back on to your right foot, everything. Superb player.'

Hirst, never one for overstatement, is equally effusive. 'Wadds was a top bloke, really top bloke. I see him every week now, we drink in the same bar and we're in a WhatsApp group together. We're still great mates to this day.

'He was an absolute superstar. It's hard to separate him and Shez as the best player I played with. Both superb at what they did. I've seen Shez open defences blindfolded and I've seen Wads skin the best full-backs in the world. Those two in the same team – as a centre-forward, you're rubbing your hands.'

*   *   *

But Hirst didn't get much chance to enjoy the silver service laid on by Wednesday's playmakers. Just five games into the season, Wednesday went to Highbury for their first dose of pain at Arsenal's hands.

Early in the second half, Hirst received the ultimate hospital pass from Paul Warhurst and was clattered from behind by Steve Bould, a challenge that would leave him with a broken ankle. Incredibly, instead of heading to the infirmary, Hirst hauled himself up and scored with his knackered foot from the resulting free kick. Only at the end of the game, which Wednesday lost 2-1, did he realise the damage that had been done. The injury would keep him out until mid-October.

Looking back on that injury, the first in a series that would blight his career, Hirst is typically sanguine. 'That's what happens in the game. If you're doing well, people are going to kick you. Teams were probably talking about that before games – "if you get a chance on the halfway line, give him one". Bouldy saw that opportunity.'

Instead of holding the defender responsible, Hirst jokes that it was Warhurst who should take the blame, 'He gave me that ball on the halfway line and it was taking forever to get to me! I could hear Bouldy coming and I knew it was going to hurt.

'To be fair though, It wouldn't have been so bad if I hadn't gone running around and spent the rest of the game trying to kick Nigel Winterburn!'

Hirst may downplay the incident now but his injury knocked the stuffing out of the team. Prior to their visit to north London, Wednesday had been unbeaten (albeit they'd drawn three of the four games). But that defeat at Highbury began a run of four losses in five league games, including a particularly woeful display against Manchester City at Hillsborough.

The UEFA Cup adventure, Wednesday's first foray into European competition since 1963, began with an 8-1 thrashing of part-timers Spora Luxembourg. But then came an altogether tougher challenge from German side Kaiserslautern. The

Rhinelanders had finished a distant fifth in the Bundesliga the previous season and their only star was the unfortunately named striker Stefan Kuntz, but they were still plenty strong enough for Wednesday. Just as they had 29 years earlier, Wednesday went out by the aggregate score of 5-3. It could have been more.

By this stage the grumbles about Francis and his regime were starting to grow. The previous season, he'd been content to sit back and allow the players to get on with it, opting for continuity rather than confrontation. Now, however, he was trying to impose himself and his men were beginning to take umbrage.

Again, it's easy to imagine a clash between football worlds ancient and modern; between an enlightened Europhile, determined to spread the austere gospel of Italian football, and a group of happy-go-lucky Anglo-Saxons desperately clinging to the old ways. This was still a time when English footballers refuelled in the bar rather than the ice bath and viewed any food that grew from the ground with a mixture of suspicion and contempt. Ronald Nilsson says that when he first rocked up in the winter of 1989 he ate chicken and rice, because that's what they did at Gothenburg. 'The players came over and asked, "What are you eating?" They were still eating chips.'

But Nilsson's team-mates are adamant they had no problem with Francis's methods. Yes, the manager encouraged them to eat more pasta and broccoli and to cut down their alcohol intake. But unlike at Liverpool, where players railed against his old mate Souness for curbing beer on the coach home from games, it doesn't appear that Francis's attempts at modernisation caused any particular friction. His players were desperate to succeed and were happy to take the new ideas on board.

Instead it was a simple clash of personalities between a manager eager to assert his authority and a group of lads who had been brought together by his predecessor precisely *because* they were such strong characters.

'The players had all been brought to the club by Ron, and they didn't look at Trevor in the same way,' Palmer says. 'But he should have just accepted it because it didn't matter. Just leave things as they are! You don't need to go to war with Carlton Palmer or any of the other players, and bring them into line. All he had to do was just sit there and go with the ride.

'But instead he went to war with strong characters and that isn't going to work. If you're going to go to war with me, that's a fucking problem.'

Perhaps Francis felt intimidated by the personalities that surrounded him. Whereas Atkinson thrived on the challenge of bringing jack-the-lads into line, his successor was an altogether more self-effacing character and may have tried to overcompensate.

Hirst certainly subscribes to this view. 'When Trevor became a manager perhaps he wasn't strong enough, given the players he was dealing with,' he says.

'Sometimes it felt that when we went training, Richie Barker was babysitting Trevor a bit. Richie would try and get his point across but Trevor didn't take it on board. Trevor wanted to be the manager, and maybe he didn't have that charisma to work it like Howard would or Ron would.'

The mood in the camp wasn't helped by the rumours surrounding Hirst himself. That autumn of 1992, Manchester United were in the market for a striker having failed in their own attempt to woo Shearer, and Hirst was their number one target. Alex Ferguson sent six separate bids through the Hillsborough fax machine and at one point he even called Francis on his car phone to bawl him out.

But Francis and Richards were unmoved. They hadn't signed Woods and Waddle only to bow down when another big club came for one of their star players. Even when United lodged a bid of £4.5m, nearly £1m more than the British record fee Blackburn had paid for Shearer, the Wednesday power-brokers decided they'd rather keep Hirst. He was, quite literally, priceless.

Looking back on that mad few weeks, the player himself says that 'I never spoke to Man United and I never spoke to Fergie. I'd heard through other means that they were very interested, but I never went into the manager and asked anything about it, nor was I in a position to. I'd just signed a new deal and I was very happy at Sheffield Wednesday.

'Then they made the bid and Trevor showed me the fax. He told me he was going to send it back, telling them that I wasn't for sale.

'Should I have knocked on Trevor's door and kicked a stink up? Probably, looking back, but that's a question I can never really answer because I don't know what the outcome would have been.

'Yes, it would have been great to have a spell at United when they were flying, of course it would. But who's to say I'd have gone there and things would have worked out? I don't dwell on what could have been and I don't regret it because I enjoyed my time at Sheffield Wednesday.

'Being honest, I didn't need to make it happen. If I'd been unhappy I could have got the move. If I'd been treated badly or anything like that, I'd have been out the door as quick as the door could open.'

Other players, however, recall that Hirst was altogether less phlegmatic at the time. Wilson, for example, says, 'I was good mates with David and I spoke to him about it. He told me how disappointed he was.' And while Hirst was admirably stoic throughout the whole affair, the constant rumour and innuendo did nothing for Wednesday's attempts to dig themselves out of their early season hole. It was the Premier League's first real transfer saga, and it was a distraction the club could certainly do without.

In the end, United got Cantona instead. And, once again, he would show Wednesday fans what they could have won.

*   *   *

As Christmas approached, things went from bad to worse. Defeat at Leeds on 12 December made it two months and seven league games without a win. Wednesday lay 17th with 17 games played, just two points clear of the relegation places.

At this critical point, Palmer claims, Danny Wilson and Viv Anderson called a crisis meeting at Hanrahan's and told the players to get everything off their chests.

'We weren't playing well, we weren't performing, we weren't getting results and it wasn't us. The camp was unhappy with Trevor. So we all had our say and we agreed, "This has got fuck all to do with the manager, this is about us, and we're better than this. We've got to sort it out, show our pride in the way we play."

'We put the onus on us to fucking sort it out. Whether we liked Trevor or not, whether we had any differences with Trevor or not, we took responsibility. We basically said, "Fuck Trevor, let's get on and do what we do." And it changed from there.'

Other players refute Palmer's account. Peter Shirtliff and Nigel Worthington, two of the most senior members of the dressing room, say they have no recollection of such a meeting. Wilson, for his part, denies calling it. 'Viv and I would never have instigated anything like that. We had too much respect for Trevor and Trevor was great with us, certainly from my perspective.'

Perhaps the truth lies somewhere in the middle. The players would gather most Tuesday nights, often to watch the reserves, and then go for a couple of quick pints. They'd have their Friday afternoon lunches and Sunday afternoon confabs in the pub. Maybe, during one of those informal get-togethers, players began to open up about their frustration and the conversation turned into an impromptu clear-the-air meeting.

Hirst's account certainly supports that interpretation. 'We had a meeting every time we went out. We all had an opinion, we'd all air our voices, sometimes we were right and sometimes we were wrong. I wouldn't say we specifically went out and said "Trevor's this, Trevor's that". But it would have been brought up while we were all having a beer, without a doubt, as it would do at most clubs.

'We certainly weren't trying to instigate a coup or anything like that. We were all winners and wanted to win. We were trying to put things right that we probably felt weren't being given to us.'

Whatever was said or not said, Wednesday's form gradually picked up. In the final game before Christmas they beat QPR 1-0 at Hillsborough, then came a crazy match against Manchester United on Boxing Day, a throwback to those barmy festive frolics of the 1950s and '60s when players would rock up stuffed to the gunnels with booze and turkey and serve up ten-goal bonanzas.

Hirst, playing against United for the first time since the transfer saga, scored after only two minutes, and with Waddle running riot, Wednesday roared into a 3-0 lead. But then United mounted the first of what would become their trademark comebacks. With just moments to go Cantona, the man whom Ferguson had signed instead of Hirst, poked in the equaliser.

Other teams would have been floored by the squandering of a three-goal lead but in Wednesday's case, the magnificence of the match seemed to inspire them. They would go a further two months and 14 games unbeaten, a run that brought the scalps of Chelsea, Tottenham and Manchester City on the road and a 1-0 victory over high-flying Norwich at Hillsborough. But it was the cup triumphs that really caught the imagination of the Sheffield public; by the time Wednesday finally lost at Coventry on 3 March they had reached the sixth round of the FA Cup and effectively booked their place in the League Cup Final.

That late-winter run was all the more impressive given Wednesday had to play almost all of it without Hirst, who received a fresh injury in freak circumstances during a League Cup tie at Ipswich on 19 January.

With Wednesday 1-0 up, Hirst nicked the ball past John Wark and raced clear despite the grizzly Scot's attempt to hack him down. A goal looked inevitable but then Hirst lofted the ball into the crowd and went down in a crumpled heap. It turned out that he had damaged his thigh muscle in taking the shot and would be out for a further two and a half months.

To lose such a key player for the second time in the season was a blow to the entire squad, of course. But it was a particular blow to the man who had joined Wednesday to play alongside him.

Mark Bright had arrived in the early season from Crystal Palace in a deal that took Paul Williams the other way. As Bright recalls, the chance to partner Hirst was a key factor in his decision to move to Sheffield.

'Trevor came to me and said he wanted a target man to play alongside David Hirst, someone to score 15 to 20 goals and hold up the ball. He said, "I've just signed Chris Waddle, he'll get you loads of chances." When I was at Palace, Hirsty was someone my mate Ian Wright and I had admired from afar, a skinny kid with a brilliant shot on him. So it was exciting to play with him. We struck up a good friendship off the pitch too – we were both single when we were at the club in those first few years so we hung around with one another. As we all know, Hirsty is good company!'

After a slow start, the pair had really clicked into gear by the time they went to Ipswich on that cold January evening. Bright had already scored 13 goals and was being talked about as a potential England striker. Now he needed a new partner.

With Gordon Watson still developing, Wednesday could easily have dipped into the transfer market to find a temporary replacement for Hirst. To Francis's credit, however, he decided on a left-field solution that would reap spectacular benefits.

* * *

When you ask the Wednesday players about Paul Warhurst, the response is universal: he was one of those players who just had *it*. Pace, strength, agility; this was a player who had been showered with gifts by the footballing Gods. And he was a top professional, a player who fit perfectly into Francis's regime.

Warhust had been bought as a long-term replacement for Peter Shirtliff at the heart of Wednesday's defence. But it was clear, right from the start, that this strapping young athlete could shine in other areas of the pitch too.

Warhurst actually made his first appearance up front in the early months of that 1992/93 season, in the wake of Hirst's injury at Arsenal. It's not entirely clear how the decision came about; Francis has claimed that he came up with the idea himself, but Roland Nilsson's account suggests the players also contributed.

'Trevor asked what we could do [to improve results] and that was an option to consider. As players, you always have a say in things. We did that in training and it became very good. So we said, "Yeah, let's try it."'

However the idea was conceived, it paid off more spectacularly than anyone could have imagined. Warhurst scored at Nottingham Forest on his full striking debut, then netted two more against Spora Luxembourg, although the second almost brought tragedy when he was knocked out in a challenge with the visiting goalkeeper and required emergency resuscitation after swallowing his tongue.

When he recovered from that horrific challenge, Warhurst moved back to defence as Hirst returned. But he'd proved that he could handle the pressure of the number nine shirt and Francis had no hesitation in switching him back after the Ipswich game. He probably thought Warhurst would hold the fort until Hirst got back and nick a couple of goals along the way. Suffice to say, Warhurst did more than that.

Not since Phil Collins ditched his drumsticks and grabbed a mic has a stand-in seized their moment with such aplomb. Warhurst scored a blinding volley at Chelsea in the first game of his new striking run and would score 11 more times in a 12-match sequence. Players have picked up international caps for less.

And it wasn't just the goals that he scored but the manner of them. These weren't bull-in-a-China-shop headers, the sort that centre-halves usually score when let loose in the opposing penalty box. These were deft dinks, dextrous volleys and finishes of slide-rule precision, scored with either foot. If you didn't know better, you could have sworn it was Hirst himself wearing the number nine shirt.

Nowadays, in an era of vast squads and rigid specialism, a Premier League club would never dream of throwing a centre-half up front in a time of crisis. It's impossible to imagine Harry Maguire, John Stones or Virgil van Dijk being shifted from one end of the pitch to the other.

Warhurst stands as a glorious relic of a bygone age. He wasn't the last utility man to grace the Premier League – Chris Sutton and Dion Dublin would both flit between the two ends of the pitch in years ahead – but he was, without doubt, the most memorable.

*   *   *

That late-winter run wasn't all about Warhurst, however. Practically everyone in the team was playing out of their skin as Wednesday sliced through one opponent after another.

Palmer was tearing into opponents with an almost maniacal zeal, playing each game as if it were his last. Sheridan and Waddle were teasing defences, luring them out of position and then springing the trap. And Bright was gorging on their creativity, providing the sort of physical presence Wednesday had lacked since the days of Lee Chapman.

And then there was a young, shy Londoner who was coming of age, revealing new parts of his repertoire with each passing week.

Chris Bart-Williams was still only 18 when he established himself in Wednesday's first team that winter, but he'd always been a man beyond his years. His parents had moved over from Sierra Leone when he was just four years old and then separated, forcing the young man to grow up with almost preternatural haste.

'With a single mum I'd had to do everything myself,' Bart-Williams says. 'Cook, clean, everything. And that meant I was always mature. I'd never been the type of guy who needed people to tell me what to do, or how to do it. I could work it out for myself.'

At Leyton Orient, his local club, Bart-Williams had been playing against semi-pro teams from the age of 13, forced to stand his ground against grown, angry men. By the time he signed for Wednesday in 1991, aged only 17, he'd already played a full season in Orient's first team.

When he met Bart-Williams, Francis may well have seen something of himself in this intelligent, thoughtful young man. He himself had been a teenage superstar, forced to grow up in the spotlight. And the pair got on right from the start: Francis may have found it difficult to control some of the older, brasher characters in the squad, but Bart-Williams is full of praise for the way his manager treated him.

'I admired Trevor. Partly because I knew he'd been through what I'd been through, coming into top-flight football at a young age, but also because he'd been great in the negotiations.

'A lot of players are put in digs when they move to a new city but that would never have suited me. I was used to fending for myself, making my own meals, doing my own laundry. So my agents said I wanted to live on my own. Trevor said "okay, fine" and I went into a hotel instead, until I could get a place on my own. That's how I met Eric Cantona!'

Bart-Williams had made his debut as a box-to-box midfielder in that 1-1 draw against Arsenal the previous year, earning rave reviews for his performance against the title-winners' heavyweight engine room. But, just as he did with Warhurst,

Francis realised that this young star could perform well in a different role, one he'd seen work to devastating effect in Italy.

'Trevor played me at ten in that second season,' says Bart-Williams. 'It was a good use of my skills. I could play off the strikers and use my passing. And of course we had Chris Waddle, too. He was so good, he would make space for people like me.'

Bart-Williams gave Wednesday a little bit of everything: he could tackle, he could pick a pass and he could score goals. And even if he hadn't been such a good footballer, his name would have made him a cult figure on the terraces by itself. The viral popularity of *The Simpsons,* in particular its spin-off LP *Do The Bartman,* meant the Wednesday faithful had an oven-ready nickname for their new playmaker, although thankfully they coined their own song, the wonderfully catchy 'We've got Chris Bart-Williams, he's worth f***ing millions.'

Bart-Williams himself was a big music fan, although his wheelhouse was more Diana Ross, Shirley Bassey and Janet Jackson than *Let's All Have A Disco.* And, appropriately enough, the Wednesday players gave him his own musically inspired nickname.

'They called me Shabba Ranks, after the dancehall musician,' he remembers with a laugh. 'I think it was because I liked the music – although maybe they just thought I wasn't very attractive!'

*　*　*

The players may not have thought much of Bart-Williams's looks, but his performance in the first leg of the League Cup semi-final at Blackburn was so beautiful it would have made Karl Lagerfeld turn his head.

The match began terribly. With just ten minutes gone Wednesday allowed Roy Wegerle to waltz through the defence and score, totally unchallenged. But then, rather than crumble, the visitors took control.

First, Bart-Williams laid on John Harkes with a perfect pirouette and cross. Then he and Sheridan combined to set up one of the most wonderfully intricate goals Wednesday can ever have fashioned. It was Sheridan at his best: a perfectly timed run, a quick one-two and then the cleverest of finishes, flicked with the side of the foot into the corner of the goal.

As Blackburn reeled, punch-drunk from the double-strike, Warhurst saw his moment. With the match still only 25 minutes old he got the ball halfway inside

Blackburn's half, burned off one defender, veered past another and drilled a low left-footed shot past Bobby Mimms. A couple of minutes later, he took a low Bart-Williams cross and rammed the ball into the roof of the net.

Although Blackburn pulled one back before that crazy first half was out, Wednesday's 20-minute burst had settled the tie. And the fact that it all happened at the away end, in front of thousands of delirious Sheffielders, only made it better. Ask any Wednesday fan who was there that night and they'll tell you it's up there with the all-time classic aways, a night when skill and passion combined to create something irresistible.

The only real blot on the evening was an injury to Nigel Pearson, who broke his tibia in the closing stages and would miss the rest of the season. For all the charisma and maturity in Wednesday's dressing room, the loss of such an influential player (and brilliant defender) would be keenly felt with so many big games coming up. And it was the cruellest of blows for Pearson himself, who had done as much as anyone to haul Wednesday out of the old Second Division and to the brink of a Wembley return.

The injury forced a rejigging of the Wednesday defence when Blackburn came for the return leg of the semi-final, a full month after the first game. Palmer, who had partnered Pearson in central defence at Ewood Park, was now paired with Anderson, who also took over the captain's armband. At first the patched-up back four were a bag of nerves; Nilsson almost scored a comical own goal early on, and then his fellow Swede Patrick Andersson put the visitors ahead.

Thankfully Wednesday had that cushion from the first leg in Lancashire, and while the atmosphere was nowhere near as relaxed or euphoric as it had been during the victory over Chelsea at Hillsborough two years earlier, second-half goals from Bright and the returning Hirst were enough to seal another final appearance.

Before that, however, the fans had another trip to Wembley, this time against the team they hated most of all.

* * *

Prior to the 1992/93 season, Sheffield's two clubs had met only eight times in 25 years. Like two yo-yos bouncing at the same time they kept missing each other, one going down as the other came up.

But even in those fallow years when their fortunes kept them apart, the flames of enmity were never quite extinguished. Fans would regularly clash in the city centre after games and sometimes the players were caught up in the crossfire.

Mel Sterland, a man who hates Sheffield United as much as anyone interviewed for this chronicle, tells a story about being ambushed by the enemy while on a night out with his big mate, Imre Varadi.

'We decided to go into Sheffield town centre and have a curry. But when we got to the restaurant this guy came up to me when Imre was in the toilet. I had a stripy shirt on and the guy said, "You look like a fucking clown." I didn't react and the guy went and sat back down with his mate. When Imre came back, I said, "I think we're going to have some trouble here."

'Eventually this guy's mate came back and said something to Imre, and Imre just stood up and cracked him! Then the first guy came back, the one who called me a bleeding clown, and I just hit him. So I'm holding him down, hitting him, and Imre's chased the second guy into the kitchen.

'Anyway I go to punch the guy, he ducks and I hit the owner of the restaurant! Meantime Imre's dragging the other guy out of the kitchen and he tells him "apologise to my pal." And, to be fair, he did.

'The restaurant was quite busy. I apologised to the owner and said, "If anyone wants a drink, I'll buy them a drink." And that was how we resolved it.'

When the two clubs finally found themselves in the First Division at the same time in 1991, the rivalry cranked up a notch. Even the 'foreigners', the ones who hadn't grown up steeped in the Steel City's internecine strife, could find themselves swept up in it.

Phil King recalls going out one night with Roland Nilsson and his wife. 'We ended up wandering into this pub that was probably more red than blue, and they just surrounded us. I thought, "Shit, we're in bother here."

'I had the gift of the gab, so I said, "Come on lads, you're doing all right, you've got some good players, let's just have a good night." But next thing we know, a drink's been thrown over Roland and I'm thinking, "Oh dear, what do we do here?"

'Then out of nowhere, like Clint Eastwood striding into the OK Corral, Billy Whitehurst appears! He just says, "Calm down lads, it's just football, on you go." They shit themselves. He was a Sheffield United legend and he was six foot five, 17 stone. Had a bit of a reputation too as I recall. I'll always be thankful to him for bailing us out.'

Occasionally, passions could spill over on the pitch too. Palmer recalls an incident in the tunnel before one game at Bramall Lane, as the teams were about to go out. 'Big Nige put his hand over the TV camera in the tunnel and suddenly everyone was it. Danny Wilson had Carl Bradshaw against the wall – it was mayhem.' The fracas, apparently, was sparked by Wednesday's suspicions that a United player had listened in to their pre-match team talk by sneaking on to the roof above the away dressing room.

Generally, however, the two sets of players got on fine. They lived in the same villages, drank in the same bars and played golf on the same courses. There was no reason for them to avoid one another just because they played for different teams.

Hirst, a man who would never let football rivalries get in the way of an ale and a yarn, recalls, 'If we'd played Sheffield United and it was all kicking off in town, we'd still be having a drink with them after the game. We were all footballers, lads who'd come up through the same system and had a lot in common.

'Yes, we played with passion. I played for Barnsley, Sheffield Wednesday and Southampton in my career and I loved playing for all of them. But as a player, it's different to being a fan. As a player, you're with a team for a certain period and then you move on. As a fan, you're with that team for life.'

Nonetheless, when the two sides were pulled out of the hat together for the FA Cup semi-final, friendships – among players, staff and supporters – were put firmly on hold. It was, quite possibly, the biggest game in either club's history, and it was certainly the biggest game in the city's history.

Neither team's progress had been particularly convincing. Wednesday had edged out Cambridge, Sunderland and Southend before beating Derby in a sixth-round replay thanks to another goal from Warhurst. United had nearly lost to Burnley in the third round before sneaking past Hartlepool and beating Blackburn on penalties. Yes they'd put out Manchester United, but only with the help of a missed penalty late on.

Both sides had reason to be confident, however. Wednesday were clearly superior and were the form team in the country going into the match. United had yet to lose to Wednesday since the two sides resumed their on-field rivalry the previous season.

The match had originally been pencilled in for Elland Road only to be switched to Wembley as part of a double-header – the first time both semi-finals had been moved to the national stadium. With Arsenal and Tottenham playing in the other tie the decision made sense, although it owed much to the lobbying of Sheffield United, who wanted to cash in on their first semi-final in either cup competition since 1961.

'That was their biggest mistake,' Palmer says. 'They could have played the game at Leeds, but they wanted to take a share of the gate receipts. On that tight pitch up there, they might have had a chance. Not at fucking Wembley.'

But Palmer himself faced a last-minute race to be fit for the game. Just four days beforehand he suffered a horrific gash while playing for England in Turkey. 'A fucking nightmare' is how he describes it now.

'Graham Taylor had phoned me and been very clear. "If everybody was fit, you wouldn't be in the squad," he told me. "But you're not only in the squad, you're going to play."

'So on the Sunday I went to Trevor and told him I'd been called up. He said, "Carlton, this is the biggest game in the club's history, I can't let you go." We ended up at loggerheads and I said to him, "Trevor, how many times have you played for your country? You know it's the pinnacle of a footballer's career. I might never get another opportunity."'

'Then I said to him, "How many times do I miss games? I'll play on Saturday. Whatever happens, I'll play. There's no way I'll miss the game, I promise." And he said okay.

'So we start the game in Turkey and I'm playing well. Don't feel any problem at all. At half-time I'm sitting down and Stuart Pearce says, "Fucking hell CP, what's happened to your foot?" I look down and there's blood pissing out of the side of my boot. Obviously with the adrenaline I hadn't noticed.

'The physio takes the boot off and it's a complete mess. Graham comes over to me at half-time and asks if I can play the second half. "Yeah, of course I can." So I get through the second half, come back in and it's an even bigger mess.

'They stitch me up, I ask the doctor if I can play Saturday and he says, "No way can you play with that." This was on the Wednesday night. Fucking hell here we go! I phone Trevor and all he says is, "You said you can play whatever."'

Palmer now faced a race against time to avoid his second bout of Wembley heartache in two years.

'We waited until about Friday to try and put a boot on. Couldn't get a boot on. Couldn't walk on it. So then we had a long chat with the doctor and the doctor said the only way we can get away with it is freezing the foot. Take the stitches out, plug it and freeze it. So Trevor goes "you said you'd play" and I said, "Yeah, that's it. If the doctor's said it'll work, fine, no problem."

'If you watch the footage of the game [Sky's extended coverage is available on YouTube], you'll see me come out nearly two hours before. The team sheet's not been handed in yet. They froze the toe and you should have seen the size of the needle. It's going through the sole of the foot! Honestly, I squealed like a baby. The boys were pissing themselves.

'I got the boot on, went out and still couldn't kick a ball. It was agony. So the doctor said, "The only way now is to freeze the whole foot, and you've got 90 minutes when I do it." I said okay, he did it, went out and I said to Trevor, "It's okay, I can do it."

'When we got going, I was winding Brian Deane up all through the game. I kept saying to him, "I've only got one fucking leg and I've still got you in my pocket!"'

*   *   *

Deane wasn't the only United player to be nullified that day. Wednesday outclassed their opponents all over the pitch. 'That game could have been five, six, seven,' Hirst says. 'I know a lot of Sheffield United fans who admit it could have been embarrassing.'

The fact that it wasn't a cricket score was down to some unusually wayward finishing and the heroics of United's talented goalkeeper Alan Kelly, who had the game of his life. But even he was unable to do anything about Chris Waddle's early work of genius.

With just two minutes gone, Waddle spotted the ball down about 35 yards from the opponents' goal. Everyone expected him to float a cross into the box, where Bright and Anderson were waiting. Instead he sprinted up and curled the ball into Kelly's bottom-left corner before sprinting away to his own fans just as Sheridan had two years earlier.

Harkes, who had practised free kicks so often with Waddle on the training pitch, remembers, 'I made a run behind the wall and he almost hit me! If you watch it, the ball goes right over my head. The players were amazed – we knew Chris was capable of course, but he didn't score a lot. He was known more for his creativity and his vision. But yeah, it was an amazing goal.'

The rest of the half was all Wednesday. Warhurst, still playing up front with Hirst not fully fit, hit the frame of the goal twice, once with the left peg and once with the right. Waddle volleyed just wide from a position almost identical to the goal.

And then, finally, a goal came.

From Alan Cork. Bloody Alan Cork. The former Wimbledon player, a man who was to football what Wurzle Gummidge was to fashion, somehow found himself clear of the Wednesday defence, played through by former Owl Franz Carr no less. His shot dribbled toward the net with the speed of a runaway mobility scooter but somehow it evaded both Woods and Waddle, who had raced back to clear the danger. Against the run of play, against the run of logic, United were level.

The second half was slightly tighter, although again Wednesday dominated. But still they couldn't score. Even the introduction of Hirst failed to break the deadlock; in fact he missed an excellent chance late on, the sort he would have buried with a bit more sharpness.

And so to extra time. For Palmer, this meant a fresh trial by needle.

'Just as it was getting to 90 minutes I could start feeling the fucking pain,' he remembers with a grimace. 'If you see me I don't go down the main tunnel, the one behind the goal, I go down the one under the main stand, where they present the trophies.

'Dr Bottomley followed me and he just said, "Carlton, I'm not going to lie, this is going to hurt, but we've just got to freeze it again." So we did it, and I continued like that more or less until the end of the season!'

Early on in extra time Hirst missed an even better chance than the one he'd had earlier, this one a seemingly open goal. After scarcely passing up an opportunity for the last four years, he had found fallibility on the biggest stage of all. Wednesday fans must have been starting to think that their grubby neighbours had put them under some kind of curse.

Then, at the start of the second half of extra time, Wednesday got a corner on the left.

'I remember running over to take that corner,' says Harkes. 'I looked up – we were exhausted by then – and just saw Mark in the middle of the box, alone. So I pinged it to him.'

The delivery was so good that it made the finish a formality. All Bright had to do was nod the ball on target. A striker as good as him was never going to squander the opportunity.

'I said to Mark after the game, "I can't do it any better, all you had to do was put your noggin on it!"' Harkes jokes. 'What I liked about playing with Mark, though, was that he'd never stop asking for the ball. He would demand a lot from you, he'd miss chances but he'd never stop running. When we needed him, he was there.'

Bright himself remembers the goal in more prosaic terms. 'Harkes to Bright, good night! What else is there to say that's not already been said. One of the greatest feelings in my life.'

United tried to rouse themselves, but they were spent. Wednesday had run them ragged, and left no one in any doubt where the Steel City's true power lay.

'We were brilliant that day,' Carlton Palmer says. 'That was us at our best. Few teams could have lived with us. The fact that their keeper got man of the match says it all.'

* * *

A team reaching English football's two major finals in the same season isn't as rare as you might think. Prior to 1993 it happened three times in consecutive seasons – Tottenham in 1982, Manchester United in 1983 and Everton in 1984. Since '93 the feat has been achieved a further six times.

But the same two teams reaching both finals in the same season? That's only happened once. And if Wednesday could have chosen one team with whom to share this unique accomplishment, Arsenal would have been right down the bottom of the list.

Arsenal were oil to Wednesday's water, a team that set out to destroy rather than create. Under George Graham's austere regime they only really had two flair players, Ian Wright and Paul Merson. The rest were fast-twitch automatons programmed to win the ball back as quickly as possible and hoof it to their twin game-breakers. Had Arsène Wenger cast his eye over the cup final rivals he'd have found a lot more kinship in Wednesday than the team he would soon take over.

But for all Arsenal's stylistic limitations, they had something of a hex over Francis and his team. In the three league games Wednesday had played against them since promotion (the fourth would be sandwiched in between the cup finals) the Owls hadn't won. That barren run included the 7-1 horror show at Highbury in early 1992.

Against such a well-drilled and ruthless side, Wednesday would need all their attacking talents to be fit and firing. As the first of the finals loomed however, major doubts remained over David Hirst, who had yet to fully recover from the injury sustained at Ipswich. Despite coming on as sub in both semi-finals, he still wasn't ready for a full 90 minutes.

Hirst's fitness problems prompted the Wednesday management team to make a decision that has enthralled football anoraks ever since.

With the same two teams appearing in both finals, the football authorities decided to trial the numbering system they were planning to introduce the following season. Players had long worn squad numbers during international tournaments, and names had been added for the European Championships in Sweden in 1992. The Premier League, sensing the merchandising opportunities, was itching to import the idea into domestic football.

When Wednesday were asked to submit their squad numbers ahead of the League Cup Final on 18 April, Francis and his brains trust faced a dilemma. Hirst was Wednesday's recognised number nine but Warhurst had done more than enough to earn the shirt and he was the only one of the pair guaranteed to play.

In the end Wednesday allowed Warhurst to keep nine and gave Hirst number five, a shirt he had never previously worn for Wednesday.

'I think it was Richie Barker who told me, "You can't start a game without a number 9,"' Hirst recalls. 'So my response was, "Give me the shirt and I'll play!"'

Hirst did play in the FA Cup Final with Warhurst restored to centre-back. Their respective numbers gave the Wednesday team a rather upside-down look, like a house with the kitchen on the roof. But Hirst says there were no hard feelings.

'It was a crazy one, for sure, but it makes my shirt pretty special! A few years ago someone was claiming to have my cup final shirt and he should have known that it couldn't have been – because it was the number nine.

'The actual shirt? I think it's up in the attic somewhere.'

* * *

But before Wednesday could try on their new shirts, they had to go to Old Trafford for a rematch with Manchester United. The game mattered infinitely more to Alex Ferguson, whose team were pushing for the Premier League title, than it did to Trevor Francis, a fact reflected in Wednesday's team selection. Hirst, Warhurst and several of their team-mates were rested, with the number nine shirt passed round to Phil King.

However Wednesday's makeshift team acquitted themselves brilliantly, and should really have won. Sheridan scored against his boyhood heroes again, this time from the penalty spot, and as United became more jittery a famous victory began to heave into view.

In the end it was snatched away by United defender Steve Bruce who scored a pair of headers, the second coming six minutes into injury time. That goal, and Alex Ferguson's subsequent pitch invasion, provided the first great televisual moment in Premier League history and remains part of its marketing spool to this day. But the magnitude of the spectacle was no consolation to Wednesday, who had led United for a combined total of 103 minutes over their two league games, yet earned only one point. 'They scored in the second leg,' Francis reflected afterwards. It wouldn't be the last time it happened to his team that season.

But Francis and his players still travelled down to London in good heart thanks to a 5-2 win over Southampton in which Bart-Williams scored a hat-trick. Wednesday remained the form team in the country; in their last 26 games they had lost only three times. Yes, Pearson was out and Hirst only half-fit, but Arsenal were without Lee Dixon and John Jensen, two players who were crucial to their defensive unit.

*   *   *

In planning the cup final weekend, Francis stuck with the routine Atkinson had created in 1991 – only without any of his predecessor's party pieces. So the players headed down on the Friday morning, stayed at the Royal Lancaster and trained out of town on the Saturday, but there was no boozing on the Friday night and there was definitely no Stan Boardman on the coach.

According to the players interviewed for this book, there were no problems with this more straitlaced approach. Yes, they'd loved the frivolities laid on by Big Ron, but by now all of them had experience of playing at Wembley and most were internationals. They didn't need a piss-up or bawdy Scouse humour to get them up for a cup final. Even Palmer says, 'The preparations were good… Trevor was organised and he knew what he was doing.' The only dissenting voice is that of Phil King, who suggests the players could have done with a bit more fun in the run-up to the finals.

'It was exactly the same as Ron's preparation, a mirror image – but no alcohol and early to bed! Same coach down, with us on one coach and partners on the other, same hotel, same restaurant. Only we had to stick to water and pasta.

'Ron's attitude had been like "go out and enjoy yourselves, I don't want anybody in bed before me".' But Trevor had been to Italy and the preparation was different. Nowadays it's commonplace to get the pastas, the carbohydrates, the fish, so Trevor was probably ahead of his time there. But it didn't really suit us. We were more about the camaraderie and the bonding – that might have been better.'

King himself had plenty of reason for nerves in the run-up to the League Cup Final. After so long out with injury, he knew he was going to start.

'I remember being sat on the bench against Sheffield United, and Nigel Worthington was one booking away from suspension. I remember him sliding in, right in front of me, and the referee reaching for his pocket. I welled up.

'Yes I was sorry for Nige, he was a great guy, but there was also some euphoria there. I was the only other left-back at the club, so I knew I'd be playing.'

The game ended up being a personal nightmare for Wednesday's ebullient defender, however.

'I was totally unfit, overweight, should never have played really.

'But I had so much desire and love for the club that I played. And I wanted to send a message to Trevor, "Give me some more money you bastard!"

'In the end I had to mark Ray Parlour, probably the fittest man in the world, and he absolutely roasted me.'

At least King had the satisfaction of setting up Wednesday's goal. From a free kick on the edge of the penalty area, the ball was pushed down the line to the left-back, who crossed hard and low. The ball deflected out to Harkes, who drilled his shot below Arsenal goalkeeper David Seaman.

'It was another of those training-ground free kicks,' the scorer recalls now. 'Shez had that deceptive little ball that he'd just lay down the line, to create the angle. He put it to Kingy on the overlap, it came to me and I just put my head down and smacked it.

'It was a great moment for me, beating a goalkeeper as good as Seaman. I had a lot of fans there from the US, 40 people in total. They told me after the game that they'd wanted to put a bet on the first goalscorer and I wasn't even on the list!'

But Harkes's and his team's jubilation didn't last. Arsenal equalised before half-time with a deflected shot by Merson and took the lead in the second half after a mistake from Palmer, who was again playing at centre-back.

Instead of clearing a cross from the left, Palmer tried to take a touch and presented the ball to Steve Morrow, who was deputising for John Jensen in Arsenal's midfield. Morrow buried the chance in what was the biggest moment of his entire career (albeit one that was tarnished in bizarre circumstances, when Tony Adams dropped him from his shoulders in the post-match celebrations and left him with a serious injury).

Looking back on the goal, Palmer admits his culpability, but adds that his positional shift was partly responsible for the error.

'If I'd been playing centre-back for three or four games, there'd have been no chance I'd take a touch. I'd have been "first time – get it out". But in midfield I wouldn't do that. I'd take a touch. And it fell to the boy Morrow and he scored.'

'If I'd have played in midfield, we'd have won that game. No danger.'

The League Cup was clearly the lesser of the two prizes on offer: both sides would have preferred the FA Cup, given its history and prestige. Nevertheless, that victory gave Arsenal a huge psychological edge going into the second instalment of the contest.

'It's like Joshua v Fury,' Palmer says. 'Whenever you've got back-to-back games, whoever wins the first one will have a great chance in the second one.'

But there was one major plus ahead of the rematch. Hirst was fit to play from the start, which meant Francis could restore Warhurst to defence and Palmer to midfield. Wednesday now had a more settled look to the back four and, crucially, they had more muscle in the centre of the pitch.

In the end, the FA Cup Final was nearly as one-sided as the semi had been. After going behind early on to a goal by Wright, Wednesday churned out chances at will, only for the brilliance of Seaman to repel them time and again.

The goal, when it came, wasn't a work of individual brilliance, like Sheridan's screamer in '91 or Waddle's worldie in the semi, but rather a beautifully worked team move. Sheridan wedged one of his postage-stamp crosses in from the right, Bright flicked it on and Harkes, arriving with his usual perfect timing, nudged it into the path of Hirst.

As he picked himself up after scoring and raised his fists in triumph, Hirst was mobbed by Bright and Harkes. Their celebration remains a defining image, a moment frozen in time when a team thought glory was within its grasp. For the scorer, however, it's all a bit of a blur.

'I have the picture of the goal with me, Brighty and Harksey, but I don't see a reaction in my face of what was happening,' Hirst says. 'This was a lad from Cudworth, playing in an FA Cup Final and scoring. When I was a kid, that would happen every cup final at half-time. Then, when I actually did it, it's like so much was going through my head that I couldn't take it in.

'The journey to getting there, all that way from Cudworth through Barnsley and Sheffield, was almost better than the event itself.'

The replay was a cagy affair. By now, the two sides had well and truly cancelled one another out. Wednesday were still the better side, but Seaman's brilliance ensured the deadlock continued.

In the end it came down to the last minute of extra time. A corner to Arsenal out on the left, swung on to the head of Andy Linighan; the header fumbled by Woods upwards, backwards, goalwards; a desperate lunge by Wednesday sub Graham Hyde, all in vain; Arsenal players mobbing one another like a gang of thieves who've busted out of prison; Wednesday players sprawled out on the turf, unable to believe they'd given so much and got nothing in return.

It's easy to blame Woods for the goal. England's first-choice goalkeeper (ahead of Seaman) should never have been beaten by such a routine attempt. But that would be to overlook the saves he had made in getting Wednesday to the final, and to ignore the fact that across the two games Wednesday had missed enough chances to win the tie two or three times over.

'Woodsy decided to catch the ball because he knew time was up,' says Palmer. 'If he'd just tipped it over, it would have been a different story. But you win as a team and you lose as a team.

'We were all over them really, particularly on the Saturday. I remember Paul Merson coming up to me after the game and saying, "We won't play as bad as that again." Sometimes these things happen.

'Did we deserve to win one of those trophies? Yes, for sure. I got man of the match in the FA Cup Final. That says everything. If you asked the Arsenal boys they'd say the same.'

* * *

Wednesday certainly couldn't be faulted for effort. During that second half of the season they'd given absolutely everything. They'd played out of position, appeared when half-fit, and gritted their teeth through the most hideous medical procedures to numb the pain.

The final act of heroism, and probably the most remarkable of all, had been provided by Roland Nilsson on the eve of the replay. For some reason, the game had been pencilled in the day after Sweden's World Cup qualifier against Austria, which meant the venerable full-back had to slog his way through two games in the space of 24 hours.

'That's something that would never happen today,' Nilsson says. 'Actually, I don't know how it was allowed to happen then. The club knew about the qualifiers and the FA had put the dates there.

'I wanted to go to the World Cup just as much as I wanted to win the FA Cup, so I was determined to play in both games. I spoke to Tommy Svensson, the Sweden coach, and we even talked about him taking me off if we were two goals up.'

In the event Sweden were only able to score once, which meant Nilsson was forced to play the full 90 minutes before flying straight back after the game and arriving in London at 1am. Somehow he got through 90 minutes and extra time (the fact that the Wednesday coaches refused to take him off seems, in hindsight, almost inhumane). By the end he was out on his feet, utterly shattered.

'I was sick for a week, just totally gone,' Nilsson remembers. 'I had nothing left in the body at all. I couldn't eat properly, the stomach just felt like lead, every time I tried to put food in it turned inside out, I couldn't concentrate. Just no power in the body at all.'

Perhaps, had Wednesday won, the suffering would have been mitigated somewhat. But instead there was just the wretched emptiness of a season that had unravelled at the very last. 'It was like you didn't want to play football anymore,' Nilsson reflects ruefully.

Little did the players know then, but the FA Cup Final would be the last time that they would all play together. Within a couple of months the break-up would begin.

14
THE BREAKUP

October 1997 was a miserable time to be a Wednesday fan. The team were bottom of the table, in the middle of a run of defeats that would cost David Pleat his job, including thrashings of 7-2 at Blackburn, 6-1 at Manchester United and 5-2 at home to Derby. Even Grimsby knocked them out of the League Cup in front of only 11,000 people at Hillsborough.

Amid all this turmoil, David Hirst's departure went almost unnoticed. The icon of the Kop, scorer of a million screamers, slunk away to Southampton in a deal worth £2m. Had Hirst been allowed to leave five years earlier, the price would have been at least double that figure and the news would have been splashed across every back page in the country.

But now Hirst was a shadow of his former self, his pace stolen from him by a litany of injuries. Since that goal at Wembley four and a half years earlier he had scored only 18 more times in Wednesday's colours.

Nonetheless, the news was saddening for the Hillsborough faithful. And not just because one of their all-time favourite players had left, but because his departure marked the final farewell to the brilliant side that took Wednesday to Wembley on five separate occasions.

The other stars had been sold off, traded in for players who weren't fit to lace their muddy Golas, but Hirst had always stuck around. Now even his reassuring permanence was no more.

Soon Ron Atkinson would be back, brought in to rescue Wednesday from the mess they'd got themselves into. But the great team he had built had left him behind.

* * *

YOUNGER FANS might not believe it, but back in the dim and distant past it was actually possible to name your club's best side in a matter of seconds.

Before the days of bloated squads and tinkering super-coaches, clubs had a first XI, a couple of dependable subs and a skeleton crew of reserves, usually made up of youngsters. The same faces appeared every week unless they were injured or suspended. 'Rest' was something players did in a Spanish *chiringuito* on their end-of-season jollies.

So it was with Wednesday in 1992/93. Barring injuries, the first XI practically never changed. Chris Woods in goal with a back four of Roland Nilsson, Nigel Pearson, Paul Warhurst and Nigel Worthington. Chris Waddle, Carlton Palmer, John Sheridan and John Harkes would be arrayed across the midfield with David Hirst and Mark Bright up front. Peter Shirtliff, Phil King, Danny Wilson, Viv Anderson and Chris Bart-Williams were on hand to step in as needed.

And that was really it. Wednesday had a few local lads in reserve (one of those youngsters, the talented midfielder Graham Hyde, actually forced his way into the FA Cup Final squad and came on in both matches) but those 16 names were Trevor Francis's bankers.

A few of them were getting on a bit but most were still in the prime of their careers, or not even there yet. They'd bloomed together at Wednesday, picking up international caps and turning the Twin Towers into their second home. The squad was settled, stable and happy.

So why was it so swiftly and mercilessly dismantled?

Well the break-up was really a combination of several factors. Age and injuries took their toll, but above all it was triggered by a series of ill-judged managerial decisions. Francis began the dissolution with a string of spats in the final two years of his reign, then David Pleat finished the job before he himself got the boot.

In the two managers' defence, few of the players they sold went on to pull up many trees elsewhere. They may claim that, in many cases, the sale represented good business for the club.

What is undeniable, however, is that both Francis and Pleat failed to replace the quality they were letting go. Just as in the late 1960s the Wednesday squad was allowed to slide away like a cliffside village, its foundations gradually ebbing and crumbling. When Hirst finally departed in October 1997 the roster was a million miles from the old Wembley wonders, both in spirit and ability.

The exodus started in 1993 with two players who left entirely of their own accord. Viv Anderson landed the manager's job at Barnsley and took Danny Wilson with him as his assistant. The latter recalls his departure without a trace of acrimony.

'Trevor was honest with me when I left,' Wilson says. 'He told me he couldn't guarantee me first-team football, and that was fine. I had a great relationship with him, he was brilliant.'

Peter Shirtliff was moved on as well, sold to Wolves for a fee of around £250,000. Looking back now, Shirtliff says Francis tried to get rid of the older players in the squad too quickly, but he is sanguine about the decision. He'd been edged out of Wednesday's regular starting team the previous season, and Wolves offered him the chance of regular first-team football.

Others, however, left in far less harmonious circumstances, running into the financial constraints that had so surprised Shirtliff when he left Wednesday first time around.

John Harkes had proved himself one of the most reliable wide players in England during Wednesday's first two years back in the top flight. Capable of playing on either flank, he worked his socks off every game and chipped in with regular goals. But Wednesday had failed to reward him.

'When I first signed for Wednesday in the autumn of 1991, Ron gave me a three-year deal on very low money,' he recalls. 'I was on £36,000 a year with bonuses and I stayed on that contract throughout my time at Wednesday.'

When Harkes requested a renewal during the 1992/93 season, Francis pitched a figure way short of what the American wanted. 'There were some players on £120,000-£140,000 and they weren't internationals,' he says. 'I was [an international].'

'Trevor made me work for everything I got at Wednesday, and I was perfectly happy with that. But Ron had promised me a better deal if I established myself in the team. Trevor didn't honour that.

'Being honest, I got the feeling that he didn't place a particularly high value on American internationals.'

The 1993/94 season should have been a golden one for Harkes. He'd established himself in the team and was getting better all the team thanks in no small part to the tutelage of Chris Waddle.

Instead he decided to drop down a division, just as Shirtliff had done back in the mid-1980s. He returned to the Baseball Ground, scene of his most famous goal, and joined Derby, who were then putting together a glamorous side under the ownership of local millionaire Lionel Pickering.

But the move didn't quite work out for Harkes. Although Derby reached the play-off final in his first season, they missed out to Leicester, and Pickering decided to stop ploughing money into the club. Several of Harkes's team-mates were sold off, including Mark Pembridge, who joined Wednesday.

In later years, Harkes would briefly return to the Premier League with West Ham and Nottingham Forest, and establish himself as an integral part of the new Major League Soccer project in his homeland. But his time at Wednesday would remain the high watermark of his period in English football, and he retains a strong connection with the city and its people.

'I loved the people of Sheffield, and the culture,' Harkes says now. 'If Trevor had honoured the promise that Ron had given me about the contract, I'd have stayed at Wednesday for life.'

* * *

The departures of Shirtliff and Harkes did at least allow Francis to make a couple more statement signings ahead of the 1993/94 season. Andy Sinton, a dashing winger who had made his name at QPR, moved north for £2.7m. In even bigger news, Des Walker was tempted back from Italy for a fee of £2.5m.

This was Wednesday planting their flag again. After the earlier signings of Woods and Waddle, Francis and Dave Richards wanted to remind the football world that they meant business. The signings made sense, too. Sinton had already collected several England caps under Graham Taylor, while Walker was a Rolls-Royce of a defender who'd been a linchpin of the England team that reached the semi-finals of Italia '90.

In truth, however, neither man captured the fans' hearts in the way their predecessors had. Sinton managed only 62 appearances and three goals across three years at Hillsborough. Walker was a key player throughout his eight years at Wednesday, but many supporters questioned his true affection for the club. When he eventually left in 2001, Wednesday were in the second tier and officials admitted they could no longer afford him.

After Walker's arrival in August 1993, fans may have envisaged him forming a jet-heeled defensive partnership with Paul Warhurst. But Francis soon put paid to that idea. At the start of the new season he sold Warhurst to Blackburn for a fee of around £3.3m.

Of all the offloads made by Francis during this period, the decision to sell Warhurst is the one that carries the clearest logic. Yes he was a thoroughbred, capable of operating with graceful efficacy in both penalty boxes. But £3.3m was a huge sum for a player who was still, essentially a work in progress. To put that into context, it's only slightly less than the fee paid that summer by Manchester United for Roy Keane, arguably the greatest midfielder in the history of the Premier League.

Again, however, the fault lies not in the sale but in the replacement – or rather, the lack of one. With Nigel Pearson again stymied by injuries Walker had no regular partner in the back four, and Hirst's increasing fitness problems meant there was a gaping hole up front, too. Warhurst could have provided crucial support on both fronts. Instead he was part of a Blackburn Rovers team that mounted a sustained push for the Premier League title and would go on to win it the following year.

Wednesday, in contrast, were on the turn. They won only one game in the first three months of 1993/94 and although they eventually recovered to finish seventh, their decline was highlighted by two games at the start of March against Manchester United, who would eventually see off Blackburn to claim the championship. First United beat them 4-1 at Hillsborough in the second leg of the League Cup semi-final and then they pulverised them 5-0 at Old Trafford, with four goals in the first half.

By the end of the season, ennui had well and truly set in around Owlerton. Wednesday finished with something of a flourish, mounting a nine-game unbeaten run to close out the campaign, but no one was fooled: crowds were down in the low-20,000s for most of the home games. The players were fed up, too, no one more so than Phil King, who had gone from being one of Atkinson's main men to something of a lost soul under Francis.

For months King had been playing on a week-to-week contract due to a dispute that stretched back to the start of Francis's time as manager. Like Harkes before him, the popular left-back felt the club's paymasters had failed to give him his due.

'I'd never earned big money,' King says. 'I signed for £600 a week – in fact in those last couple of years, I earned more in bonuses than I did in wages.

'In the last season under Ron, he'd said, "Look, you're behind on other players' earnings, but you prove your worth and we'll sort it out." That year we won the League Cup, and I was going to go to Big Ron and discuss a new contract with him. But he left.

'So I went to see Trevor and I remember his words when he came back to me. "Kingy, I want you to be first-choice left-back, here's a new contract." But I looked at it and said to him, "That's less than what they're earning in the reserves." It was true – I knew some of them were on more than that. He said, "That's what I've put together, that's all you're getting," so I said, "Okay then, no negotiation."

'It got to the stage where Trevor wouldn't pick me because I refused to sign the contract. But I felt I couldn't sign the terms they'd offered. I got player of the year in 1991/92 and won an England B cap, and yet they were giving more money to lads who couldn't even get in the team.'

King spent the whole of 1993/94 in purgatory, given opportunities only when Worthington was injured. Then, in the close-season, Ron Atkinson gave him a call and persuaded him to give Aston Villa a try.

'I remember Dave Richards phoning me and he asked, "Why are you going? We love you!"' King recalls with a wry chuckle. 'I said, "Well I love you too, but Trevor wouldn't give me any more money!" He asked me what the problem was, and I told him we were arguing over something like 300 quid a week. "Three hundred quid?" he said. "I'll pay you that out of my own pocket." And I'm like, "You're telling me this now but I'm about to go down and sign for Villa!"'

King's spell in Birmingham would begin brilliantly. In September 1994 he scored the winning penalty in a shoot-out against Inter Milan in the UEFA Cup, a feat that earned him cult hero status among the Villa fans. However the football fates soon returned to bite him on the arse. In November Atkinson was sacked, and King would find himself marginalised under new manager Brian Little. His career then took him on a round-the-houses tour of English football's lower reaches until he retired at local club Bath City in 2001.

Like Harkes, he wishes now that he'd been able to stay at Wednesday. 'I was devastated when I left that football club. It's my biggest regret in football, not signing that contract. I wish I'd signed it, got on with it, cemented my place as left-back and the financial rewards would have come from there. But at the time I couldn't accept the terms on offer.

'I have no hard feelings towards Trevor and have some sympathy for him. Ron was a hard act to follow, for sure. But he didn't have a clue how to man-manage and he seemed really keen to get rid of the players we had.

'I just felt he bought names. Ron bought players who would fit into the system, but I thought Trevor was more about the big-name signings. It just seemed a bit weird and he certainly didn't need to do it. He had the nucleus of a good squad. And he had such respect as a player, so he didn't need to impose himself.

'When teams have been successful, clubs try and keep the players for as long as possible to ensure they pass on the experience – look at Wes Morgan at Leicester, for example. But we'd had a great run under Big Ron and it seemed like Trevor wanted to get rid of that experience.'

A quick look at Francis's other transfer dealings in 1994 lend weight to King's observation. Five senior players were allowed to leave that summer, a cull that finally ripped the heart out of the cup final team.

Of the departures, Nigel Pearson's was the easiest to understand at the time. The club captain, Herculean figure though he was, had played only a handful of games over the past two seasons and Middlesbrough offered a perfectly good fee of £500,000 to take him up the M1.

But it was Boro and their new manager Brian Robson (who presumably knew a leader when he saw one) who would have the last laugh. Pearson would resurrect his career on Teesside and captain the side to promotion before reaching two cup finals in 1997.

If the decision to get rid of Pearson looks rash in the rear-view mirror, the decision to let Roland Nilsson slip through the Hillsborough exit door looked barmy even when it happened. In the four and half years since he signed, Nilsson had been the most consistent right-back in Britain. That summer of 1994, as he prepared to leave Hillsborough, he reached the semi-final of the World Cup with Sweden.

There were extenuating circumstances in Nilsson's departure; a close relative was sick, so he wanted to go back to Sweden to be closer to his family. The fact that he signed for Helsingborg, rather than one of European football's powerhouses, suggests this was a personal rather than a professional decision.

Even here, however, it appears the Wednesday power-brokers are partly culpable for what happened.

'Things happened in the 1993/94 season that I wasn't pleased with,' Nilsson says. 'Mainly around my role in the team. In fact we'd discussed me getting the captaincy, and that didn't happen.

'A member of my family was ill too, so in the end I spoke to Trevor, spoke to the chairman and we agreed that I would play out the 93/94 season and then go back to Sweden.'

Just like Pearson, Nilsson would enjoy an Indian summer in the Premier League. In the summer of 1997 he signed for Coventry, then under the management of Ron Atkinson's protege Gordon Strachan, and over the next two years he would play a further 60 games, elevating the Sky Blues' defence with his unflappable elegance.

Annoyingly, it should have been Wednesday he returned to. 'I was supposed to come back to Sheffield that summer. Dave Richards and David Pleat came over and I was thinking about coming back. David Pleat was like, "Dave has said you're a good player, we'll just have to see how it goes when you come over." But he didn't even know what kind of player I was! I just thought, "If he doesn't know who I am and what I do, why should I travel back?" I didn't want to come over and prove myself again.'

It's the sort of blunder that would shock you, if so many other players hadn't told similar stories.

*   *   *

As Roland Nilsson upped sticks for Sweden that summer of 1994, his old full-back partner Nigel Worthington made a move much closer to home. Worthington signed for Leeds and was reunited with Howard Wilkinson.

Like his international colleague Danny Wilson, Worthington says he got on well with Francis, and it is clear there was no bad blood in the lead-up to his departure. In fact it was one of those rare deals that worked out well for everyone: Worthington got to play out his top-flight career under his old mentor, Leeds got a hugely capable and reliable full-back, and Wednesday more than doubled their money on the player's original transfer from Notts County, ten years and 400 games earlier.

But Worthington wasn't the only Owl flying the nest for Elland Road.

Carlton Palmer had just signed a five-year contract when Wilkinson called for him. But his relationship with Francis was deteriorating fast.

The player had infuriated Francis with that injury on England duty before the FA Cup semi-final, and in November 1993 another major row had erupted after an international break, the one that marked the end of Palmer's England career and forced Graham Taylor to resign as manager.

'I'd played for England against Holland on the Wednesday night, and Graham asked me to play on the right,' Palmer says. 'To be honest, I thought he had better players for that job, but I'm not going to refuse to do that for my country. So I did it and, although we lost, I played well.

'So therefore Trevor decided that's what he wanted me to do in the next game, against Wimbledon at home. He put Bart-Williams inside and me on the right. Now with all due respect to Bart-Williams, I'm an England international!

'Anyway, we're struggling in the game and I changed it. I told Bart to fuck off out on the right-hand side, went inside, then I had an argument with Brighty because he said, "You can't do that, you need to do what the manager says." I said "Brighty, we're struggling here, if you want me to go back out on the right it's not happening."

'After the game Trevor wasn't happy and really that was the beginning of the end. I said, "Trevor, listen, I will always help the club out in different positions if there are injuries and I've played in lots of different positions in the past. But I'm not a right-sided player. I did it because I was playing for my country. If you're not going to play me centre-back or centre-midfield there's going to be a problem." And that's how it all ended up going tits-up.'

The incident is revealing in itself. The very fact that Palmer was willing to undermine his manager's authority shows the mistrust in their relationship, and points to a lack of respect for Francis's regime. It's hard to imagine a player reacting to one of Atkinson's tactical instructions like that, isn't it?

Despite the growing frostiness, Palmer and Francis limped on together until the summer. The player even signed a new contract, although like many of the others interviewed for this story, Palmer believes Wednesday's management of the situation could have been better.

'I was pissed off that they'd brought in Des Walker, Chris Woods, people like that, yet I was one of the top players and they didn't come to me and redo my contract. But I'm not one of those who goes to the manager and says "so-and-so's earning more than me, I'm not happy." I wait my time.

'I was going to sign a new contract, but at the same time I wait until the time is right and then you pay me what I'm worth. In the end, Dave Richards gave me an unbelievable contract.'

Just days after signing the deal, however, Palmer says he received a call from Francis informing him that he was about to be sold.

'Villa and Leeds actually came in around the same time. When Trevor phoned me, he was actually at the World Cup, and he said he'd had a big offer. He didn't even know I'd signed a new contract! You tell me what happened there.'

When Leeds eventually won the bidding war, the fee stood at £2.6m. On paper it looked like another great deal for Wednesday, given that Palmer was already 28 and had come to the end of his England run.

But what Palmer brought to the team was really irreplaceable. The drive from midfield, the aerial presence, the ability to rouse the rabble around him when things were going pear-shaped – no other midfielder in the country offered such a complete package. Yes there were more skilful players around at that time (including a couple in his own team) but as a box-to-box man there were few who could touch him.

Of all the players who left Wednesday during this period, Palmer enjoyed the best post-Hillsborough career. He played 100 games for Leeds, then went to Southampton and played an integral role in keeping them in the Premier League. His last hurrah came, like Nilsson's, at Coventry. In 1999/2000, the year Wednesday were relegated, he played 30 games as the perennially perilous Sky Blues finished 11 points clear of the drop zone.

*   *   *

To fill the gap left by Palmer and the rest, Francis made a boat-load of signings that summer. In came Peter Atherton and Ian Nolan, defenders snaffled from Coventry and Tranmere respectively, as well as the World Cup stars Dan Petrescu and Klaas Ingesson, opening the door for a wave of foreign signings in the years ahead.

The British signings were pretty good, particularly Nolan, who became a regular and dependable starter until a horrific leg-break against Spurs in 1998 curtailed his stay at Hillsborough. But neither Petrescu nor Ingesson, who tragically died from cancer in 2014, stayed long enough to make a real impression.

The rejigged side never found any momentum. It was a season that had a beginning and end with nothing much in between. There was no cup run or string of good results to punctuate the apathy. And as the campaign ground on, rumours began to circulate that players were briefing their media friends against the manager.

In April 1995 the Francis regime plumbed its lowest depths with a 7-1 home defeat by Nottingham Forest, who could have scored even more as the home side downed tools. 'We want Trevor out,' chanted the crowd as the goals flooded in at the Kop End. Within a month, they got their wish.

Looking back on his dismissal, Francis has suggested that Richards and the board acted too hastily and should have given him more time to build a new squad. And it's certainly easy to sympathise with him, up to a point.

Replacing Atkinson was always going to be a thankless task given the outgoing manager's charisma and popularity. In the circumstances, Francis did pretty well overall. He stuck with the lovely passing game bequeathed by Big Ron and his 1992/93 team was full of vim and attacking flair, a credit to his managerial principles.

Not all of his signings worked out but at least they were mostly good footballers; unlike his old mate Graeme Souness, who brought in players like Julian Dicks and Neil Ruddock, Francis never forgot what Wednesday stood for. And while big-name signings like Waddle and Walker made the headlines, he actually operated on a budget for most of his three years in charge. During his tenure the net spend was only £1m.

Still, it's hard to escape the impression that Francis never quite got to grips with his inheritance. Having taken on a dressing room full of characters he tried to tame them rather than giving them the space they needed. It was the behaviour of a man who wasn't truly secure in his position.

Yes, perhaps he would have come into his own with a new team made up of players loyal to him, but the very fact that he needed to meddle with the old team is a damning indictment in itself.

Palmer, looking back on his time with Francis, has nothing but praise for the character of his former sparring partner. 'I like Trevor, and I don't want people to think otherwise. I like him as a bloke. I stayed at his house in London, he had me seeing specialists that he knew [when Palmer was injured]. I respected him then and I still do to this day.'

However, when asked about the imprint Francis left on the squad, his comments are cutting.

'It was always Ron's team, in truth. It was never Trevor's team, at any stage. But still, had Trevor just got on with it, there'd have been no problems whatsoever. The dressing room was so experienced, so full of winners, that everything would have been fine. All he needed to do was make a little tweak here, a little tweak there, keep everybody happy, and the lads would have done the rest.

'But Trevor let that get to him and he didn't need to. He wanted people to say it was his team rather than Ron's. But honestly, who gives a fuck whose team it is as long as it's winning?!'

'I don't feel sorry for him, in truth, because I didn't want to leave Sheffield Wednesday. My home was there, I had a great rapport with the fans and it was cut short. Trevor wanted to put his stamp on it, but if you look at the players who left around that time, I'm going to Leeds United at the age of 28, I'm in my prime! Crazy.

'He broke the team up and what happened? He ended up getting the sack.'

*　*　*

In June 2020, to mark the 25th anniversary of David Pleat's appointment as Sheffield Wednesday manager, the *Star* newspaper ran a profile entitled 'The Man to Break Up Greatness'. And that's pretty much how most Wednesday fans viewed Pleat; as a man who took a silk purse and turned it into a sow's ear.

During Pleat's time at Hillsborough, the quality of the playing staff steadily declined. By the time he was sacked the squad included Dejan Stefanovic, a £2.7m signing who would soon leave Hillsborough having not played enough games to gain a work permit, and Andy Booth, who managed only 28 goals in five seasons after costing £3.5m. And he'd offset these white elephants by casting off the rest of the 1992/93 team.

Again, it's important to retain a sense of perspective here. Francis may have sold off some of Wednesday's stars a little early but by 1995 several of those who were left were clearly coming to the end. Francis rebuilt out of choice; Pleat did so out of necessity.

The new manager also inherited some contractual disputes from his predecessor, none more damaging than the snafu in which Chris Bart-Williams had become tangled up. The midfielder had played 38 games in the 1993/94 season (he had yet to reach his 21st birthday) and won an England B cap. Yet, like so many before him, Wednesday had bungled the negotiations over a new deal.

'I felt forgotten at Wednesday,' says Bart-Williams. 'They'd had me for four years and not even given me a new contract. I'd been to two cup finals, got England caps [at youth and B level]. I felt really let down by the club. When Trevor finally talked about a new contract I thought, "Nope, too late. If you wanted me you'd have signed me ages ago."'

In the end Pleat opted to sell Bart-Williams to Nottingham Forest for a fee of £2.5m. With the player determined to leave and Wednesday liable to lose him for nothing the following year under the new Bosman ruling, it may be argued that the manager had no option.

But if Pleat was largely powerless in the departure of Bart-Williams, even his staunchest advocates would admit that his handling of the subsequent reconstruction was clumsy in the extreme. Nilsson's account is damning, but it's hardly isolated.

Take the testimony of Mark Bright, who left Wednesday in January 1997 when the overhaul was at its most frenzied. Having turned 34 he knew he was reaching the end of his shelf life as a top-level footballer, and he does not dispute the decision to dispense with his services. What rankles, however, is Pleat's lack of clarity.

'He wasn't honest with me,' Bright says. 'He said I would play and I didn't. Knowing what I know now, I would have said my goodbyes and moved on, but I got messed about playing reserve-team football when I still thought I could score in the Premier League.'

Waddle and John Sheridan, the two creative fulcrums of the 1993 side, had already moved on. Waddle, who had been released in the summer of 1996, has kept his counsel about his departure from Wednesday. Sheridan, however, has been highly critical of the way the club handled his own departure, claiming no one even said thank you when he departed for Bolton.

Then, of course, there's the other charge levelled at Pleat: that he replaced good players with average ones and allowed the Wednesday squad to become clogged up with mediocrity. Again, it's hard to mount a case for the defence.

Pleat signed over 20 players during his two and a half years at Hillsborough, and only a handful can be described as successes when you look down the list. There were the captures of Benito Carbone and Paolo Di Canio, who dazzled the Hillsborough crowd, albeit briefly. And there were the solid signings like Pembridge and goalkeeper Matt Clarke, who did decent jobs without ever quite eclipsing the players they replaced.

But soon you run into Patrick Blondeau, a £1.5m signing who played less than ten games for Wednesday. Or Wayne Collins, a midfielder who scored only six goals for the Owls and never played for another top-flight team. Many fans still bristle at the thought of Stefanovic and the way he left the club but if anything sums up the mismanagement of Wednesday on Pleat's watch, it was the signing of his fellow Serb, Darko Kovacevic.

The striker arrived in January 1996 for £2m but lasted only six months before being offloaded to Real Sociedad. Then he exploded, earning moves to Juventus and Lazio and becoming one of the most feared strikers in Europe. Wednesday had struck gold and cast it off like scrap.

Gradually these transfer blunders began to take their toll. Wednesday started the 1996/97 season superbly, winning their first four games, but by the end they were being tonked by West Ham and Blackburn. Everyone could see that the faecal matter was about to hit the fan, and it would end up splattered all over Pleat's face.

As widely predicted, Wednesday began 1997/98 appallingly, winning only one league game by the end of September. With Ron Atkinson ready for a return to football, Pleat's time in charge was clearly coming to an end. But the soon-to-be-ex-manager had one final decision to make.

'They called me in one day and told me they'd been offered £2m by Southampton,' David Hirst recalls of his departure from Hillsborough. 'I said, "Yeah, I'll get out of your way."

'I'd had a number of injuries, I wasn't getting in the team, Pleaty wasn't that bothered and I think he wanted me out. When the club receives a bid and the manager and chairman accept it, there's no point fighting it because they want you out.'

Hirst admits that it was a huge disappointment to leave Wednesday after 11 years and more than 300 games. And although he is more reluctant to criticise Pleat now than he has been in the past, he alludes to major problems in their relationship.

'We had a personality clash, for sure. I was opinionated, he didn't like it and he's the one who picks the team.

'I didn't appreciate some of the things he did. During the time Pleat was there, I was injured a lot and I was left with the physio, as I had been previously. But whereas Big Ron would come and ask "are you fit to play Saturday" he wouldn't do that. It just all felt a bit more distant.'

In a perverse kind of way, Pleat completed his mission when he sold Hirst. He had been asked to oversee a rebuilding job and he had done so. Unfortunately he'd knocked down the footballing equivalent of an ageing imperial palace and built a Soviet tower block in its place.

No one can say with any certainty where Wednesday would be now had that great team been handled and replaced with the care it deserved. Perhaps they'd be a Leicester City, a prosperous club happily perched on the edge of the elite. Perhaps they'd be a Chelsea or a Manchester City, propelled to footballing utopia by foreign billionaires. Then again, maybe they'd have just drifted away anyway, like Blackburn, Derby and Nottingham Forest all have.

It's just a shame we were never allowed to find out.

15
WHAT HAPPENED NEXT

EVERY AFTERNOON, the bank of Perth's Swan River becomes a highway of heavenly bodies. Locals and expats, drawn to the Australian city by its porcelain beaches and year-round sunshine, converge on the waterfront to run, cycle, stretch and generally hone their physiques.

In among all these perspiring fitness junkies an old man trundles along the cycle path, a picture of contentment. He can't run anymore but he still gets out on his bike as much as he can to keep fit and bask in the healthy glow of his adopted city. It's not quite Hillsborough or Goodison Park on a Saturday afternoon, but it'll do.

'I love it here in Perth,' says Mick Lyons. 'It's great. Lovely atmosphere and lots of Brits. My knees are knackered from football but thankfully I've still got the bike, and I go to the gym a lot too.

'They love their sports here – Aussie Rules is the main sport, but they also love the Premier League, so I can watch all the games live. Only trouble is they don't think it's proper football!'

Lyons has ended up in Perth after a rather nomadic journey that started out in Grimsby – a place with practically nothing in common with the Australian city apart from the fact that both are on the coast.

In 1985, Lyons left Wednesday to become manager of Grimsby Town. His route to the dugout was almost pre-ordained; with his physical presence, effervescent charisma and leadership skills, it seemed like this posting by the North Sea was but the first step on the road to greatness.

It never quite worked out for Lyons the manager, however. His team finished 15th in his first season and were relegated in his second, whereupon he left his position. Although he subsequently took up a coaching role at Everton he never received another managerial job in English football.

Typically, however, Lyons turned the setback into a positive. He embarked upon a tour of football's exotic outposts, taking managerial postings in Brunei, Canada and finally settling in Australia, where he now lives in semi-retirement.

For a man raised in the backstreets of Merseyside, it's been quite an adventure. During his time in Brunei, before his knees finally gave way, Lyons would go running in the jungle with the Hash House Harriers, an international running group for exiled Brits (one assumes all those hill runs under Howard Wilkinson served him well). When he talks about his post-playing career, it's clear there are no regrets.

'Brunei was a real eye-opener – but it was great. I had a swimming pool and thankfully there was no alcohol ban! The British army were there, so I had plenty of company. Then someone offered me a job in Australia and it's just so laidback. The weather helps too, of course. It's not quite Middlewood Road on a January morning!'

Lyons hasn't coached a senior team since 2011 but he still keeps his hand in, even at the age of 69.

'I take kids' football teams training on Mondays and Wednesdays. I don't really get recognised but I've always got my shirts on, from both Everton and Wednesday. I still wear them even now!'

It's lovely to hear Lyons talk so enthusiastically about his new life, a life hard-earned and richly deserved. Nonetheless, as a fan, it's difficult to escape the feeling of what might have been.

Had things gone slightly better for Lyons at Grimsby, had another English club taken a punt on him, he might have blossomed into the manager everyone thought he would be. Maybe he would have taken over from Ron Atkinson in 1991 and built on his foundations, melding the steeliness of Howard Wilkinson with the flair Big Ron had left behind.

But then you can say the same about many of the players featured in this book. Wednesday's teams of the mid-'80s and early '90s were so packed with winners and intelligent football minds that it seemed inevitable many would go on to be successful managers. Better yet, some would go on to be successful *Sheffield Wednesday* managers.

In fact, only two of those players have gone on to manage the club – and both of them were left thoroughly chastened by the experience.

Danny Wilson was first to try his luck, hired in the summer of 1998 after an excellent spell with Barnsley during which he delivered promotion to the top flight for the first time in the club's history.

Wednesday were already in trouble when Wilson took over, however. The club was saddled with a mediocre squad and a bloated wage bill, forcing Wilson to shed a host of senior players as soon as he arrived. Just a few games into his reign the problems were compounded when Paolo Di Canio pushed referee Paul Alcock in a game against Arsenal. The Italian never pulled on the stripes again.

Wednesday actually did quite well in Wilson's first season, finishing 12th. The following year, however, was an omnishambles. Wednesday took only one point from their first nine games, including an 8-0 defeat at Newcastle, and by Christmas they were effectively relegated. Wilson was dismissed in March, but not before a group of MPs led by Cabinet minister David Blunkett had mounted a campaign for his removal.

Perhaps unsurprisingly, Wilson is reluctant to get into specifics about his time as manager. He insists, however, that there were mitigating circumstances to the nightmare he endured.

'Wednesday were sliding when I took the job,' he says. 'They were having a bad time. You don't get someone in when you're having a good time, do you?

'They lost a lot of players during the time I was there. I was promised funds, I was promised this, that and the other and it never materialised. The money wasn't available. We managed to stay up in that first season, but it became quite unsavoury after that.'

Many fans maintain that Wilson was out of his depth as manager, a view that has been given substance by criticism from Di Canio, who in his autobiography called Wilson a 'frustrated nobody' who wasn't strong enough to deal with the characters in his charge – echoing the commnents many have levelled at Francis in this book.

Wilson admits, 'I could have done things differently, we all make mistakes.' However, he adds, 'At that moment in time we were fighting for our lives with a team that wasn't good enough.

'There's been a lack of investment for years. Trevor Francis had the same problem. Instead of investing in the squad when things were good, they let it weaken.'

On the MPs who tried to oust him, Wilson has nothing but contempt. 'The government at the time were trying to get people into jobs and, with that protest, we had four MPs trying to get people out of jobs. You'd think they'd have bigger things to worry about.'

By the time Chris Turner took charge in November 2002, the slide had become an avalanche. Wednesday's financial problems were now acute and the squad was being pared to the bones. Relegation from the First Division (now the Championship) looked, if not inevitable, then certainly likely.

Turner came armed with plenty of experience, both good and bad. At Leyton Orient he'd watched with horror as co-manager John Sitton launched into a bizarre half-time rant at the players which was immortalised in a fly-on-the-wall Channel 4 documentary ('I was always against them filming that,' he reflects ruefully). Then he'd had a fine spell at Hartlepool, setting the north-east club on the way to promotion from the Third Division before Wednesday came calling.

This grounding, however, did nothing to prepare him for what he found on his return to his boyhood club.

'I couldn't believe the state they were in, to be honest. I'd been top of the league at Hartlepool with a great bunch of lads, built a team up over three and a half years. But at Wednesday there was no money around in those days. Loads of players had left but the club was still £7m in debt and they were trying to sell the training ground. There were all sorts of things happening off the field.

'We still had a lot of players under contract from the Premiership days and they didn't give a toss. Lots of managers had left because they couldn't stem the flow. I remember a quote from Dave Allen, the former chairman, that it was either get rid of the players or get rid of Paul Jewell [in 2001], and they chose the latter. Other managers had had the same problem.

'I remember that we got Gerald Sibon playing well, and he was a tremendously talented player. But we couldn't afford to keep him and it was cheaper for us to let him go and pay him about £150k to leave.'

Turner points out, quite reasonably, that he actually did well in his first half-season in the job. 'I was manager for about 24 games and if you tally up the points I got in that first year, we would have finished in the top ten of the Championship if you average it out over a full season.' Nonetheless, he was unable to arrest the slide into the Second Division, and in his only full year in charge Wednesday finished 16th, reaching depths not plumbed since the days of Len Ashurst.

Like Wilson, Turner has been criticised by Wednesday fans for his part in the club's decline. However he believes he took on a thankless job and did the dirty work that no one else was prepared to do.

'When Peter Shreeves left, the season before I took over, I saw Howard. He told me "the next manager of Sheffield Wednesday will not be the successful one. It will be the one after that, because you've got to clear everyone out." He was right.

'They'd stuck players on three and four-year contracts, on decent money – four, five, six grand a week, which was a lot back then – and they wouldn't go. All the contracts seemed to expire in 2004 and I had to endure the players who were under those contracts.

'That summer of 2004 [after Wednesday finished 16th] I let 15 of the 16 players whose contracts had expired go. I then bought in 11 or 12 new players that I felt would be successful in that league. Unfortunately I only had nine games. Won three, drew three, lost three.

'If you look at the players I brought in, they played a massive part in getting the club back into the Championship that year. The goalkeeper David Lucas, Lee Bullen, Steve MacLean who scored 20 goals, Glenn Whelan, Chris Brunt; when we got promotion, Paul Sturrock very generously gave me a lot of credit.'

After leaving Wednesday both Wilson and Turner suffered further relegations, with MK Dons and Stockport respectively (Turner left the Cheshire club bottom of the Football League). However the two men then reunited at Hartlepool as manager and director of football respectively, and rebuilt their careers by guiding the north-easterners to promotion. Wilson subsequently took Swindon to a play-off final (his brief spell at Sheffield United didn't work out so well) while Turner held the position of CEO at Chesterfield for five seasons, a period that brought both promotion and record turnover from player sales.

Nowadays these two old friends hold very similar roles. They both work as consultants, a rather nebulous role within the football industry which is part-mentor, part-fixer and part-talent spotter. Wilson is also a driving force behind The Fans Agency, a talent network owned by football supporters. Turner, meanwhile, is working to set up the first professional football club in Wakefield. With so much experience of how *not* to run a football club, one assumes he'll organise it on the right lines.

* * *

It's hard to imagine that any of those great 1980s and '90s players will follow Turner and Wilson in returning to Hillsborough. Nigel Pearson would be the outstanding candidate, given the success he enjoyed at Leicester, but he has said that he doesn't want to jeopardise his relationship with the people of Sheffield (where he still lives) by taking the job.

Certainly, none of those interviewed for this book appear likely to come back. Nigel Worthington and Peter Shirtliff have both enjoyed excellent careers in coaching and management, the former guiding Norwich to promotion to the Premier League in 2004 and the latter working as coach and assistant manager at various clubs. It's been several years, however, since either man has held a senior managerial role.

Then there's the curious case of Roland Nilsson. The classy Swede seems ideally suited to modern management, given his flawless professionalism and urbane sophistication. However his transition from player to coach has not gone as smoothly as many would have predicted.

Nilsson's only experience as a manager in English football came in a brief stint at Coventry at the start of the millennium, which ended in dismissal when the team failed to make the Championship play-offs. Since then he's held various roles in Sweden's age-group sides and managed the under-21s, but his time in club management has been patchy. A few months before this book went to press he was sacked by IFK Gothenburg, a team which, like Wednesday, endured a purple patch in the '80s and early '90s before falling on hard times, hamstrung by bungled transfers and muddled decisions at board level.

Despite these chastening experiences, however, Nilsson feels he still has plenty to offer as a manager, and is very candid when asked if he would be open to returning to Wednesday one day. 'It's definitely a thing that I would consider,' he says. 'And if things were right, then I would say yes to that.'

There *is* one former Wednesday player flourishing in big-time football, however. Martin Hodge has never coached or managed since he hung up his boots but he's credited as one of the architects of Burnley's remarkable emergence as the Premier League's great overachievers.

As chief scout at Turf Moor, Hodge has unearthed a string of golden nuggets including Chris Wood, James Tarkowski and Nick Pope. Their success has enabled Burnley to survive in the Premier League for five years and counting while spending roughly a tenth of the amount splurged by Chelsea and the two Manchester clubs. Hodge's ferocious professionalism and unwavering eye for detail make him the perfect fit for the talent-spotting role.

'We look at players at all different levels,' says Hodge. 'We get to know them and then we go and watch them live. Sometimes agents will throw names at you, but we don't rely on what people send us – we go on what we think. You can have all the data you want but, to me, live scouting is the answer. My eyes are my guide. The youngsters of today do look at *FIFA* [the video game] and get their knowledge from there, but there's no substitute for seeing a player in the flesh.'

Hodge has worked at Turf Moor for over five years at the time of writing, but still lives in Sheffield and doesn't see that changing any time soon.

'My neighbours are all season ticket-holders, and I like going to Sheffield United too. I'm good friends with Simon Tracey and I like Chris Wilder and Alan Hill. But Wednesday will always have a special place in my heart.

'Wednesday is one of the best-supported clubs around. If they spit you out, you won't last five minutes. But if they take you in, they take you in.'

*   *   *

While Hodge continues to find bargains at the sharp end of world football, other players interviewed for this book have built lives well away from the scrutiny and Twitter-driven innuendo that occasionally sullies the highest levels of the game.

In fact, three of our interviewees have set up camp on the south-eastern tip of the United States, where football is fast breaking free of its minority status. Unsurprisingly John Harkes has led the way, taking the role of head coach and sporting director of North Carolina's Greenville Triumph in the United Soccer League, which sits below Major League Soccer. Just down the coast, Paul Williams and Chris Bart-Williams are training junior players in Florida, shaping a generation that US bosses hope will finally turn their national team into a global superpower.

Then there are those who have opted for careers in the media, a path that has become ever-more lucrative with the explosion of interest since the formation of the Premier League.

Lawrie Madden was first to go down this rarefied path, working as a journalist for a string of outlets and as a pitchside reporter for IMG, the international arm of the Premier League. 'I actually started doing media work before I finished playing,' he says. 'I had a lot of contacts. Trying to get access to people was getting more difficult but I had more access than most!'

More recently Mark Bright has become a hugely respected commentator, pundit and all-round housewife's favourite. In 2019 he published his autobiography, *My Story – From Foster Care to Footballer*, to critical acclaim. Although he has been drawn away from Sheffield, Bright says he enjoyed '99 per cent' of his time in the city.

John Pearson has a regular commentary gig on Wednesday Player, the club's in-house streaming service, and supplements his media work with a day-to-day role as a community organiser for Sheffield Wednesday. 'I do a fit club, walking club, walking football and a general health club now, which is great,' he explains when asked about his current endeavours. 'Everyone is welcome… even if they're United fans! I also do events, dinners with the likes of Ron Atkinson and Gary Megson… all sorts.' With Pearson's natural warmth and gregariousness, there could be no finer ambassador for the club.

Andy Blair might have been expected to follow the media route given his skills as a raconteur. In fact, the former midfielder was hosting events even when he was still a Wednesday player.

'For some reason the commercial manager asked me to host an evening with Tommy Docherty, and it went from there,' Blair recalls. 'In fact I remember hosting Miss Sheffield Wednesday – don't ask me how they came to be hosting that! Howard was one of the judges. Early on I said that I didn't think our manager was a religious person, but whenever I get the ball he says, "Oh my God!" He said the next day, "Very good, son, I think you've missed your vocation in life." I didn't realise what he actually meant at the time.'

However Blair took a lower-profile route after leaving football, launching his own school uniform shop back in Coventry. 'I clearly struggle to take instruction from others, so I went into business myself,' he explains.

Down in Cornwall, meanwhile, Blair's old pal Gary Bannister has moved into hotel maintenance, where he can be alone with his thoughts without anyone barking instructions at him every five minutes. In London Andy McCulloch has managed his own cleaning company, although he says he misses the more down-to-earth life he enjoyed up north.

'I had a lovely place in Sheffield. A place called Millthorpe, near Chatsworth. Down south it's all rush and go, but in Sheffield the people were so much more relaxed,' McCulloch says. 'Wednesday were my favourite club, without a doubt. My daughter was born in Sheffield and she's very much a Yorkshire lass.'

Tony Cunningham, the man who was brought in to replace McCulloch all those years ago, has stayed closer to Sheffield. But his career has taken him even further away from the football field, into the murky waters of the English justice system.

Cunningham always possessed an inquisitive mind and a relentless desire to succeed. 'When I played I poured my heart and soul into it,' he says. 'I didn't go out drinking or playing snooker, I stayed back in the afternoon to do extra work. It took over me. Whatever I've done, I've dedicated myself to it.'

When the bell finally tolled on his career, aged nearly 37, Cunningham says he felt unfulfilled 'because I realised there was more to life and more I wanted to do.' So he decided to follow his wife into the legal profession, and with the support of a PFA grant he studied at Huddersfield and Nottingham universities before getting his first job in 1995. More than 25 years on he remains with the same firm, based in its Lincoln office.

Cunningham specialises in crime, which seems an ideal fit; as a player he was hard but fair, happy to go toe-to-toe with the most dastardly centre-halves. In person, however, he is gentle and softly spoken, a world away from the behemoth who would terrorise opposing defences. While others interviewed for this book revel in their footballing memories and the chance to step back into their old personas, Cunningham is desperate not to be trapped in the stereotypes of his old profession.

'I've had it many times since I finished playing football,' he explains. 'They think footballers aren't intellectual, that they're thick. I've had people say to me many times, "Ah, you were just a footballer." Even judges of the court have indicated that I'm not educated enough because I was 'only' a footballer.

'Even now I don't think that's gone away. The fact that I was a footballer, and quite a successful footballer, has followed me around. After 25 years they haven't forgotten. Some people think that being a footballer and being a solicitor are mutually exclusive. I still have work-related problems because of the football I played.

'I'm a fiercely determined person, though. Some people might think that's because of my upbringing, but no, that's just how I am. And I don't shirk challenges.'

* * *

Each of these stories is hugely impressive, of course. The fact that so many players have built successful new lives away from the football pitch is a credit to them, and to the managers who nurtured them.

But no story is more impressive than that of Carlton Palmer.

The lung-busting midfielder didn't even hang up his boots until he was nearly 40, which suggests that the odd pint the night before a game isn't as ruinous as the dieticians would have us believe. He even came back to Wednesday in 2001 as a favour to Ron Atkinson, playing 22 games to help the club avoid relegation (albeit briefly).

'We had to win ten of the last 14 games to stay up, which was a tall order, but Ron had asked me to do it,' he remembers. 'I looked at the games and I knew we were getting in Trond Soltvedt, my pal from Southampton, so I thought "we can do this."

'We beat Tranmere one Tuesday night and I got everyone out on the lash afterwards. Proper good night, like the old days, lads just bonding with one another over a beer. And I knew we were going to stay up then.'

Mission accomplished, Palmer tried his hand at management with Mansfield Town, taking Shirtliff as his assistant. The job was only available because Mansfield's controversial chairman, Keith Haslam, had suspended Keith Curle over allegations of bullying, which were later proved unfounded in court. As a friend of Haslam, Palmer was on a hiding to nothing from the start and he lasted less than a year in the job.

That was the last British, or indeed world football saw of Palmer the manager. He and his second wife Lucy, a teacher, embarked on a new career in Shanghai, where Palmer rose to become sporting director at Wellington College, an elite private school for the children of Western workers. He still holds the position to this day.

With his natural wariness of authority (and love of a country pub) it's hard to imagine Palmer teaching pampered kids in a city of 24 million people. But like everything he has done in his life, Palmer has attacked the job full-on.

'When I played for Wednesday, there were no limits to the culture. When we played or when we went out on the piss, there were no fucking limits, we were all in. Everybody to a man was like that. If you weren't like that, you wouldn't survive. I'm still like that now.'

Alongside his work in education, Palmer continues to provide regular punditry on Asian TV as well as appearing on a string of British radio shows and podcasts. His trenchant opinions and post-watershed language have brought a steady stream of controversy, never more so than in 2004 when he leapt to the defence of Ron Atkinson after his former manager was heard using a racist epithet while working for ITV.

Palmer has since attracted further criticism for suggesting that racism will never be eliminated, despite movements such as Black Lives Matter. When asked to expand on this view, he suggests much of the recent talk of progress has been overstated.

'Racism was bad when I played. I experienced some of the worst abuse you can imagine, and I actually think it's become a little bit worse, because it's been highlighted by the media. It's like everything – if you've got a spot on your face, as soon as people see it, they start pointing at it.

'People say things are changing, but they aren't. I hear people say, "Oh there's going to be a black manager interviewed for all jobs," but you look at some jobs and you can see there hasn't been a black manager interviewed.'

Rather than letting the abuse overwhelm them, Palmer says that black players have to rise above it through their skill and determination.

'Ultimately, it's about making yourself the best. Then you force people to make decisions. I've got four kids, and I want them to be educated and be the best. That's how things will change. That gives you a voice.'

*　*　*

Of course, it wouldn't be a book about ex-footballers without a couple of stories from the hospitality trade. Back in the 1980s and '90s it was common for former players to open pubs and bars; it was a job that didn't require a huge amount of training and allowed them to monetise their fame. So it's no surprise to find that two of our interviewees have gone into this particular line of work.

Lee Chapman went in at the high end of the industry. He and his wife have opened a string of restaurants and nightclubs in London, and at the time of writing they are scoping out potential sites for a place in Ibiza, where they have a base.

Phil King, on the other hand, operates at the other end of the scale: a spit and sawdust boozer in the centre of Swindon, sandwiched between a car park and a working men's club. The pub does a roaring trade, however, and the blokey banter makes it an ideal working environment for an extrovert like King (or at least it was until the hospitality industry was forced to shut down in 2020 due to the coronavirus pandemic). The pub is also round the corner from Swindon's County Ground, where he works as a host on matchdays.

Life after football hasn't always been easy, however. In 2011 King appeared in court, accused of cashing scam cheques. He was eventually cleared and says now that it was all an innocent misunderstanding.

'It was common for lads to cash their work cheques in pubs, and the guy was the fiancé of one of my staff,' he explains. 'I didn't see a problem with it. But over time the cheques got bigger and I ended up getting arrested.

'It was horrendous. I was in court for 23 days. All I did was say my name, over and over again. In the end they realised that I had nothing to do with it, but what a fucking nightmare. There was no way I'd have got involved in anything bad, I just thought I was doing someone a favour! I certainly never cashed any cheques after that.'

Then he developed a serious gambling problem. 'It wasn't horses or anything like that – it was roulette machines in the bookies.

'The government has called it the crack cocaine of the gambling world. I just got hooked on it.

'I don't know exactly when it started, but it almost took everything off me. I reckon I did over £200,000 over a period of years. I was hiding it from my wife, kids, everything. I'd be up until three and four in the morning, playing roulette online, sweating. My accountant would say, "Jesus, Phil, there's 15 grand come out of the business account here," but I didn't tell anyone.'

Eventually King joined Gamblers Anonymous and managed to turn his life around. At the time of writing he says the problem is under control, although he recognises that, 'you're only one bet away from slipping back into it', and adds, 'I hope my story serves to help other people. I'm happy to talk about what happened to me and maybe it will be useful to someone else who's going through the same thing. What happened to me could happen to anyone.'

King isn't the only player interviewed for this book to hit turbulence after quitting football. Mel Sterland, another ebullient personality, went through his own ordeal after being forced to retire prematurely in 1994.

'I'd got injured at the start of the 1992/93 season, the first one in the new Premier League, and then the following year I had to pack it in,' he recalls. 'I was still only 32 at the time so I should have had three or four years left in me.

'I was in a bad place. I couldn't accept that I'd been forced to retire from football so young. I didn't know what to do. I thought I was letting my wife and kids down. I was getting pissed, going to the bookies and losing my money, then going back for another pint.

'I could lose two grand in a day, easy. I even bought my own horse. My wife nearly killed me! King Cracker it was called, it had more shoes than she did. I paid £13,000 and sold it for £1,500, then it went and won.

'It got so bad that I nearly committed suicide. I'd set everything up, ready to go. As I was in the car I heard a voice, "What are you doing you stupid bastard? You've got a wife and kids." So I came back, had a drink and reconsidered.'

Although things have got brighter since then, Sterland recently had a major health scare when a deep-vein thrombosis developed in his foot and turned into a pulmonary embolism, a life-threatening blockage of the lungs. The illness forced him to take early retirement, although he remains comfortable enough.

Looking back now, Sterland can reflect happily on a life well lived both on and off the pitch. He even has a film credit; in 1996 he was asked to appear in the Sean Bean movie *When Saturday Comes*, about a Sheffield pub player who rises from obscurity to become an overnight sensation – with United.

Sterland laughs when asked how he ended up wearing the shirt of his hated rivals. 'I know Sean Bean well, and Jimmy Daley, who produced it. I was managing Boston United at the time, so I was nearby.

'Jimmy wanted some players to come and do some filming, so I did that, and he turns round and asks, "Why don't you be captain of Sheffield United?" I told him to fuck off! I said, "I'm not putting a Sheffield United shirt on." So then he said, "I'll give you £1,500," so I said okay! But, for all the fans reading this, I want them to know that I had a Wednesday shirt on underneath!

'It was quite funny actually. Sean Bean was a crap footballer. I took him up to Sheffield Wednesday's training ground to take some penalties, and he did his hamstrings! That knackered him for a week. He wouldn't be able to hack the training we did in our day, certainly not when you smoke 100 fags a day like him!'

* * *

Then, of course, there's David Hirst, arguably the most popular player of all those interviewed for this book.

Hirst could have cashed in his fame by becoming a media personality or writing a book of his own. He could have tried his hand in management and used his playing profile to get fast-tracked into a job in the lower divisions.

But Hirst likes the quiet life far too much to pursue either of those options. After touching the heights of superstardom as a player, he prefers to keep a much lower profile these days. He's done a bit of work in hospitality at Wednesday and is now part of a player management company, a role he augments with regular bookings on the after-dinner circuit, where he remains in high demand.

'I always tell a story about what I would have got had I gone to Manchester United,' he says. 'I really go to town – "they offered me £100,000 a week, a Ferrari, a Range Rover, a house in Barbados, and a boat." It's all bullshit of course. Then I break down crying to really ramp it up!'

It's easy to imagine Hirst being frustrated, not only with Wednesday's refusal to sanction that move to United in 1992 but with the spate of injuries that took away his pace over the next few years and forced him to retire in 2000, aged just 32 – the same age Sterland was when his own career was terminated.

Not a bit of it, however. Hirst appears totally content with his lot and is excited by the progress of his son George, who started out at Wednesday and is now at Leicester. With the sums being thrown at footballers today, the mind boggles at what Hirst would be worth were he playing now. But the man himself says he's happy to have played in an earlier era, when players were allowed to kick lumps out of one another and then patch things up over a pint afterwards.

'Yeah the money is great now, but I watch games and it's horrendous,' Hirst says. 'Honestly, the game's dying. If I was playing now I probably wouldn't be on the pitch five minutes. And if you're offside with your big toe – there's no way strikers are going to score.

'The spirit was great in our day, too. The pranks we used to play on one another – they still make me laugh now. I remember once throwing a bucket of water over Big Ron when he was in the toilet, because Shez had tricked me into thinking Nigel Pearson was in there. You should have seen Ron's face when he came out – his fringe was practically down to his waist!

'That's the sort of thing I remember. We had a great side but more than anything, we had a great set of lads who could have a laugh but then go out and support one another on the pitch. Yes we could have won more trophies, but that camaraderie makes up for it.

'I don't regret anything, in truth. Not even the injuries.'

Perhaps, as fans, we should take a pinch of this attitude ourselves. Rather than grumbling about how that golden era was allowed to rust we should be thankful that it happened in the first place.

In the time period covered by this book, Wednesday went to three major cup finals (four if you count the FA Cup replay) and a further two semi-finals. They beat Liverpool and Manchester United not just once but several times. And in David Hirst, Terry Curran, John Sheridan and Chris Waddle, they had four of English football's great entertainers.

Will we see their like again? Who knows. But the main thing is that we saw them at all.